Prophesies of Godlessness

Prophesies of Godlessness

Predictions of America's Imminent Secularization, from the Puritans to the Present Day

EDITED BY CHARLES MATHEWES AND CHRISTOPHER MCKNIGHT NICHOLS

OXFORD
UNIVERSITY PRESS

2008

OXFORD
UNIVERSITY PRESS

Oxford University Press, Inc., publishes works that further
Oxford University's objective of excellence
in research, scholarship, and education.

Oxford   New York
Auckland   Cape Town   Dar es Salaam   Hong Kong   Karachi
Kuala Lumpur   Madrid   Melbourne   Mexico City   Nairobi
New Delhi   Shanghai   Taipei   Toronto

With offices in
Argentina   Austria   Brazil   Chile   Czech Republic   France   Greece
Guatemala   Hungary   Italy   Japan   Poland   Portugal   Singapore
South Korea   Switzerland   Thailand   Turkey   Ukraine   Vietnam

Published by Oxford University Press, Inc.
198 Madison Avenue, New York, New York 10016

www.oup.com

Library of Congress Cataloging-in-Publication Data
Prophesies of godlessness : predictions of America's imminent secularization,
from the puritans to the present day / edited by Charles Mathewes and
Christopher McKnight Nichols.
    p.   cm.
Includes bibliographical references and index.
ISBN 978-0-19-534253-6; 978-0-19-534254-3 (pbk.)
1. United States—Religion.   2. Secularization—United States.   3.   United
States—Forecasting.   I. Mathewes, Charles T., 1969–
II. Nichols, Christopher McKnight.
BL2525.P76 2008
200.973—dc22   2007040444

9 8 7 6 5 4 3 2 1

Printed in the United States of America
on acid-free paper

*For the Institute for Advanced Studies in Culture
at the University of Virginia*

Acknowledgments

This book simply would not be, if it were not for the Institute for Advanced Studies in Culture (IASC) at the University of Virginia. It was at a seminar of the Institute that the coeditors first thought of the idea for this book, and when we began to come to grips with the range of scholarly competencies we would need to compose it, we were able to walk its halls and pick our authors almost entirely from the colleagues and friends located therein. The Institute has sustained us in many ways; it has given us food and time and skeptical and rigorous readers, providing a home for this book project and for many of the scholars involved in this and other serious studies of the relationship between meaning and moral order, past and present. We thank IASC for the financial support and interdisciplinary intellectual community provided here, and for the good fortune we have had to be a part of it.

Despite the names that appear on the title page, it is the authors of the various chapters who did the fundamental work of making this book. Thanks to Wilson, to Johann, to Matt, to Wayne, to Andrew, to Kevin, to David, to Slava, to Joe and David, and to Josh. Without them, the book would never have moved beyond a pipe dream. Thanks to them for managing to grasp something solid of our rather airy vision, and then making something substantial of it.

Crafting a single argument out of many voices is never easy; in fact, when you look at edited volumes, it is a task more often avoided than undertaken. Certain individuals helped a great deal.

In smoothing the writing style of our many authors from various disciplines, in several stages, we enlisted the editorial services of John Paine, who was invaluable in molding and streamlining this book into a cohesive narrative. Susan Witzel and Christy Hall at the Institute also deserve acknowledgment and thanks, for their invaluable aid with fiscal management for the book and in varied efforts on the manuscript and in organizing our Prophesies Conference in 2006. Andrew Witmer must also be acknowledged for his exemplary work on the index. We also thank Jennifer Geddes for reading and commenting on parts of this manuscript. We owe a special thanks to Karen Guth for her editing and formatting assistance. And of course, many thanks to Cynthia Read and her crack staff at Oxford University Press, and OUP's anonymous book reviewers, for their excellent comments and suggestions.

Finally, however, it is to the people who make up the IASC that this book owes the most. The executive director of the Institute, James Davison Hunter, deserves more than our thanks. He has backed this work from its earliest flickers, and he has consistently championed it through its publication. We still do not know whether he would agree with all we argue here; but we never doubted that he would give us his full support. All in all, creating a book is relatively easy; creating a space where people can create books is something else altogether. Many people know James as an author and thinker; we are more fortunate, for we know him also as a supporter and friend. At the institute we were also supported by the directors, three of whom—Joseph Davis, Slavica Jakelić, and Joshua Yates—not only helped organize our work sessions on the draft chapters, but were so thoroughly involved that they became contributors as well. May this book be a token of our gratitude to all of them, and to the Institute that they enable to exist.

Contents

Contributors

The Editors

Charles Mathewes, associate professor of religious studies at the
University of Virginia, specializes in religious ethics. His books in-
clude *Evil and the Augustinian Tradition* and *A Theology of Public Life*.
Through 2010, he is editor of the *Journal of the American Academy of
Religion*, the flagship journal in the field of religious studies.

Christopher McKnight Nichols, fellow at the Institute for Advanced Studies in Culture at the University of Virginia, is a special-
ist in United States intellectual, cultural, and political history from
the late nineteenth century through the twentieth century. He is
revising a manuscript for publication titled *From Empire to Isolation:
Internationalism and Isolationism in American Thought*. Nichols has
received several teaching awards and has published articles in leading
academic journals and public newspapers on the United States
and the world, political philosophy, foreign policy, and religious
thought.

The Contributors

Wilson Brissett is a postdoctoral fellow at the Institute for Advanced
Studies in Culture at the University of Virginia, where he also completed his Ph.D. in English focused on early-American literature and

culture. His dissertation, "Beauty among the Puritans," traces the centrality of aesthetic sensibility in the religious culture of colonial Massachusetts.

David Ciepley is assistant professor of political science at the University of Denver. He is the author of *Liberalism in the Shadow of Totalitarianism* (2006) and of several articles dealing with the transformation of the American self-understanding during the ideological struggle against totalitarianism. He is a former Mellon postdoctoral fellow at Washington University and former postdoctoral fellow in the Center on Religion and Democracy at the University of Virginia. Ciepley's current work focuses on nongovernmental forms of governance, and especially on the history and theory of corporations understood as governance institutions.

Joseph E. Davis is research director of the Institute for Advanced Studies in Culture and research associate professor of sociology at the University of Virginia. He is the author of *Accounts of Innocence: Sexual Abuse, Trauma, and the Self* (2005), and editor of *Stories of Change: Narrative and Social Movements* (2002) and *Identity and Social Change* (2000). In his current work, Davis is exploring questions of suffering and culture, medicalization, and the growing use of psychoactive medications by both children and adults.

David Franz is a doctoral candidate in sociology at the University of Virginia and a dissertation fellow at the Institute for Advanced Studies in Culture. He studies the cultural influence of business corporations on conceptions of the good and on the language used to articulate such conceptions. His dissertation, titled "The Ethics of Incorporation," examines the rising importance of business management theory in American culture since the 1980s.

Wayne Wei-siang Hsieh is assistant professor of history at the United States Naval Academy. His research specialties include nineteenth-century U.S. military history, especially the Civil War. He has published two chapters in edited collections: "Christian Love and Martial Violence: Baptists and War—Danger and Opportunity," in *Virginia's Civil War* (2005), and an essay on Lee's decision to secede, in *Crucible of the Civil War: Virginia from Secession to Commemoration* (2006). Hsieh is currently working on a book based on his dissertation, titled *The Old Army in War and Peace: West Pointers and the Civil War Era, 1814–1865*.

Slavica Jakelić is research assistant professor of religious studies at the University of Virginia and co-director of the Program on Religion, Culture, and Democracy at the Institute for Advanced Studies in Culture. Her work explores the importance of religion for people's collective identities. She has written numerous essays on the theories of religion, the public role of religions in modern societies, secularization and secularism, religion and violence, and religious dialogue. Jakelić is presently working on a book titled *Religion as Identity: The Challenge of Collectivistic Religion in the Contemporary World*.

Matthew Mutter is a doctoral candidate in English literature at Yale University and a graduate fellow of the Institute for Advanced Studies in Culture at the University of Virginia. His dissertation is on the meaning of secularization in modernist poetry and philosophy, particularly in the work of George Santayana, Wallace Stevens, and W. H. Auden. He has written on Don DeLillo and ordinary language philosophy and teaches British and American modernist poetry and fiction, Romantic poetry, and contemporary American fiction.

Johann N. Neem is assistant professor of history at Western Washington University in Bellingham, Washington. He specializes in the early American Republic and intellectual history. Neem is the author of *Creating a Nation of Joiners: Democracy and Civil Society in Early National Massachusetts* (forthcoming).

Kevin M. Schultz is assistant professor of history and Catholic studies at the University of Illinois, Chicago. He teaches courses in American history focusing on ethnoracial history, religious history, intellectual history, and questions of American identity. He has published articles in the *Journal of American History, American Quarterly*, and *Labor History*, among other places. Schultz's first book is tentatively titled *The First Multiculturalists: Catholics and Jews in Postwar America* (Oxford University Press, forthcoming).

Andrew Witmer is a doctoral candidate in the Corcoran Department of History at the University of Virginia and a dissertation fellow at the Institute for Advanced Studies in Culture. His publications include several essays on the history of religion and race in the nineteenth-century United States. Witmer recently published a chapter on African-American and white Virginia Baptists during the Civil War, in *Crucible of the American Civil War: Virginia from Secession to Commemoration* (2006).

Joshua J. Yates is research assistant professor of sociology at the University of Virginia and associate director of the Institute of Advanced Studies in Culture. He has written on the cosmopolitanism of American global elites, international humanitarianism and world culture, the challenges of a globalizing modernity to religion, the worldwide spread of democracy, and the antiglobalization/global justice movement. Yates is currently working on a book titled *To Save the World: Humanitarianism and World Culture*.

Prophesies of Godlessness

Introduction: Prophesies of Godlessness

Christopher McKnight Nichols and
Charles Mathewes

Imagine two scenes, each playing out many times over the last three centuries.

Scene 1: An American intellectual—a public figure—sits alone at his desk, writing to a correspondent. Both author and recipient are anxious about the American public order. The intellectual writes to comfort his colleague. Surely institutional religious organizations are declining, he writes; surely they are on their last legs. Soon they will decay into merely loose affiliations of more liberal-minded individuals. All we need do is wait, the man writes. The future, he firmly believes, belongs to us.

Who was that man? It was Thomas Jefferson writing in the 1820s; or perhaps Thomas Paine in the 1780s, Walter Lippmann in the 1910s, or it might have been Ralph Waldo Emerson in the 1840s. It could have been Walt Whitman in the 1860s, or John Dewey in the 1930s. More recently still, such an intellectual skeptic might have been John Judis or Ruy Teixera, writing to recommend their well-regarded *The Coming Democratic Majority*, published in 2002.

Scene 2: A man—a renowned religious leader—stands before a crowd. The future looks grim, he says. Americans are losing their faith. Where has their deep reliance on the God of their fathers gone? Civic energies are atrophying. American character is decaying. We stand in the last days—of the republic, of the idea of America, of the vast gamble that was, and is, our ultimate mission. Unless we receive a miracle or make a concerted effort to change our current situation, he disclaims, soon we will see the crumbling of the great and noble effort we represent.

This could have been Cotton Mather in 1700, Jonathan Edwards in the 1740s, Samuel Hopkins in 1800, or Edwards Amasa Park in the 1870s. Or William Jennings Bryan in 1920. It might have been Hal Lindsey or Jimmy Carter in the 1970s, or Jerry Falwell in the 1980s. Or—absent the clerical garb—Christopher Lasch in the 1970s, Robert Putnam in 1990s, or Ann Coulter in the new millennium.

These are powerful examples of what any casual observer of America knows: America has always been a religious country anxious about its own religiosity. From the Puritans until today, American public life has had a decidedly religious cast. Despite many battles and challenges, the national motto is "In God we trust." Yet the First Amendment is treasured for protecting citizens' right to worship, or not, in whatever way they deem proper. Americans have neither affirmed a state religion nor sought to expel faith from public life. And few doubt that the swerving course of Americans' thought about God is central to the history of the United States in general. To be an American, even for unbelievers, means having a view about America's God.[1]

But they are not just examples of such views. For along with having a view about America's God, Americans seem compelled to have a view about the nation's future. America's destiny has seemed both singularly messianic and singularly precarious. As philosopher Stanley Cavell accurately discerned, America has a unique sense of history. Other countries remembered a time before their current political configurations, so that

> before there was Russia, there was Russia; before there was France and England, there was France and England; but before there was America there was no America. America was *discovered*, and what was discovered was not a place, one among others, but a setting, the backdrop of a destiny. . . . Its present is continuously ridiculed by the fantastic promise of its origin and its possibility, and because it has never been assured that it will survive. Since it had a birth it may die. It feels mortal. And it wishes proof not merely of its continuance but of its existence, a fact it has never been able to take for granted. Therefore its need for love is insatiable.[2]

This is not self-congratulatory "American exceptionalism" but an acute insight into the nature of American self-identity. Virtually alone among the nations of the world, the United States has had a tangible sense of tenuous temporality stemming from the singular moment of the founding to the present.

Accompanying this powerful awareness of the past is the strong intuition that everything could change in an instant: The United States, once "made," could be unmade. Unlike the nations of Europe, with historical sensibilities that antedate their governments and civic institutions, America manifests few such pretensions of endurance. The nation *is* its ideals; without the one, many Americans believe, the other cannot long endure. And not only is religion an essential element of these national ideals, and not only are the ideals themselves often collectively held with religious fervor, but the very idea of America's destiny has often been expressed in a messianic frame. America's anxiety about its present has been tied up with its future, and has been typically framed in religious terms.

At the confluence of thought about religion and about the future, then, lurks a hidden but powerful current of reflection about the future of American religion—the future of American religion as perpetually imperiled. This is the story we tell in this book. Our narrative reveals the recurrent, and recurrently wrong, predictions of America's coming loss of faith: the history of America's prophesies of godlessness.

Prophesies of Godlessness

Every generation of Americans, from the nation's colonial past to its postmodern present, has witnessed and given rise to new predictions of the coming "godlessness" of American society. Major thinkers from each period in United States history have voiced surprisingly similar expectations about religious and moral change.

The differences among these predictions are significant. Sometimes members of the same generation disagreed vehemently: some favored the foreseen future, some dreaded it. Nor are these predictions the property of any single ideology, denomination, or political party. Both the Right and the Left have made myriad prophesies of the nation's pending godlessness. They have been presented as part of an explicitly political or social agenda; thundered in jeremiads from pulpits, both churchly and bully; proposed as putatively scientific or scholarly analyses; proclaimed in tones of anticipatory excitement and anticipatory despair.

Yet their similarities are crucial as well. Such prophets have often heightened their rhetoric to the point that it suppressed genuine dialogue, instead favoring polarizing debates; many have made the issue of coming godlessness or rising godliness seem to be the most pressing issue at stake in society. And in every generation, those issuing such statements often believed they lived at a unique and pivotal moment; catastrophes or utopias seemingly always have been on the horizon for these prophets.

In the end, for our purposes, what most crucially unites them all is that they share a history: their various senses of the future are as old as America, and their stories are intertwined with the nation's social, intellectual, political, moral, and religious development. Their beliefs, and the ways they have viewed, questioned, and prophesied the role of religion in American life, have profoundly shaped the public language of their times. They continue to shape how we approach these subjects today. Religious and moral predictions, for and against godlessness, are as ingrained, continuous, and contentious in American society as they have ever been. And they are as commonplace, and as necessary to living, as the shared belief that the sun must rise tomorrow.

This is a perennial feature of American society. For example, Jefferson believed that all Americans would become Unitarians; more recently, Ruy Teixera argued that the "new" Democrats will find greater political appeal because they see government and "modern science, nurtured by government, as a tool of progress rather than as a threat to biblical religion," so in turn they project a rise in so-called secular liberals in the coming decades.[3] Yet the society, always seemingly on the brink of becoming denuded of believers, has neither collapsed nor become less religious in three centuries; indeed, some argue that the United States today is a more religious country than it was in 1776.[4]

In American history, prophesies of godlessness are as American as American godliness itself. That is the curious fact that prompted this book.

The Puzzle

Why, given America's patent religiosity, do leading Americans of every generation prophesy, fearfully or hopefully, a coming godlessness? Why is this so common that Americans practically come to expect these prophesies? And why, in our eagerness and anxiety to hear them, have we not realized that they sound so similar—in content, tone, and quality of expectation—across the centuries?

Answering these questions is this book's goal. While leading thinkers' visions of America's past, present, and future differ in many ways, their predictions of the nation's moral and religious future have been strikingly consonant; they have traveled along well-carved rhetorical grooves. There are patterns, what we call scripts, that ideologically and rhetorically shape observers' expectations about the relationship between the nation's moral and religious past, present, and prospective direction. These scripts affect how most people express their expectations, and how others hear them.

What we see as the most salient scripts are collections of ideas or modes of evaluating the present with an eye toward the future, collections that reveal shared uses of language and common symbols to respond to rhetorical conditions and cultural contexts. We will explain the specifics in the next section. However, what is most significant is that these scripts reach from the Puritans to our age. While they have taken a sinuous and at times subterranean route to the present, when anyone thinks about the future of America, that thinking—even today, among atheists and those who predict optimistic techno-utopias—employs symbols, images, and tropes that would be familiar to Puritans sitting in pews in the 1630s, revolutionaries at town meetings in the 1770s, abolitionist evangelicals at camp meetings in the 1840s, and social scientists at conferences in the 1950s. Americans continue to invoke and re-orient these scripts in ways consistent with advanced by thinkers from past centuries. This book illuminates the contours of these potent scripts.

Of course, things are more complicated than this (or any) brief overview can detail. And these scripts are obviously not the only means of understanding American religiosity. But these patterns are worth study, for they have been surprisingly resilient over the centuries. There are interesting discontinuities between what Americans apparently expected to happen and what actually has happened, regarding American religiosity. On the other hand, there are extraordinary *continuities* within these expectations, across generations.

Scholars thrive on noting trends and torturing them to look for larger significance. But this particular continuity has been the subject of surprisingly little direct reflection. In fact, as far as we can see, it has produced no reflection at all: No one has noticed that people have been predicting religion's demise in America since America's beginnings. This book, that is to say, is among the first efforts by scholars to investigate and emphasize the importance of this subject.

Scripts and Themes

We cannot but be aware of the bewildering diversity of thought about religion, and so we confess that we have eschewed comprehensiveness and preferred illustration. We focus on people and their particular predictions to elucidate patterns in the latter and tendencies in the former. Our approach resembles Lytton Strachey's approach to the Victorian era, in *Eminent Victorians*:

> It is not by the direct method of a scrupulous narration that the
> explorer of the past can hope to depict that singular epoch. If he is
> wise, he will adopt a subtler strategy. He will attack his subject in

unexpected places; he will fall upon the flank, or the rear; he will shoot a sudden, revealing searchlight into obscure recesses, hitherto undivined. He will row out over that great ocean of material, and lower down into it, here and there, a little bucket, which will bring up to the light of day some characteristic specimen, from those far depths, to be examined with a careful curiosity.[5]

Each chapter is guided by Strachey's "careful curiosity." Each attends to a particular era and is organized around a focal individual, a community of thought, and changing conceptions of secularization. And each chapter uses that analysis to discuss, largely indirectly and by example, how such predictions are part of thinking about "the good society," and how such thinking structures our apprehension of the present. Because we decided early on to select several representative figures that are ideal-typical for ranges of thought in their eras, we make no pretensions to total comprehensiveness, and aim to avoid preemptive generalizations.

Two Caveats

In conceiving and writing this book, we have sought to avoid two faulty yet remarkably resilient mistakes thinkers make in reflecting on religion and America: one about religion, one about America.

First of all, we reject the received notion of secularization, at least as it is commonly understood: as decreasing levels of belief in supernatural entities. There are many problems with this notion. One is that it has turned out to be wrong; the world does not seem set on a path of steadily declining commitment to religion.[6] Another is that it assumes a seductive yet misleading Eurocentrist teleological trajectory of inevitable secularization. Often we assume that the final question is, "When will America finally become like Europe?" But secularization, modernization, and becoming like Europe are not the same thing, nor does the march of History necessarily end with all nations becoming like Holland. Nor must secularization lead to secularism. "Secularism"—the political or philosophical view of public or social life that affirms that the less public religiosity there is, the greater the benefits for society—and "secularization," which is the sociological process of religious privatization, religious decline, or something else, are different things altogether. Such assumptions seriously distort our ability to see the real changes on the ground; they slot our thinking into well-worn grooves down which thought travels too easily, steadily diverging from an accurate assessment of whatever changes it discerns.

The proper meaning of "secularization," as well as its veridicality on *any* determinate meaning, is hotly debated in the sociology of religion and in the modern history of religion. For the purposes of this book, however, we broaden the definition of individual-level religious decline by arguing that secularization and thinking about a "godless" present and/or future explicitly refer to perceptions of a decline in religious authority. In that vein, this book speaks implicitly to the ongoing scholarly reassessment and reconstruction of theories of secularization. Yet ours is fundamentally a descriptive and not an analytic-normative project: We are interested centrally in our thinkers' understandings of secularization, not in the proper meaning of "secularism" or in measuring processes of secularization.

Second, we follow several decades of American historiography in resisting the New England–centrist understanding of the origins of American intellectual life and culture in general, For a long time, everyone thought, like Tocqueville, that the "state of departure" in understanding America and the peculiar religiosity of the United States began with the New England Puritans. Many astute observers found the essence of early American thought in how the Puritans gave shape to the jeremiad, as well as covenant theology, and later the New England democratic village system with town meetings. There is much to be said for this tradition of thought. Its insights are powerful and largely persuasive. But it can occlude the full story of America in trying to get at (what it sees as) the *true* story of America—leaving much of the rest of the nation not fully "American."[7]

Yet the Puritans were not the only story in early America. In contrast to New England, the colonies located across the middle swath of the eastern seaboard did not have strict religious components to their founding ideals; their overt inspirations were more capitalist (mercantilist trading corporations) or royalist (British Crown sponsorship). This "Chesapeake model" did not solicit from its inhabitants the predictions for a pious religious future in the same way the models to their north did. The profound influence of Methodism and other, more affect-centered forms of Protestantism in the American South gave prominence to a distinctively non-Puritan Christianity and a concomitantly different approach to the question of the prospects for the future of belief. As we will see, this tradition had its own distinct influence on the course of these prophesies, in episodes such as the Civil War, the Scopes trial, and the reemergence into the public square of more conservative (and emotivist) forms of Protestantism in the 1970s and 1980s. Furthermore, "godless" Virginian founders like Thomas Jefferson and James Madison pushed for the Virginia Statute for Religious Freedoms, urged no mention of God in the Constitution, and secured the Establishment Clause of the First Amendment. The people of the mid-Atlantic did, of course, consider their future in religious terms, yet not so incessantly as their northern brethren, nor did they do so quite so thoroughly in the declensionist manner the Puritan jeremiad demanded.[8]

Nonetheless, while the Puritans were only part of a larger pandemonium of actors in the American colonies, their contribution was inescapable; and by the time of the Founding Fathers, everyone was engaged in these issues—and all shared the Puritans as intellectual ancestors, if not actual ones.

Guiding Ideas

To preface our investigations, we begin with some of the ideas that have guided us in our approach to this book.

First of all, "godlessness" for us does not necessarily mean the complete extinguishing of religious belief. Rather, we mean especially to identify predictions about the loss of *visible* religiosity, especially in regard to *public* religiosity, which often is termed or seen as religious deinstitutionalization. In fact, many of the predictions of "godlessness" are just as much expectations of true godliness, enabled by the escape from the dead weight of traditional institutions. Jefferson was interpreted as godless, even though his Unitarian vision of America's religious future held out, he thought, the best hope for true piety, unmuddied by entanglements with dimensions of human life fundamentally distinct from religion (see chapter 2). Even many self-proclaimed defenders of the faith have wanted to keep their faith out of the public sphere, not so much for the sake of the public sphere as out of interest in preserving true religion; and audiences not attuned to such individuals' arguments often have accused them of promoting godlessness. As the chapters that follow reveal, this was as true for Ralph Waldo Emerson as for more contemporary scholars, including Harvey Cox, who have experienced the same difficulty of getting their message heard for what it is (see chapters 3 and 9). It is hard, in American history, to find an atheist gleefully anticipating the death of God, although the so-called Great Agnostic, Robert Ingersoll, represents one such exemplar of "atheistical" prophesying (see chapter 6). Even in the Puritan jeremiad tradition, a faithful remnant would remain, if only to witness to God's wrathful judgment. Prophesies of godlessness, then, were typically prophesies about the dominant and visible religion.

Second, we study *prophesies* of godlessness, not ultimately the prophets who pronounced them. We have chosen to examine these prophetic predictions about public religiosity as they developed over time. Our main characters, that is, are scripts, not people, although each chapter focuses on key individuals and groups. The unity of our story rests as much in how the scripts were heard as in how they were spoken. We therefore constructed our study to begin with the Puritans and to continue through to the present day. In this way, we aim to provide a long view of these scripts and how they have developed and changed yet in remarkable ways remained consistent over the last four centuries.

Third, as prophesies, these are pictures of history and so imply a vision of history's full scope—past, present, and future. They are thus as much about the past and the present as the future. Furthermore, in keeping with broadly Judeo-Christian cultural understandings of time, these scripts typically assume an apocalyptic sense that history has certain pivotal moments and an end point of sorts. Such a sense of linear trajectory as a way of constructing knowledge has meant that Americans have a very deep sense of history's fragility; that is to say, events leading up to and through the present take on greater meaning and have been amplified by Americans' own particularly self-conscious understanding of their nation's founding moment as precarious and under threat both internally and externally. If the past is subject to interpretation and cannot be secure, then the "present and future prospects of the past" are crucial to its meaning. Hence the past is not fixed; the future also bears the weight of the past, because of the American apocalyptic sensibility—secular as well as religious—that everything might change in an instant.

Three Background Traditions

American thinkers did not, of course, spring de novo from the virgin soil of the New World, with minds untainted by "Old Europe." For good or ill, they inherited three major traditions of thought about the nature and destiny of human political association that shaped and oriented their discussions of whether their society was becoming morally and religiously better or worse, was in ascent or decline (variously defined). These traditions changed over time, as Americans have revised them in light of new cultural contexts and with new rhetorical situations; have combined in various fashions in particular moments and for particular voices; and yet they remain distinctly identifiable even today.

1. *The jeremiad tradition*, and more generally the tradition we sometimes refer to as Protestant covenantalism, was integral to the Puritan "city on the hill" concept, as well as the underlying morality for the first democratic forms of social contracts, a la the Mayflower Compact. This tradition in America

differed from that in Europe—it was largely based on the sense of a shared mission in the New World, which itself was seen as a *tabula rasa*, where there was little need to reform preexisting socioreligious conditions. Pointing to signs of depravity and immorality, or providential omens, over time the jeremiad became a call to reform more than a just an invocation of mission in the Americas as well. Jeremiads often assumed the form of declension narratives, but not necessarily.

2. *The tradition of civic republicanism.* As a political philosophy, in America at least, civic republicanism combined civic liberalism (the theory of rights, elaborated by thinkers like John Locke) and republicanism (the theory of virtuous citizenship, from Aristotle through the Italian Renaissance to Jean-Jacques Rousseau). This tradition united a concern for establishing the prerequisites of citizenship with protecting rights to life, liberty, and property (the Jeffersonian "pursuit of happiness"). Yet it also encouraged and sustained expectations of decline, expectations that equally (if typically covertly) express a nostalgia for a noble republican past of virtue and sacrifice in contrast to a present-day nadir of luxury and lassitude. In many ways, U.S. anxiety about decay is in part driven by an understanding of what led to the fall of earlier republics, most famously Rome; thinkers as early as Polybius, the second century BCE Greek witness to the Punic wars, argued that all republics followed a cycle of virtuous youth followed by prosperous maturity before declining into luxurious antiquity. From the days of John Winthrop to the present, civic republican concerns have returned again and again to haunt the American religiopolitical imagination.

3. *The Enlightenment rationalist tradition in its American form* is a referent for virtually all prophesies of godlessness. Seeking to use reason to scrutinize previously accepted doctrines and received wisdom, many of the Founding Fathers broadly worked out of an Enlightenment rationalist perspective to develop their critique of monarchy and aristocracy, based on a shared understanding of natural rights. One enduring legacy of American Enlightenment rationalism in its American setting has been the search for "rational religions," which gave rise to Deism. Perhaps most significant to the historical and prophetic assessments we track throughout this book, Enlightenment rationalism has had a tendency to think in terms of a "march of reason," which in turn reinforces a sense of linear progress in human history.

These traditions have joined, inflected, and resisted each other in myriad ways. Yet they have provided, and continue to provide today, the basic frameworks for many of America's prophesies. A considerable amount of discussion about the present character and future prospects of religion in the United States finds a place in this framework.

Ascension and Declension

Given these charged frameworks of interpretation, the most enduring thematic scripts we have found are those of progress and regress. To be sure, there are more nuanced possibilities—of better and more godlessness, more and less religiosity—that can be represented by the vast middle ground, or complex arena of shades of gray. But nuanced analysis does not make for powerful rhetoric, and whatever else they do, these prophesies reach always for rhetorical power. Those who have attempted to chart a subtle path have lost their flocks in the underbrush of obscurity; those comfortable with starker proclamations, blazing a clear trail, have tended to be much more persuasive.

Representing both historical judgment and future prediction, ascension and declension narratives provide potent material to make a forceful call for change. Where we were and where we are going is critical to ascent or decline and adds urgency to the present moment. From this base, most prominent prophets delineate their versions of the nation's trajectory. They stake out how bad it has become, or how good, and then set a point of departure and a mechanism for change toward their proposed goals, either greater godlessness or godliness.

The first major prophetic vision to appear was the godlessness-as-declension narrative, derived in large measure from the Puritans and the jeremiad tradition, as well as from the other religious heretics and commercial adventurers settling in America. Following on that script, however, was an influential counter narrative, one premised on ascension, which may be seen to be a product of Enlightenment thinking and of the American illuminati of that intellectual orientation. Both of these narratives are as much a way of constructing an understanding of group and national history as a means of evaluating the present and projecting visions for the future.

Please note that we do not intend this book to be polemical. We do not assume that either of these interpretive scripts—the ascensionist or declensionist—carried the day, or should carry the day; rather, we see them as two of the most distinct and broad scripts, or traditions, in the American intellectual tradition of thinking about the nation's religiosity, regardless of the religious and political beliefs of those who promoted them. In the chapters that follow, we have no favorites.

Some Critical Themes

In studying these scripts, we have often returned to several crucial ideas that repeatedly appear and have been contested throughout prophesies of both coming godlessness and rising godliness over time. We argue that the three most potent of these themes are "America"; "the creedal nation"; and "modernity."

The first is, in one sense, not surprising. America was and is at issue in prophesies of godlessness, because there is a connection between the inner meaning of America for these prophets and the possible final answer to the question whether the nation is "really" religious or not. For some—say, descendants operating in the declensionist tradition of the Puritans—America is "really" religious and needs to get back to being so; for others—say, descendants of Jefferson or Paine and a more ascensionist narrative—America is "really" not religious and must cast off its religiosity to finally realize itself. Either way, America's identity seems curiously and self-consciously implicated in its religious identity as well.

America's religiosity is well known. It is pervasive, feverish at times, and a matter of energetic commitment yet prone to rapid alteration individually and communally. Few other nations' citizens seem so susceptible not just to belief but also to believing many things, sometimes serially and sometimes simultaneously. In America, an equally remarkable velocity has complemented the remarkable volume of faith. Change and pace of change are crucial to the ways Americans have viewed the relationship of present morality and society to those to come in the future. Americans can conceive of things changing radically in a short period of time because of the revolutionary nature of American religiosity and of the added sense of agency inherent across much of U.S. society. Americans appear to demonstrate an almost apocalyptic sense of the velocity of their own agency. Does this make Americans more religious, or only superficially so? Just what is the character of American religion, after all? What answer one gives to these questions is a matter of contestable judgment; but that religion has been a central challenge to the meaning of America in the past and for the future is undeniable.

Second, American ideals have been crucial to virtually every prophet and every prophecy—all tend to share certain fundamental beliefs. From its republican cradle in the 1770s, the United States was always what has aptly been termed a creedal nation. It is, as the earlier cited passage from Cavell proposed, a project. Most Americans have perceived their nation to be without core blood ties, a constructed entity. Thus, to be American was really a matter of assenting to the creed. A creedal nation is particularly sensitive to the state of its adherence to its core beliefs and is particularly in need of interpreting and managing creeds properly. But because creeds require voluntary appropriation, they are inherently subject to interpretation and change. This instability in meaning is at the heart of all the prophesies we study, thus animating many of the creedal predictions in this book.[9]

There is a connection between creedal ideals and prophesies of godless-ness or godliness at times of regional and national disaster. September 11, 2001, was only the latest such moment; a number of pivotal situations—including the Civil War, the Scopes trial, the 1929 stock market crash, and Pearl Harbor, to name just a few of the most prominent—also stand out because of the way Americans have responded to them. Immediately after the World Trade Center and Pentagon attacks, for example, Americans addressed the situation in keeping with how they responded in the past; that is, events were rapidly interpreted in terms of America's present religious and moral situation, along with a reinterpretation of history in an attempt to determine "how we got here." Some asked: Were the attacks brought on because Amer-icans are grubby materialist secularists? Did this happen because American foreign policy has been caught in the grip of ignorant Christians committed to a messianic alliance with Israel? Has the American response to the attacks been too Christian or not Christian enough? These and other questions have all been debated. This should not be surprising. With so much at stake in war, catastrophe, and depression, prophesies take on a particular importance at these times. Yet, paradoxically, as some chapters here argue, moments of relative peace also provide some of the most fruitful periods of dialogue on the state of religion and morality in society. In storm or calm, the debate goes on, and it is as much about America as about religiosity.

Third, modernity is a crucial theme. For good or ill, the nature of mo-dernity itself has been at issue in these prophesies. As both idea and process, modernity has been integral to how Americans since the seventeenth century have viewed the changing state of their society. The relationship between modernity and social change has been critical to most of the rhetorical patterns we can discern; and it has been particularly evident in predictions made during the twentieth century. Insofar as America is the paradigmatic modern state/ society, the question of the fate of religion in the U.S. is all the more a live issue in understanding the nature of modernity. Linked to ideas about America and modernity is the important yet distinct issue of "progress," and how reli-gious beliefs might be best integrated, or not, into personal, local, and national progress (variously defined). By the late Industrial Revolution in America, "progress" was the catchword individuals used to seize on the challenges of the emerging commercial, military, and urban might of America; people heralded, decried, or otherwise viewed modernity and progress as intrinsically inter-connected. To be modern was to have a view of progress; this is as true today as it was in 1900, and in some ways as true as it was for Americans living before the Civil War.

What is most intriguing about the recurrent theme of modernity is how fraught with tension it has been. Between the predictions of ideological modernism and the complex realities of the actual process of modernization, Americans of all persuasions have struggled to find a way to view modernity and progress without completely stripping it of meaning. For example, the notion of progress often has been subject to the multidirectional pulls of those viewing it as inevitable, versus a variety of groups arrayed against perceived forms of progressive change. Similarly, calls to return to national or religious origins or ideals have often been cast and reinterpreted in terms of antimodern sentiment—a nostalgia for a multiplicity of perceived halcyon days, eras, or beliefs—or simply as a call to achieve specific objectives in coming years. Such flexibility seems inherent in the idea; however dangerous this flexibility may be, it has certainly been a cause of modernity's fruitfulness for thought.

Of course, these are not the only themes discussed in the following pages. Nor are they equally visible in every chapter. In preparing this road map for the book, we have made every effort not to impress scripts or themes on the material but to let them naturally emerge from the prophesies themselves. We mean to provoke readers to new thought, not lead them to an anticipated conclusion.

Conclusion

Innumerable transformations have altered American society over the past four centuries. Successive generations of Americans viewed their nation's moral and religious future in manifold and diverse ways. Yet certain continuities are, when noticed, profound and telling. The Revolution, the Civil War, industrialism, and America's rise to preeminence in the twentieth century—to take only the most prominent examples—all challenged Americans' understanding of their moral and religious condition; yet time and time again, the changes and challenges have called forth similar interpretations, analogous predictions, and comparable calls for response from the parties involved. This merits study, and we have tried to study it.

The authors of this book met together over the past several years, and it took shape from their conversations. It began in an exchange between the editors in a seminar about secularization. As we first imagined the book, we gathered a dedicated and diverse group of scholars to examine these prophesies, scholars whose expertise spans fields ranging from history and sociology to English literature and religious studies. The interdisciplinary scope of our inquiry is crucial to this book, and is due to the vibrant intellectual environment at the Institute for Advanced Studies in Culture at the University of Virginia, in which most of the authors have been involved at one time or another in recent years. This book has been conceived, discussed, and researched by a group of scholars who are passionately interested in its topic. Each chapter has been constructed and crafted, in several stages and many drafts, in consultation with the editors, and in conversation with all the other authors, for the purposes of this book alone. Unlike those in most edited collections, these chapters were not produced for conferences, articles, or other projects. Energetic and caffeine-infused arguments over the course of the past year have strengthened each chapter, as well as the coherence of the whole. From these discussions, fresh themes and insights have emerged that we hope will illuminate for the reader in an unprecedented way the historical patterns in Americans' predictions (opposing or embracing) of a coming godlessness.

Ultimately, our aims for this book are ambitious. We think it appears at an especially important moment—a time when religion and politics have once again become particularly charged issues under scrutiny in the American public square. We hope to contribute to the current public debates over the "proper" role of religion in the public square, made pressing by the recent trends in national politics, and expressed dramatically by the recent presidential elections, as well as decisions by the Supreme Court. We do so by uncovering a surprising history of serial predictions of secularization—each era's predictions echoing already refuted expectations, built on the foundation of common rhetoric, or calling on the lessons of those few predictions from the past that have proved more or less accurate.

We have conceived and written this book as a work of historical scholarship, an exploration of patterns in rhetoric and in the predictions of imminent secularization during America's past, and we have constructed it with civic aims in mind as well. We have gone about our scholarship always faithful to the evidence. In noting these patterns of prophesying, and the scripts that reappear in them, we hope to help advance public debate beyond the stale dichotomy of secularization as good or bad. Indeed, at their most extreme, received understandings of "secularization" are often rooted in an apocalyptic either/or conception of true piety set against utter godlessness; far from being an innocent analytic tool, the category may obscure more than it illuminates. Further discussion, scholarly and nonacademic, of religious and moral change will be better served by a more thoroughly demythologized—that is, fine-grained and cold-eyed—approach to the evidence.

The velocity of change and the contested meaning of America have given added significance to current predictions of coming godlessness and questions of pending change in religiosity. This book offers an under-appreciated historical view of how Americans have imagined and disseminated prophesies for and against "godlessness" in the past, in the hope that we may do better in our reflections in the future.

The fact that expectations about America's future character and piety are often infused with profound emotional assessments of these future prospects, whether anxious or hopeful, is not accidental. Metrics such as worship attendance or church membership cannot fully measure these expectations and their powerful traveling companion, predictions. As we will show, for many Americans something other than—perhaps more than—church attendance records is at stake in these issues. In fact, prophesies of godlessness are absolutely essential to how citizens have defined the meaning of America, the practice of democracy, and ultimately the nation's future. This has been so in the past; it remains so today; and we are confident such prophesies will continue in the years to come.

NOTES

1. See Alfred Kazin, *God and the American Writer* (New York: Knopf, 1997). For excellent overviews of the history of American religion, see Jon Butler, Grant Wacker, and Randall Balmer, *Religion in American Life: A Short History* (New York: Oxford University Press, 2003), Edwin Gaustad and Leigh Schmidt, *A Religious History of America: The Heart of the American Story from Colonial Times to Today* (New York: HarperOne, 2004), and Roger Finke and Rodney Stark, *The Churching of America, 1776–2005: Winners and Losers in Our Religious Economy* (New Brunswick, N.J.: Rutgers University Press, 2005).

2. Stanley Cavell, "The Avoidance of Love: A Reading of *King Lear*," in *Must We Mean What We Say? A Book of Essays* (Cambridge: Cambridge University Press, 1976), 344–45.

3. John Judis and Ruy Teixeira, *The Emerging Democratic Majority* (New York: Scribner's, 2002), 5.

4. See Finke and Stark, *The Churching of America*.

5. Lytton Strachey, *Eminent Victorians* (New York: G.P. Putnam and Sons, 1918), preface, 5.

6. See Peter Berger, ed., *The Desecularization of the World: Resurgent Religion and World Politics* (Washington, D.C.: Eerdmans, 1999), and José Casanova, *Public Religions in the Modern World* (Chicago: University of Chicago Press, 1994). See also Casanova's essay "Rethinking Secularization," and the other articles collected in the special double issue of *The Hedgehog Review* 8, 1–2 (spring/summer 2006).

7. In constructing this book, we have made a conscious effort to concentrate on American prophesies of godlessness and godliness. We were tempted to devote more attention to Alexis de Tocqueville, as anyone who works on religion in America must be tempted; but as our theme is American prophets and then, secondarily, those

others (such as Auguste Comte) who had a discrete influence on American thinkers about these matters, extended attention to Tocqueville had to be forgone. One unexpected result of our research, in fact, is that we found that Tocqueville was more like other European observers of the American scene, including, for example, James Bryce, whose views were widely disseminated yet appear to have had relatively little distinct effect on American thinkers or voices in terms of prophesies about American religiosity. We must leave more study of Tocqueville to other books, and other scholars. It surprised us that Tocqueville did not play more central a role in this book; but the fact of his relative unimportance is itself telling.

8. See Jack Greene, *Pursuits of Happiness: The Social Development of Early Modern British Colonies and the Formation of American Culture* (Chapel Hill: University of North Carolina Press, 1988).

9. This is akin to the argument of historian Louis Hartz, who famously claimed that America is not a nonideological country; rather, he said, it is *entirely* an ideological country. See Louis Hartz, *The Liberal Tradition in America* (New York: Harcourt, Brace, 1955).

I

Puritans and Revolution: Remembering the Origin: Religion and Social Critique in Early New England

Wilson N. Brissett

The Puritans of New England remain famous for their prophesies of godlessness. Ministers in the Massachusetts Bay colony regularly preached sermons rebuking their congregations for sinfulness and predicting the disintegration of society if sinners were not willing to repent and reform. This type of preaching was so common in early New England that scholars have developed a name for it—the jeremiad tradition—that refers to the archetypal warning of moral declension identified with the ancient Hebrew prophet Jeremiah. It was such a narrative of the social deterioration of Europe that initially drove many of the first settlers to depart for Massachusetts. It could be said that the act of departing for the New World was itself a jeremiad; the history of the colony begins with a retreat from the corruptions of Europe to the wilderness of the New World to establish a society founded in purity and righteousness. This sense of an errand into the wilderness determined one powerful and influential interpretive framework for how many scholars and citizens have viewed the subsequent trajectory of American culture and history.

This essay aims to present these cultural forms within their initial context—that of seventeenth-century English covenant theology—and suggest how the jeremiad managed to stay relevant beyond the era of Puritan dominance.

The original Massachusetts project was tightly focused on the covenant goal of establishing the true worship of God on earth, and that remained its moral and civic force for at least 150 years. As such, the Puritan commonwealth provided a highly structured cultural system designed to promote godliness and discourage godlessness. The jeremiad is the primary literary artifact of that system, and its distinctive language illuminates the moral logic undergirding the Puritan civil project. In the eighteenth century, the powerful Enlightenment trends of political liberalism, Romantic aestheticism, and common-sense moralism would dismantle the Puritan "New England Way." But only once we have properly recognized the character of the initial Puritan ambition will we be able to identify the cultural modes that survived the founding era and endured, albeit in altered form, through American history.

Covenant Theology and the Jeremiad

In early Massachusetts, the dominant form of social critique was the jeremiad—that mode of sermonizing in which the preacher catalogued the sins of the community and threatened the congregation with the specter of divine punishment in order to call the people back to obedience. Over the first century of New England life, the jeremiad became a cultural ritual: a minister's response to a natural disaster, a wave of crime, or a change of political or military fortunes became an occasion for a collective warning intended to convince the congregation of their sins and bring them back to righteousness. Despite the overwhelmingly negative tone of the jeremiad sermons, their purpose remained the positive one of setting the community back on the straight and narrow path.

The jeremiad was the natural outgrowth of the Puritans' idea that their society was founded on a series of binding covenant agreements, the most fundamental of which was made with God himself. The sense of obligation to maintain these covenants, and the moral strictures they detailed, led to New England ministers' intense interest in taking the spiritual pulse of the community. The jeremiad sermons did not invoke an arbitrary set of moral rules but recalled the originary covenant agreement. In a moment of crisis, the jeremiad called the community back to its beginnings, to rededicate itself to the collective civic mission of the commonwealth. It was a very public strategy of prophesying godlessness in the hope of producing godliness as a sobered response from repentant audiences.

In Sacvan Bercovitch's classic study *The American Jeremiad*, the jeremiad is described as the cornerstone of a developing American middle-class ideology that optimistically hailed progress as it ritually ignored real social problems.[1]

Actual jeremiad texts, however, were a good deal less fantasy-driven than this thesis admits. The promised blessing in the jeremiad tradition of preaching was always conditional on repentance and reform. Subsequently, the jeremiad was appropriated in diverse ways, and did in some instances serve the bourgeois ideology Bercovitch defines. Preachers in later generations of Puritan New England, however, remained doggedly committed to advocating concrete reforms in their sermons, as we shall see, and later, post-Puritan crusaders insisted as well on the necessity of social transformation. If covenant theology regarded the misfortunes of the commonwealth as chastisement from an aggrieved deity, this did not prevent ministers from insisting on a response of social and personal reform in addition to one of prayer and repentance. Nor did it prevent early New Englanders from employing the jeremiad for purposes that seem today decidedly pragmatic and unreligious. In the end, the jeremiad served the dual purpose of remembrance of the past and reform for the future. It recalled the original covenant in order to correct the errant path of the present—a protection against the enticements of godlessness.

The Jeremiad at the Origin

Scholars disagree about the motivations underlying the Puritan migrations to New England, but clear documentary evidence remains of the stated goal of the members of the original Massachusetts Bay group.[2] They wanted to move to the new world in order to form a commonwealth that would support a fully reformed church, which many Puritans felt was lacking in seventeenth-century England. There may have been other goals, such as the possibility of altered economic and legal arrangements, but the promotional writings in support of relocating to Massachusetts make the religious motivation primary. Puritans argued that the Church of England had stymied the real goals of the Reformation, which included freeing the church from what they saw as superstitious ritual and a corrupt hierarchy. In 1620, John Winthrop wrote:

> All other Churches of Europe are brought to desolation, and our sins, from which the Lord begins already to frown upon us, and to cut us short do threaten evil times to be coming upon us, and who knows, but that God hath provided this place to be a refuge for many whom he means to save out of the general calamity, and seeing the Church hath no place left to fly into but the wilderness, what better work can there be, then to go and provide tabernacles and food for her against she comes thither.[3]

This statement frames the moral position of the covenant. The language of retreat into the "wilderness," which is a "place of refuge," in order to "provide tabernacles and food," is eschatological language that harks back to the ancient Israelite exodus from Egypt.[4] As the Israelites left Egypt for the wilderness to worship God, so the Puritans would flee the corruption of Europe to establish truly reformed worship in the wilderness of America. The first thing the Israelites did after they left Egypt was to form a covenant with God that promised blessing and protection in return for obedience to the Mosaic Law. The migration to America would be premised on a similar covenant, and the true church in the New World would be marked by its covenant faithfulness.

One of the more influential invocations of this covenant is in Winthrop's sermon "A Model of Christian Charity." He reportedly delivered this sermon to the first group of emigrants en route to Massachusetts:

> When God gives a special Commission he looks to have it strictly
> observed in every Article....Thus stands the cause between God and
> us, we are entered into Covenant with him for this work, we have
> taken out a Commission, the Lord hath given us leave to draw our
> own Articles[,] we have professed to enterprise the Actions upon
> these and these ends, we have hereupon besought him of favor and
> blessing: Now if the Lord shall please to hear us, and bring us in
> peace to the place we desire, then hath he ratified this Covenant and
> sealed our Commission, and will expect a strict performance of the
> Articles contained in it, but if we shall neglect the observation of
> these Articles which are the ends we have propounded, and dis-
> sembling with our God, shall fall to embrace this present world and
> prosecute our carnal intentions, seeking great things for ourselves
> and our posterity, the Lord will surely break out in wrath against us
> be revenged of such a perjured people and make us know the price of
> such a Covenant.[5]

This passage comes near the end of the sermon, beginning the famous section that includes the exhortation that the colonists be aware of their position as "a City upon a Hill" (42). At first glance, the passage looks almost simple-minded, arguing that if the ship arrives safely in the New World, they can be sure they have received God's blessing. But Winthrop's language is multilayered; he also connects the settlers' ocean crossing to the biblical pilgrimage of the chosen people to the Promised Land.[6] God has given the settlers a "special Commission," Winthrop says, just as God called Israel out of Egypt as a peculiar people, and these sorts of extraordinary callings are cemented with God in solemn agreements called covenants. In the covenant, God agrees to bless the people, and the people agree to follow the "Articles" laid out in the covenant. If they live up to these purposes, they will receive God's blessing; if they fail, God's wrath will be poured out on them.

Among the many reasons Winthrop gives for the emigration are escape from the corruption of European churches, revival of education, service of the greater Protestant church, the reduction of England's swelling population, the continuing opposition to the Catholic Church, and evangelizing the American Indian population.[7] Winthrop views these individual reasons as serving the greater end summed up in the original covenant agreement of the first Boston church: "To walk in all our ways according to the rule of Gospel."[8] Winthrop's use of the "City on a Hill" phrase from the Gospel of Matthew signals the proper scope of the gospel vision many of the Puritans embraced as their civic ideal. Many modern readers have understood Winthrop's use of this phrase as an exhortation that the colonists should aspire to build a civilization great enough to be emulated by other peoples around the Christian world. Winthrop's reference, however, strives first to describe a reality before it advocates any course of action—he realized that the Massachusetts community would be watched for good or ill, whether they succeeded or not. They would be watched because they were audaciously claiming special providence to achieve, more than any civilization that had gone before, a holy city that approximated true worship and just social order in obedience to God's commands and in an attempt to model the divine being in the very constitution and outworking of the society itself. It is precisely this sense of a providential civic undertaking that defined the serious moral matrix through which the Puritans understood the various crises (social, military, natural) that beset their community—and dictated the jealousy with which they guarded the godliness of their commonwealth.

But how was godliness defined? If gospel obedience is to be the end the colony labors toward, Winthrop argues in his sermon, love will be the measure of its success. The great danger in the Puritan experiment was the possibility of being "seduced [to] worship other Gods our pleasures, and profits, and serve them" (42). In this way, the people might "fall to embrace this present world and prosecute our carnal intentions, seeking great things for ourselves and our posterity" (41). The temptation is not the achievement of material success, since Winthrop anticipates prosperity as a sign of the ongoing blessing of God on the community. The primary motivation to be avoided in the drive for success is a primary concern with the establishment of one's personal prosperity at the expense of others'. For Winthrop, the theological doctrine of love indicates the necessity of social interdependence in the construction of a thriving godly commonwealth. In the middle part of the sermon, Winthrop explains how love forms the bonds that hold a society together. Only a true affection for others based in the "Sympathy of parts" (36) felt between members of the body of Christ is powerful enough to establish a "habit in a Soul" (35) where love orders every thought and action toward the benefit of neighbor and community. This civic connectedness will be the defining characteristic of Winthrop's glorious civilization, a society, bound by covenant, that continually points back to its larger dependence on the God who called its people to this project initially. Only this love, Winthrop insists, can motivate the citizens of Massachusetts to work for the common good in a way that glorifies God.

If this all sounds a bit too heavenly for the basis of a working society, Winthrop also gets down to details: the theological imperative of love is to be embodied socially in the commitment to economic justice.[9] He counsels the settlers to avoid narrow self-interest by practicing the three facets of the "duty of mercy": "Giving, lending, and forgiving" (30). The prosperous persons in the society are to labor for themselves and for others: "If thy brother be in want and thou canst help him, thou needst not make doubt, what thou shouldst do, if thou lovest god thou must help him" (32). So Winthrop's jeremiad, far from supporting a bourgeois mentality of personal gain, argues instead for a radical approach to economic relations that takes the theological virtue of love as a basis for material interdependence. In this way, the exhortation to charity in economic relations serves as a bulwark against Winthrop's fear of a possible decline into economic individualism and social disintegration.

Traditional Dissent

Although the covenant occupied a central place in early Massachusetts, not all Puritans shared the same view of its meaning. Even within the founding generation, the jeremiad was employed to advocate positions that differed dramatically from Winthrop's. In 1646, a pro-English group of dissenters brought a "Remonstrance and Petition" against Winthrop and other Massachusetts leaders, accusing them of exercising power in an arbitrary fashion. Their complaint, which was presented to the General Court as a legal document, takes the form of a jeremiad:

> The hand of our good God, who through his goodness hath safely brought us and ours through the great ocean and planted us here, seems not now to be with us, yea rather against us, blasting all our designs, though contrived with much deliberation, undertaken with

great care, and proceeding with more than ordinary probability of successful events, by which many of good estates are brought back to the brink of extreme poverty, yea at this time laying his just hand upon our families, taking many away to himself, striking others with unwonted malignant sickness, and with some shameful diseases.[10]

After this litany of misfortune, the writers quickly move on to address "the special causes of the Lords turning his face from us" (189). They decide that they "cannot, according to our judgment, discern a settled form of government according to the laws of England" (190). A set of reforms are suggested that would encode the laws of Massachusetts in better correspondence to English law. The petitioners end their discourse with a list of the blessings—including changes of fortune in regard to "merchandizing and shipping," "fishing," "husbandry," "mechanical traces," "staple commodities," and "foreign enemies"— that would ensue on acceptance of their proposed legal reforms: "These things being granted, by the blessing of God to us in Christ, we hope to see the now contemned ordinances of God highly prized, the gospel much darkened, break forth as the sun at noon day, christian charity and brotherly love, almost frozen, wax warm" (195).

This legal petition takes the classic form of the jeremiad, with its interpretation of a current social crisis as the result of corporate sin, its recommendation of changes that will bring the community back into the path of original obedience and avoid further judgment, and its description of the blessings to be enjoyed once obedience is secured through the enactment of the jeremiad's prescriptions. Even for those who diverged from the main course of church and state in early Massachusetts, preferring older English modes of governance and ecclesiology, the method of dissent was to make an appeal within the logic of covenant morality. In this way, the jeremiad served as a relatively flexible instrument for advocating various (sometimes contradictory) social reforms.

The Form Expands

The jeremiad would prove to be even more malleable in the coming years, both within Puritan culture and in the era of transition toward America's political independence. The jeremiads of the second and third generations in Massachusetts, for instance, maintained a similar balance of remembrance and reform, while often lionizing the founding generation as exemplars of covenant-keeping. Among these later ministers, the prophetic call to reform looked back not only to the original covenant but also to this golden age of faithfulness. The Halfway Covenant of 1662—by relaxing standards for church membership—became a flash point for such nostalgia. In some churches, membership came to be based on family connections instead of proof of conversion, and traditionalists felt the heart of Puritan religion had been attacked. Their response was to insist more emphatically on the necessity of heartfelt conversion, and before long a fresh religious movement arose that became instantly controversial for its renewed focus on emotionally charged religious experience.

In the 1740s, the revivals of this Great Awakening split New England clergy between those who supported the movement as a work of God and those who detested it as so much emotional claptrap. Jonathan Edwards found himself right in the middle of this battle, not only because of his central preaching role in the awakenings, but because he vigorously defended the spiritual movement in print. His major work on the subject, *Some Thoughts Concerning the Present Revival of Religion in New-England* (1743), attempted to be conciliatory; he refused, however, to soften his position on the importance of the revival:

> At a time when God manifests himself in such a great work for his church, there is no such thing as being neuters; there is a necessity of being either for or against the king that then gloriously appears: as when a king is crowned, and there are public manifestations of joy on that occasion, there is no such thing as standing by as an indifferent spectator; all must appear as loyal subjects, and express their joy on that occasion, or be accounted enemies.[11]

As is clear from both this work and his *History of the Work of Redemption* (1739/1774), Edwards regarded the awakenings as a unique movement of the spirit of God and a key prelude to the onset of the millennial reign of Christ on earth; those who did not support the revival and recognize the conversions it produced were opposing God.[12]

Nor was the revivalistic line of thinking revisionist in Edwards's mind. He understood the emphasis on lively preaching and emotional conversions as consistent with traditional Puritan teaching and practice. His own father and his maternal grandfather had each presided over similar revivals on a smaller scale—if the awakenings of the 1740s were more widespread than in the past, it was simply a sign that God's spirit was being poured out with more liberality and the age of the millennium was approaching more rapidly. This was cause for celebration, not censure, for supporters often saw the awakenings as a reformation from contemporary godlessness and a return, through experiences of true conversion, to the spiritual sincerity of the founding generation.

Edwards for a time was even convinced (and delighted) that God had chosen the American colonies as his springboard for the great push toward the dawn of the millennial age. In this he extended the conception, so firmly established by Winthrop, of America as a project of civilizational holiness, intended primarily to avoid the entrenched godlessness of Europe:

> God has made as it were two worlds here below, the old and the new (according to the names they are now called by), two great habitable continents, far separated one from the other. The latter is but newly discovered; it was formerly wholly unknown, from age to age, and it is as it were now but newly created: it had been till of late wholly the possession of Satan, the church of God having never been in it, as it has been in the other continent, from the beginning of the world. This new world is probably now discovered, that the new and most glorious state of God's church on earth might commence there; that God might in it begin a new world in a spiritual respect, when he creates the new heavens and new earth. . . . America has received the true religion of the old continent; the church of ancient times has been there, and Christ is from thence: but that there may be an equality, and inasmuch as that continent crucified Christ, they shall not have the honor of communicating religion in its most glorious state to us, but we to them. . . . And 'tis worthy to be noted that America was discovered about the time of the Reformation, or but little before.[13]

The stakes, as far as Edwards was concerned, could not have been higher. The civic projects under way in the American colonies, and especially in the godly commonwealth of Massachusetts, made up the vanguard of the coming kingdom of God on earth. The awakenings stood as the key movement of God in initiating this new age, and so opposition from those who were wary of the excesses of the revivals was read as advocacy of godlessness, plain and simple.

Edwards's warning to pastors against standing aloof during the awakenings should be understood as a condemnation of those who thought they could weather the storm by not taking sides. If the millennial work of God is hindered by the reluctance of his people to respond to it, Edwards warns, woe unto those who make up the faction of the unwilling. America stands on the brink, as it were, and the choice lies before its people to participate centrally in God's renewal of the entire earth, or to sink into the same corruption that is plaguing Europe—whose people, Edwards asserts, were broadly responsible for the crucifixion of Jesus. The scope of the original covenant in New England is vastly expanded in Edwards's writings, as befits the expanded historical consciousness of the dawning Enlightenment era; but this vision is still cast within the jeremiad framework—in this case, the protection of the redemptive role of America in an expanding world that is increasingly tied together by transatlantic networks of learning, science, and evangelical religion.

Antislavery Jeremiads

If Edwards's millennial optimism was notably intellectual rather than practical, his theology nonetheless had vast influence on one of the more politically engaged Calvinists of the revolutionary era.[14] One good example of his intellectual legacy lies in Revolutionary-era debates about American slavery. Samuel Hopkins studied with Edwards for eight months after his graduation from Yale, and for seven years held a pulpit in a town only seven miles away from Edwards's Northampton. Before he took up a call from a church in Newport, Rhode Island, Hopkins shared Edwards's view that slavery was justified as long as slaves were treated kindly and evangelized. Newport, however, gave Hopkins a closer view of both the realities of the slave trade and the thinness of the arguments that Rhode Islanders, living richly off its exploitation of black labor, made for its justification. By the 1770s, Hopkins was a leading antislavery spokesman.[15]

Hopkins did not need to search for a new mode of discourse to frame his antislavery arguments; he had the perfect vehicle already at hand in the jeremiad tradition. A sermon he preached in August 1776 employs, in part, Edwardsian ideas as well as liberal political thought to support his arguments; he even quotes from the newly written Declaration of Independence. But the moral vocabulary for his diatribe against the people is strictly traditional:

> True Religion depends on Just notions of the Deity, but the master
> is daily giving his Slaves, and Whole house false notions of God.
> 'tis the care of every Religious Householder to represent God to
> his Household as infinitely king gracious and merciful, full of good
> will to them and Loth that they Should be miserable, and persuade
> them by the Mercies of God to present their bodies a living Sacrifice
> holy acceptable &c—but Master represents God as cruel, unmerci-
> ful and unkind, having made creatures to make them miserable,
> which is a character worse then the Devil's. . . . Can we wonder that
> Religion is done to decay in our Land, that vice and profaneness have
> overspread the whole Land, when the Ever glorious God has been
> blasphemed openly in the practice of Slavery among us for So long a

time? or can we wonder that God is now breaking us down and plucking us up, and thretning Soon to make us no people who have So long blasphemed his holy name that is Seases now to be any longer a refuge for us, affords no plea in our favour, but is really against us, God being obliged for the Glory of his own name now to destroy us from being any Longer a people if we will not reforme.[16]

Hopkins marshals the jeremiad's remarkably flexible net to catch the problem of slavery at once within both the Calvinist moral language of collective sin and the emerging American liberal political discourse of equal rights and republican self-rule. He invokes the original gospel mission of New England to establish a people set apart for God, worshiping God in purity, for the purpose of bringing greater glory (that is, truer representation) to God's name around the world. The broad civic awareness of this mission becomes clear in this case, where prophetic judgment understands the integrity of the social fabric as bound irrevocably to the eradication of the moral evil of slavery.

Underwriting the New Order

We have seen how the tradition was flexible enough to allow expression of serious dissent from the dominant Puritan position but stable enough to maintain the core of moral and religious identity. The flexibility of the form, an aspect that arguably kept it vital during the time of the Puritan ascendancy in New England, also rendered it useful during the massive social and cultural transformations of the Revolutionary era. If Samuel Hopkins's sermon tied the fate of the nation, in the Revolutionary era, to the maintenance of the New England covenant, most revolutionaries found ways to employ the jeremiad form of social critique without insisting on its Puritan context. Up to this point, the vicissitudes within the jeremiad tradition have not taken us very far from the essential commitments of the Puritan founders.

Yet that would soon change. In fact, a large aspect of the necessary cultural work of the Revolution, at least in the Northeast, was the transferal of the originary imagination of American society from its basis in the godly covenant of Massachusetts to a new focus on the social contract of liberal political thinkers. In this respect, the *novus ordo seclorum*, or new order of the ages, that signaled for many the great transition into the era of liberal democracy, also involved a profound cultural shift whereby the rhetoric of national destiny, which had been significantly shaped by the gospel-oriented covenant logic of Puritan

Massachusetts, was newly centered around the autonomy of the people to determine their own best form of government.[17] The covenant language would often be retained, but the developing rhetoric of social critique in republican America would shift the jeremiad significantly away from much of its original Puritan context. Before the dawn of the nineteenth century, indeed, the great power of Enlightenment strands of thought had taken their toll on Puritan culture more broadly, loosening the grip of traditional thinking.

But still, new jeremiads attempted to buttress the moral purity of American society against new forms of godlessness. The jeremiad tradition of remembering the origin in order to correct the trajectory of the present resurfaced as a useful tool in the political liberalism of Thomas Jefferson and the Romantic individualism of Henry David Thoreau, to name two prominent examples. It would also become central to Abraham Lincoln's political project of maintaining national unity in the wake of civil war. In these later jeremiads, the origin has completed the shift that began in Hopkins's dual reliance on covenant and Declaration—the shift from foundational religious covenant to primary political documents. What remains is the power of the strong moral language of the jeremiad tradition to maintain a viable mode of social critique that seeks to avert the possibility of a slide into godlessness by issuing a call of faithfulness to the binding commitments of the founding moment.

NOTES

1. See introduction to *The American Jeremiad* (Madison: University of Wisconsin Press, 1978).

2. For a nice summary of some dominant scholarly positions, see Emory Elliott, *Early American Literature* (New York: Cambridge University Press, 2002), 31–32.

3. From "Reasons to Be Considered, and Objections with Answers," *Winthrop Papers*, vol. 2 (Boston: Massachusetts Historical Society, 1931), 138–39. I have modernized the spelling in this and all other passages quoted in this text.

4. See, for example, Exodus 3:12, 5:1, 8:1, 9:1, 9:13, 10:3.

5. John Winthrop, "A Modell of Christian Charity," in Michael Warner, ed., *American Sermons* (New York: Penguin Putnam, 1990), 41. (Subsequent references are cited by page number in the text.)

6. See especially p. 43 for the drift of Winthrop's language toward the Exodus narrative.

7. A full list can be found in Winthrop, "Reasons to Be Considered," 138–40.

8. Quoted in Francis J. Bremer, *John Winthrop: America's Forgotten Founding Father* (Oxford: Oxford University Press, 2003), 192.

9. I use "economic justice" in its familiar contemporary sense, even though it is probably anachronistic to the Puritan context.

10. Thomas Hutchinson, *Collection of Papers* (Boston: Thomas and John Fleet, 1769), 188–89. (Subsequent references are cited by page number in the text.)

11. *The Works of Jonathan Edwards*, vol. 4, ed. C. C. Goen (New Haven: Yale University Press, 1972), 349.

12. Jonathan Edwards' *A History of the Work of Redemption* originally issued as a series of thirty sermons in 1739; uncompleted during Edwards' lifetime, the sermons on his expansive vision of salvific history were subsequently published in expanded form in 1774 in Scotland.

13. Ibid., 354–55.

14. On Edwards's influence more broadly in the abolitionist movement, see Kenneth Minkema and Harry S. Stout, "The Edwardsean Tradition and the Anti-slavery Debate, 1740–1865," *Journal of American History* 92, 1 (2005): 47–74.

15. Jonathan D. Sassi, " 'This whole country have their hands full of Blood this day': Transcription and Introduction of an Antislavery Sermon Manuscript Attributed to the Reverend Samuel Hopkins," *Proceedings of the American Antiquarian Society* 112, 1 (2002): 42–49.

16. Ibid., 70.

17. Nathan O. Hatch, *The Democratization of American Christianity* (New Haven: Yale University Press, 1989), 17–46.

2

The Early Republic: Thomas Jefferson's Philosophy of History and the Future of American Christianity

Johann N. Neem

On June 26, 1822, from his home at Monticello, Thomas Jefferson wrote a letter to Dr. Benjamin Waterhouse in Massachusetts prophesying America's religious future. In his letter, Jefferson laid out the main tenets of his Unitarian faith—a Christianity purified of mystery and compatible with reason—and then proclaimed that all Americans would soon embrace similar beliefs: "I trust that there is not a *young man* now living in the United States," Jefferson wrote, "who will not die an Unitarian." Nearing the end of his life, Jefferson imagined a glorious future in which a Christianity based on reason rather than faith would become America's civil religion.[1]

Jefferson's prophecy was mistaken. To understand how he could be so confident, and so wrong, it is necessary to probe Jefferson's philosophy of historical progress, which itself proved inaccurate.

Jefferson, while more extreme in his religious views than many other American founders, is representative of their ideas of history and its meliorating effect on religion. As Alexis de Tocqueville observed just a few years after Jefferson's passing, "The philosophers of the eighteenth century had a very simple explanation for the gradual attenuation of religious belief. Religious zeal, they said, was bound to dwindle as liberty and enlightenment increased. Unfortunately, the facts do not bear this theory out."[2] This chapter will examine the tenets of Jefferson's philosophy of history to explain why Jefferson and others of his generation believed that the religion of the future would be less prone to fanaticism and more compatible with the tenets of Enlightenment reason.

Every Human Excellence

Jefferson's religious beliefs have been a source of much controversy. In his own time, his opponents called him an infidel and atheist, even claiming that a vote for Jefferson was "rebellion against God." Jefferson's private correspondence suggests, however, that he considered his opponents the true enemies of Christianity. They perverted Jesus' true teachings and relied on a complex artifice of lies and mystery to keep the people in ignorance. To Jefferson, most of America's ministers were "the real Anti-Christ."[3]

Jefferson considered himself one of Jesus' true disciples. He proclaimed, "I am a Christian, in the only sense he [Jesus] wished one to be; sincerely attached to his doctrines, in preference to all others; ascribing to himself every *human* excellence." Jefferson was a very different type of Christian from most Americans then or today. To him, Jesus embodied the perfect human being but nothing more. Jesus' excellence was "*human* excellence." The only reasonable explanation for popular belief in Jesus' divinity, Jefferson thought, was the long alliance between ministers and the state that kept the people in ignorance. Jefferson, like Tom Paine, was a Deist. He believed in a god who created the world and humanity and who established the laws of nature, including those of human nature. Deists considered faith an unreliable foundation for religious belief. Instead, religious questions, like any other questions, should be placed under the microscope of reason.[4]

In a 1787 letter to his nephew Peter Carr, written while Jefferson was the American ambassador in Paris, he advised Carr to "shake off all the fears & servile prejudices under which weak minds are servilely crouched. Fix reason firmly in her seat, and call to her tribunal every fact, every opinion." This questioning extended to religion: "Question with boldness even the existence of a god; because, if there be one, he must more approve of the homage of reason than that of blindfolded fear. . . . But those facts in the bible which contradict the laws of nature, must be examined with more care, and under a variety of faces." It was more likely that the Bible and ministers were incorrect than that the laws of nature would change. For example, Jefferson noted, the book of Joshua says that the sun stood still for several hours, but any reasonable person knows that this cannot be true. The same is true of the Immaculate Conception. Is it really possible, Jefferson wondered, that Jesus "was begotten by god, born of a virgin" in a manner that "suspended & reversed the laws of nature"? Such a preposterous claim must be dismissed for the more likely one that he was "a man of illegitimate birth, of a benevolent heart, enthusiastic mind, who set out without pretensions to divinity." Jefferson concluded, "Your own reason is the only oracle given you by heaven, and you are answerable not for the rightness but uprightness of the decision."[5]

Jesus' teachings were the "the purest system of morals ever before preached to man," Jefferson believed, because they were compatible with human nature. Following thinkers of the Scottish Enlightenment, Jefferson considered people naturally virtuous. The Creator had endowed each person with an innate moral sense capable of distinguishing between right and wrong. To Jefferson, "the Creator would indeed have been a bungling artist, had he intended man for a social animal, without planting in him social dispositions." In 1813 he wrote Carr: "Man was destined for society. His morality therefore was to be formed to this object. He was endowed with a sense of right & wrong merely relative to this. This sense is as much a part of his nature as the sense of hearing, seeing, feeling; it is the true foundation of morality." Jesus taught us what we knew to be true when we listened to our moral sense.[6]

Because each person has a moral sense, it mattered little whether or not a citizen believed in a god. As Jefferson (in)famously wrote in his *Notes on the State of Virginia*, "It does me no injury for my neighbor to say there are twenty gods, or no god. It neither picks my pocket nor breaks my leg." He repeated this claim in an 1814 letter. Belief in a god is not the basis of morality, since "if we did a good act merely from the love of God and a belief that it is pleasing to Him, whence arises the morality of the Atheist?" He continued, "It is idle to say, as some do, that no such being exists." The only conclusion was that atheists' "virtue . . . must have some other foundation than the love of God," namely the moral sense.[7]

Monkish Ignorance

Like other late eighteenth-century Enlightenment thinkers, Jefferson considered human reason the moving force of history. Over time, reason replaced ignorance and inherited custom with true knowledge of the natural and human worlds. As historian Henry May writes, many Enlightenment thinkers "were sure they lived in a new age. For them, Enlightenment was an unsparing sunrise, revealing the wickedness and folly of ancient ideas and institutions, illuminating also the fundamental goodness of man." The American Revolution was a case in point. Through reason, humanity sundered the chains in which monarchs had kept them bound for so long. Once the chains were broken, humanity was free to organize society according to, as Jefferson put it in the Declaration of Independence, "the laws of nature and of nature's God." Jefferson was so confident that the Revolution had purified the past and revived natural man with his innate moral sense that he suggested, "State a moral case to a ploughman & a professor. The former will decide it as well, & often better than the latter, because he has not been led astray by artificial rules." Stripped by reason of their tyrannical power, neither politicians nor priests, nor professors for that matter, could corrupt pure American citizens.[8]

Like many other Americans, Jefferson considered the Revolution the harbinger of a *novus ordo seclorum*, a new order of the ages. The Revolution, Jefferson believed, had wiped away past custom and "presented us an album on which we were free to write what we pleased." In 1826, he looked back at the Revolution as initiating a process in which "all eyes are opened, or opening, to the rights of man." The Revolution had taught "the mass of mankind" that they had "not been born with saddles on their backs, nor a favored few booted and spurred, ready to ride them legitimately, by the grace of God." Jefferson was thankful that Americans had "burst the chains of monkish ignorance and superstition" that had kept humanity in darkness for so long and looked forward to a future characterized by the "unbounded exercise of reason and freedom of opinion."[9]

Not all Americans agreed with Jefferson. While many Americans considered the Revolution the beginning of a new order, they were uncertain how to adapt their religious heritage to their republican future. Ministers had given vital support to the Revolutionary cause, especially in New England, where they considered the fight against Britain part of their larger effort to revitalize covenantal theology. In an election sermon the Rev. Samuel Cooper preached the day Massachusetts's new post-Revolutionary government went into effect, he reminded the elected leaders that Massachusetts had been settled "as a refuge from tyranny." Like the people of ancient Israel, the Puritans had been "led into a wilderness" and "pursued through the sea, by the armed hand of power." In the New World, they engaged in "a covenant, a compact a mutual stipulation" to live under God's laws. Cooper admitted that "we want not, indeed, a special revelation from heaven to teach us that men are born equal and free." This idea could be gained through the use of reason, itself a gift from God. But it was also revealed in Scripture. Like Joshua, the rulers of Massachusetts now entered into "a solemn renewal of this covenant."[10]

Although most states disestablished the church after the Revolution, New England continued to provide taxes to promote public religion—until 1818 in

Connecticut, 1819 in New Hampshire, and 1833 in Massachusetts. John Adams defended Massachusetts's tax-supported church as the most efficient way to ensure a virtuous citizenry. Outside New England, Pennsylvania's famous education reformer Benjamin Rush, a friend of both Adams and Jefferson, argued that Christianity was necessary to maintain public morality. In Jefferson's home state, Patrick Henry urged citizens to maintain tax support for churches, even as Jefferson and James Madison were pushing for the complete separation of church from state. Despite these disagreements, Jefferson remained confident that history would prove him correct.[11]

The Only Effectual Agents against Error

Jefferson's confidence grew out of his philosophy of history. So long as the freedom of speech is protected, Jefferson argued, reason will defeat error in the public sphere. Once we are freed from error, or enlightened, human nature will lead us to Jesus' pure morality. But progress is never certain. Citizens must vigilantly protect the separation of church and state to prevent backsliding. This final claim was crucial. Jefferson did not believe that historical progress was inevitable; it was up to people to ensure that history moved forward.

It is worth contrasting Jefferson's conception of history with those of two of his contemporaries, both philosophers of history: Immanuel Kant and Jean-Antoine-Nicolas de Caritat, marquis de Condorcet. In his "Idea for a Universal History" (1784), Kant sought "to discover a regular progression" in history that transcended what seems "confused and fortuitous" to individuals. Kant was confident that the human race was "unwittingly guided in their advance along a course intended by nature." What, he asked, is the relationship between our freely willed actions and progress? He answered that history is moving toward universal enlightenment, guided by social processes beyond any person's control. The end of history would be a "universal *cosmopolitan* existence," that is, a global civil society ruled by law. Kant admitted that his philosophy of history was not a substitute for "empirical" study but rather a perspective on the past according to which "it may be assumed that nature does not work without a plan and purposeful end, even amidst the arbitrary play of human freedom." Although Jefferson shared Kant's goal of a peaceful world order under the rule of law, he could not share Kant's belief that this was Nature's inexorable plan.[12]

Jefferson would have viewed with equal skepticism the words of his Parisian friend Condorcet. Even more than Kant, Condorcet was certain that the progress of science over the past two centuries was proof of history's ultimate trajectory. We can prophesy "the future on the basis of the past," Condorcet argued. In the natural world, the observation of phenomena gives rise to scientific laws. So, too, in the human world. An empirical examination of human progress over the past two centuries proved beyond a doubt that history was moving toward "the true perfection of mankind." Condorcet anticipated a time "when the sun will shine only on free men who know no other master but their reason; when tyrants and slaves, priests and their stupid hypocritical instruments will exist only in works of history, and on the stage."[13] In a 1799 letter, Jefferson agreed "with Condorcet" that humankind's "mind is perfectible to a degree of which we cannot yet form any conception." When Jefferson examined the past, he also saw the progress made by science. He considered it "cowardly" to believe that "the human mind is incapable of further advances," adding that this false belief is the doctrine of "despots." But history taught Jefferson another lesson as well: how easily progress can be thwarted. Progress depends on human beings, not on universal laws. Nowhere in Jefferson's writings does one get a sense that the eighteenth-century revolutions in knowledge, politics, and religion are inevitable and secure. Instead, one often senses Jefferson's fear that progress could easily be turned back if the wrong people come to power.[14]

In *Notes on the State of Virginia*, Jefferson wrote: "Reason and free enquiry are the only effectual agents against error. Give a loose to them, they will support true religion, by bringing every false one to their tribunal, to the test of their investigation. They are the natural enemies of error." He continued, "Reason and experiment [in the sciences] have been indulged, and error has fled before them. It is error alone which needs the support of government. Truth can stand by itself." Jefferson was confident "that truth is great and will prevail if left to herself." Reason, guaranteed its freedom in the public sphere by the First Amendment, would divest Christianity "of the rags in which they [the ministers of the established churches] have enveloped it."[15]

Reason would restore Christianity to its "original purity and simplicity." More colorfully, Jefferson wrote that "abstracting what is really his [Jesus'] from the rubbish in which it is buried, easily distinguished by its luster from the dross of his biographers, and as separable from that as the diamond from the dunghill, we have the outlines of a system of the most sublime morality which has ever fallen from the lips of man." Strip away all the things that are incompatible with reason—miracles, the Immaculate Conception, the Trinity—and we are left with a noble code of ethics. The Bible, after all, was written by humans and embodies human errors. In 1823, Jefferson wrote confidently that "the day will come when the mystical generation of Jesus, by the supreme being as his father in the womb of a virgin will be classed with the fable of the generation of Minerva in the brain of Jupiter. But we may hope that the dawn of reason and freedom of thought in these United States will do away with all this artificial scaffolding, and restore us to the primitive and genuine doctrines of this the most venerated reformer of human errors."[16]

The key to progress was the separation of church and state. In his 1802 address to the Baptists of Danbury, Connecticut, Jefferson called for a "wall of separation" between church and state. Progress was possible only if ministers could not use the state to propagate their lies. As historian Joyce O. Appleby writes, Jefferson believed that "if the authoritarian institutions of the past"— none more so than the established church—"could be reformed, then a different and happier future could be imagined." To Jefferson, the separation of church and state was a necessary means toward his ultimate end: a Christianity premised in reason and compatible with human nature. Committed to the purification of Christianity through the free exercise of reason, Jefferson wrote a friend soon after his election to the presidency, "I have sworn on the altar of god, eternal hostility against every form of tyranny over the mind of man." If Jefferson had his way, ministers of the church would never again be allowed to use state power to limit free inquiry.[17]

According to Jefferson, Americans must consciously protect the separation of church and state for progress to occur. Progress was the work of human activity, not of impersonal historical processes. Decades before Hegel, Comte, and Marx, Jefferson prophesied the future on the basis of past experience, not an abstract faith in historical necessity. In fact, he worried that if the separation of church and state was not maintained, Americans would fall back into ignorance. Enlightenment required constant human vigilance.[18]

Vigilance was all the more necessary, Jefferson believed, because progress was not a law of history but a fact of recent American history. His skepticism may have had to do with his grounding in English Whig thought. English Whigs, trained in the tradition of classical republicanism, believed that liberty is fragile and that all free societies are prone to what eighteenth-century writers called "corruption." The history of earlier times, particularly that of Rome, proved that free societies lose their freedom when citizens and their leaders value their own interests more than the common good. The history of all societies was cyclic. At first, citizens value their liberty and are willing to sacrifice for the common good. In time, however, they turn inward, valuing their own material welfare over others', and the common good is abandoned. In Gordon S. Wood's words, American colonists believed that "the history of particular nations and peoples, whatever may have been the history of mankind in general, was not a linear progression, but a variable organic cycle of birth, maturity, and death, in which states, like the human body, carried within themselves the seed of their own dissolution." History was filled with examples of liberty gained and lost. Jefferson constantly worried that the cycle would repeat itself in the new United States.[19]

Jefferson hoped to break the classical cycle and redirect history toward sustained progress. He was hopeful about the future. He condemned those who espoused the "Gothic idea that we are to look backwards, instead of forwards for the improvement of the human mind." In his final letter, written just days before his death, Jefferson looked back on the years of his life and, thinking of the American Revolution in particular, wrote: "All eyes are opened, or opening, to the rights of man. The general spread of science has already laid open to every view the palpable truth" that people are born free and capable of governing themselves. The light of human reason had illuminated the essential truths, the "laws of nature and of nature's God," and it was up to human beings to embrace these laws and ensure continued progress toward political and religious liberty.[20]

Jefferson's philosophy of history was influenced by the Scottish Enlightenment's theory of historical stages. According to Scottish thinkers, especially Adam Ferguson, history demonstrates that societies develop over time, moving from the barbaric stage through the agrarian stage to the present stage of polite commercial society.[21] Jefferson invoked Scottish stages of history theory in reference to Native Americans. In an 1824 letter, he commented that the North American continent exhibited peoples at various stages of development. Starting at the Rocky Mountains and moving east, a traveler would first observe peoples "in the earliest stage of association living under no law but that of nature." Continuing, the traveler would find Indians in "the pastoral state," relying primarily on agriculture. Reaching the American frontier, the traveler would be confronted by "our own semi-barbarous citizens, the pioneers of advanced civilization." If the traveler continued east, "he would meet the gradual shades of improving man until he would reach his, as yet, most improved state in our seaport towns." This survey, Jefferson asserted, "is equivalent to a survey, in time, of the progress of man." Reflecting on how his own Albemarle County had changed since he was a youth living on what then seemed the edge of civilization, he concluded: "Barbarism has . . . been receding before the steady step of amelioration; and will in time, I trust, disappear from the earth."[22]

Jefferson's survey of "the progress of man" does not imply that history will inevitably advance. As his concerns about corruption demonstrate, forward movement requires human effort. Jefferson urged Native Americans to move from the "earliest stage" of civilization to the advanced stage reached by the United States, but it was up to them, not to the forces of history, to do so. As Jefferson put it in his Second Inaugural Address, Americans must prepare Indians "for that state of society, which to bodily comforts adds the improvement of the mind and morals." But Indians had to *choose* progress. Jefferson told Native Americans in 1808: "It depends on yourselves alone to become a numerous and great people." Jefferson urged Indians to give up their savage ways and become yeomen. Otherwise, they would be overwhelmed by white settlers moving west. In essence, Jefferson told Native Americans to get on the right side of history or be annihilated—a threat Andrew Jackson would later fulfill.[23]

Jefferson favored the modern age over the past. He considered modernity to be the result of conscious human action. Native Americans could embrace the modern world or live in the past, he asserted. American citizens had the same choice when it came to religion. They could erect a "wall of separation" between church and state, allow free inquiry to purify Christianity, and establish educational institutions that would promote rather than hinder scientific knowledge. Or they could continue to allow the ministers of the church to keep the people in ignorance. It was up to them.

The Only Safe Depositories

Ultimately, Jefferson believed, the people are the "only safe depositories" for power. Thus only the people could protect and promote progress. Politicians and ministers would always advance their own interests, so public oversight was essential. Only the people could break the dangerous historical cycle that led to corruption and tyranny. That is why Jefferson feared the federal government's expansion under George Washington and John Adams during the 1790s. Jefferson saw in the Federalists a conspiracy to rob the people of the liberties won in 1776. This conspiracy was made more dangerous by the alliance between Federalist politicians and the New England clergy. Virtuous citizens must stop the Federalists from moving history backward, Jefferson argued.[24]

In Jefferson's opinion, the election of 1800 pitted the forces of the future against those of the past. On the one side were Federalist politicians and ministers, apostles of "bigotry in Politics & Religion" who would "bring back the times of Vandalism, when ignorance put everything into the hands of power & priestcraft." Federalists had "hood-winked" American citizens "from their principles." Despite Federalist efforts to crush free inquiry with the 1798 Sedition Act, Jefferson and his Republican allies had awakened the people to the impending danger. The election of 1800 demonstrated that "the band is removed, and now they [the people] see for themselves." In his 1801 inaugural address, Jefferson argued that Americans must constantly strive to remain true to the "natural" and pure principles of 1776. No innate law of history had freed humanity from the shackles of the past and given them political and religious liberty; instead, "the wisdom of our sages and blood of our heroes had been devoted to their attainment." History was a product of human agency, and it was equally possible to move backward as well as forward. When we stray from the path, Jefferson urged, "let us hasten to retrace our steps and to regain the road which alone leads to peace, liberty, and safety."[25]

The greatest threats to political and religious liberty were the evil intentions of political and religious leaders. The only way to ensure historical progress was to protect free inquiry by separating church and state. But a problem remained. If the people were the only check against progress's enemies, and they had been "hood-winked" once, might they be hoodwinked again? This was a serious conundrum for Jefferson, one he devoted much intellectual energy to resolving. One answer was to insulate citizens as much as possible from power. Believing that each person was born with a moral sense, Jefferson sought to protect people's natural virtue from corruption. For this reason Jefferson celebrated the yeoman. God had made yeomen "his peculiar deposit for substantial and genuine virtue," Jefferson wrote. On his own farm, not owing his livelihood to any other, each yeoman would remain independent of politicians, ministers, and the relations of dependence created by mercantile commerce. His independence would be his salvation. "Those who labour in the earth are the chosen people of God," concluded Jefferson.[26]

Jefferson also believed that citizens should be educated. If ignorance was the source of tyrants' power, education would be the tool of liberty. Following the Revolution, Jefferson proposed an ambitious program to educate all boys in Virginia at public expense. Although people are born with a moral sense, it can be weak, and thus "minds must be improved to a certain degree." Education in a republic would be different from "the education of our ancestors," however, because it would embrace the knowledge gained by reason. American educational institutions must break from the past and remove from the professoriate the ministers of the church who had kept people in the dark for so long. As Virginia's governor, Jefferson had wanted to remove all professors of theology from his alma mater, the College of William and Mary. "Science is progressive," he argued, and "what was useful two centuries ago is now become useless, e.g. one half of the professorships of Wm & Mary."[27]

Giving up on his alma mater, Jefferson turned his sights to establishing a new university to teach scientific knowledge about the natural and human worlds. He considered this institution, which would become the University of

Virginia, one of his crowning achievements. Jefferson's call for a secular university was radical at a time when almost all American colleges remained tied to a denomination. Jefferson was certain that progress depends on the victory of science over faith. He faced much resistance from Baptists and Presbyterians in his home state, but this was one battle he was determined to win. In his 1818 report to the commissioners supervising the establishment of the university, he condemned the view "that to secure ourselves where we are, we must tread with awful reverence in the footsteps of our fathers." To ensure that the university served its public mission of promoting truth, Jefferson wanted "no professor of divinity; and the rather as the proofs of the being of a God, the creator, preserver, and supreme ruler of the universe, the author of all the relations of morality, and of the laws and obligations these infer, will be within the province of the professor of ethics." Rather than support a particular faith Jefferson hoped that his university would promote as "the general religion a religion of peace, reason and morality."[28]

A Threatening Cloud of Fanaticism

Jefferson's fear of corruption tempered his faith in progress. In his 1822 prophecy to Waterhouse, he moved quickly from confidence to concern. "I fear," Jefferson wrote, "that when this great truth"—the pure teachings of Jesus as espoused by Unitarians—"shall be established, its votaries will fall into the fatal error of fabricating formulas of creed and confessions of faith." History might repeat itself if free inquiry was not continuously protected. If Unitarians became the sole keepers of the faith, they would destroy "the religion of Jesus" as the church ministers before them had done. But Jefferson sensed a more immediate threat to progress: the growth of evangelical Christianity in America. He worried that evangelicals would destroy what he and the Revolutionary generation had sacrificed to create. "The atmosphere of our country is unquestionably charged with a threatening cloud of fanaticism," he commented sadly.[29]

In this instance, his prophecy would prove well founded. Jefferson made his Unitarian prophecy at a time when the United States was undergoing one of the most intense and transformative moments in its religious history. American Christians were abandoning the shackles of the past, not to embrace Unitarianism and reason but rather to encourage the revival of faith-based Christianity. In what has come to be known as the Second Great Awakening, evangelical Christians from various denominations argued that religion, while

voluntary, is the foundation of American civil society. Forgoing their past reliance on the state, they claimed that religion would prove more powerful if it
was officially separated from the state. They did not seek a "wall of separation"
as impermeable as Jefferson's, to be sure, but they concluded that competition
and voluntary choice would effectively promote the cause of faith. They were
correct. The number of Americans attending churches rose dramatically during
the 1820s and after. Some historians have argued that it was only during the
Second Great Awakening that America became a "Christian nation." Needless
to say, this was not the historical process Jefferson had envisioned.[30]

One of the leaders of the Second Great Awakening was the New England
Congregational minister Lyman Beecher. Beecher had been a minister in
Connecticut, where he had opposed disestablishment of the church in 1818.
But Beecher discovered that voluntarism was a blessing in disguise. Connecticut's ministers could no longer rest on their laurels but, "cut loose from
dependence on state support," had to rely "wholly on their own resources and
on God." In 1826, Beecher took over Park Street Church in Boston so as to
attack the cancer of Unitarianism at its source. He vigorously recruited new
converts, and he relied on voluntary associations to bring more people into the
church.[31]

Despite his ambition and confidence, Beecher feared that he would lose
the battle if American Protestants did not redouble their efforts. He was particularly concerned by the growing number of Catholic immigrants. Many
American voters and politicians also remained hostile to his effort to increase
Protestant Christianity's public influence. Jacksonian Democrats, for example,
spurned Beecher's effort to enforce the Sabbath, accusing him of seeking a
union between church and state. Beecher concluded that as the center of the
American population shifted west, unless Americans on the frontier could be
brought into the church, the progress of American Protestantism would falter.
In his famous sermon entitled "Plea for the West" (1835), Beecher called on all
American Protestants to help support missionaries and plant new churches
and seminaries on the frontier.[32]

Beecher was another important American prophet of godlessness. He
worried that America would become less religious unless Christians worked
hard to further the cause of faith. Beecher's efforts proved more successful
than Jefferson's. He helped pioneer the voluntary association as a tool for both
personal salvation and the moral reformation of society. In voluntary associations, Americans signed up to battle sin and in the process affirmed their
commitment to their god. Beecher discovered that he could embrace the Jeffersonian commitment to the separation of church and state, because "voluntary efforts, societies, missions, and revivals . . . [allowed ministers to] exert a

deeper influence than ever they could by queues, and shoe-buckles, and cocked hats, and gold-headed canes." In the 1810s and after, Americans' efforts to fight godlessness took on cosmic proportions, as ministers and their congregants formed and joined thousands of voluntary associations. Americans joined Sabbatarian societies to ensure respect for the Sabbath, Bible societies to spread the Word to every household in America, and temperance societies to aid Americans in avoiding the sinful dangers of drink. Beecher transformed the voluntary association into a popular agent of change and empowered thousands of ordinary citizens to participate in public life. And despite Jefferson's prediction, the majority of Americans celebrated their freedom by promoting faith rather than abandoning it.[33]

Thanks in part to Beecher's efforts, America became a more Christian nation and remains today an outlier among Western nations that experienced the Enlightenment. Perhaps ironically, Jefferson's "wall of separation" protected Christianity from the state as much as it protected the state from Christianity. In another way, however, Jefferson was correct. The progress of reason was not inevitable. If anything, Americans became more religious during the years of the early American republic. No historical processes inevitably ensure the victory of reason over faith. Humans make their own history.

Jefferson's misguided prophecy, like those of others discussed in this book, was not the product of ignorance. Rather, it suggests the power of ideas in shaping the ways intellectuals view the world. Jefferson was an acute observer of the world and was committed to basing his conclusions on empirical evidence. Yet he remained confident that America would become Unitarian. He certainly noticed the growth of evangelical Christianity, but his own theory of progress, premised on his study of history and the experience of the American Revolution, confirmed his belief that reason would overcome error. His misplaced confidence in a future based on reason reminds us that ideas shape our perceptions of reality as much as the other way around. To Jefferson, like other Americans before and after him, the future of Christianity in America could only make sense as part of a larger theory of history.

Future American writers would continue to draw on the lessons of history that Jefferson articulated. While some would reinvigorate the Puritans' declension narrative, many others would, like Jefferson, assume a universal conflict between reason and faith, and hope that the end of history would see the victory of one over the other. But what Jefferson saw as an ongoing human struggle between enlightenment and ignorance others would soon transform into a law of history, exhibiting a certainty that Jefferson's experience would never let him share.

NOTES

I thank the editors and contributors to this book, Peter S. Onuf, and Allan Megill for their guidance.

1. A Thomas Jefferson to Benjamin Waterhouse, June 26, 1822, in *Thomas Jefferson: Writings*, ed. Merrill D. Peterson (New York: Literary Classics of the United States 1984), 1458–59. (All Jefferson citations hereafter refer to page numbers in this volume.) On Jefferson and civil religion, see Thomas E. Buckley, "The Religious Rhetoric of Thomas Jefferson," in Daniel L. Dreisbach, Mark D. Hall, and Jeffrey H. Morrison, eds., *The Founders on God and Government* (Lanham, Md.: Rowman and Littlefield, 2004), 53–82. For general studies on religion in this era, see: Nathan O. Hatch, *The Democratization of American Christianity* (New Haven: Yale University Press, 1989); Jon Butler, *Awash in a Sea of Faith: Christianizing the American People* (Cambridge, Mass.: Harvard University Press, 1990); Isaac Kramnick and R. Laurence Moore, *The Godless Constitution: The Case against Religious Correctness* (New York: Norton Press, 1996).

2. Alexis de Tocqueville, *Democracy in America*, trans. Arthur Goldhammer (New York: Library of America, 2004), 340. Tocqueville himself prophesied that most Americans would eventually join the Catholic Church. Given that Catholicism is America's largest Christian denomination today, perhaps his prediction has come true, but for reasons different from those he provided. To Tocqueville, citizens in a democracy seek equality above all else, and they are willing to accept conformity in order to ensure that no person is different from, that is, unequal to, another. Catholicism, Tocqueville ventured, is the ideal democratic religion because it is "unified and uniform." Either Americans would reject religion altogether or they would embrace a common religion, Tocqueville hypothesized, in *Democracy in America*, 510–11.

3. Thomas Jefferson to Samuel Kercheval, January 19, 1810, 1213–15. On the rhetoric of Jefferson's opponents, see Robert M. S. McDonald, "Was There a Religious Revolution of 1800?" in James S. Horn, Jan Ellen Lewis, and Peter S. Onuf, eds., *The Revolution of 1800: Democracy, Race, and the New Republic* (Charlottesville: University of Virginia Press, 2002), 173–98; Philip Hamburger, *Separation of Church and State* (Cambridge, Mass.: Harvard University Press, 2002), 111–20; Frank Lambert, " 'God and a Religious President . . . (or) Jefferson and No God': Campaigning for a Voter-Imposed Religious Test in 1800," *Journal of Church and State* 39, 4 (autumn 1997): 769–89.

4. Thomas Jefferson to Benjamin Rush, April 21, 1803, 1122–26; Thomas Jefferson to Benjamin Rush, September 23, 1800, 1081. On Jefferson's religious beliefs, see Edwin S. Gaustad, *Sworn on the Altar of God: A Religious Biography of Thomas Jefferson* (Grand Rapids: Eerdmans, 1996); Jean M. Yarbrough, *American Virtues: Thomas Jefferson on the Character of a Free People* (Lawrence: University Press of Kansas, 1998), 182–93; Kramnick and Moore, *The Godless Constitution*, 88–109; Charles B. Sanford, *The Religious Life of Thomas Jefferson* (Charlottesville: University of Virginia Press, 1984).

5. Thomas Jefferson to Peter Carr, August 10, 1787, 900–905.

6. Thomas Jefferson to Samuel Kercheval, January 19, 1810, 1213–15; Thomas Jefferson to Thomas Law, June 13, 1814, 1337; Thomas Jefferson to Peter Carr, August 10, 1787, 901–2. On the influence of moral sense theory on Jefferson, see Yarbrough, *American Virtues*; Daniel Walker Howe, *Making the American Self: Jonathan Edwards to Abraham Lincoln* (Cambridge, Mass.: Harvard University Press, 1997), 48–77; Yehoshua Arieli, *Individualism and Nationalism in American Ideology* (Cambridge, Mass.: Harvard University Press, 1964), chaps. 6–8; Adrienne Koch, *The Philosophy of Thomas Jefferson* (Gloucester, Mass.: Quadrangle Books 1957), 15–22. Jefferson's clearest expressions of his moral sense theory are in two letters: Thomas Jefferson to Martha Jefferson, December 11, 1783, 784–85; Thomas Jefferson to Peter Carr, August 10, 1787, 900–905. Lord Kames, like Jefferson, marveled at the Creator's genius in implanting a moral sense as "part of the human system" to make it possible for humans to "to live in society; and because there can be no society among creatures who prey upon one another, it was necessary, in the first place, to provide against mutual injuries. Further; man is the weakest of all creatures separately, and the very strongest in society. Therefore mutual assistance is the principal end of society." See Henry Home, Lord Kames, *Essays on the Principles of Morality and Natural Religion*, 2 pts. (Edinburgh, U.K.: R. Fleming, for A. Kincaid and A. Donaldson, 1751), 67.

7. Thomas Jefferson, query 14 in *Notes on the State of Virginia*, 284–85; Thomas Jefferson to Thomas Law, June 13, 1814, 1335–39. See also Thomas Jefferson, "A Bill for Establishing Religious Freedom," 346–48.

8. Henry May, *The Enlightenment in America* (New York: Oxford University Press, 1976), 153; Thomas Jefferson, "A Declaration by the Representatives of the United States of America, in General Congress Assembled," July 4, 1776, 19 (see also Thomas Jefferson to John Cartwright, June 5, 1824, 1490–96); Thomas Jefferson to Roger C. Weightman, June 24, 1826, 1516–17; Thomas Jefferson to Peter Carr, August 10, 1787, 901–2. In *The Philosophy of the Enlightenment* (Boston: Beacon Press, 1951), 220, Ernst Cassirer notes that the Enlightenment's notion of progress was about removing the cultural debris that interposed itself between reason and the social world: "History shows how reason gradually overcomes these obstacles, how it realizes its true destiny." On Jefferson's conception of the role of the Revolution in creating a new future, see Peter S. Onuf, *Jefferson's Empire: The Language of American Nationhood* (Charlottesville: University of Virginia Press, 2000); Joyce O. Appleby, "What Is Still American in the Political Philosophy of Thomas Jefferson?" *William and Mary Quarterly* 39, 2 (April 1982): 287–309; Carl Becker, *The Declaration of Independence: A Study in the History of Political Ideas* (New York: Harcourt Brace, 1922).

9. Thomas Jefferson to John Cartwright, June 5, 1824, 1490–96; Thomas Jefferson to Roger C. Weightman, June 24, 1826, 1516–17.

10. Samuel Cooper, "A Sermon preached before His Excellency John Hancock... being the day of the Commencement of the Constitution and Inauguration of the new Government" (Boston, 1780), in Ellis Sandoz, ed., *Political Sermons of the American Founding Era, 1730–1805* (Indianapolis: Liberty Press, 1991), 627–56. For the way theological, republican, and Enlightenment ideas merged in

American religious thought, see Mark A. Noll, *America's God: From Jonathan Edwards to Abraham Lincoln* (New York: Oxford University Press, 2002); Harry Stout, *The New England Soul: Preaching and Religious Culture in Colonial New England* (New York: Oxford University Press, 1986); Nathan O. Hatch, *The Sacred Cause of Liberty: Republican Thought and the Millennium in Revolutionary New England* (New Haven: Yale University Press, 1977).

11. On the religious beliefs of other founders, see Dreisbach et al., *The Founders on God and Government*.

12. Immanuel Kant, "Idea for a Universal History with a Cosmopolitan Purpose" (1784), in *Kant: Political Writings*, ed. Hans Reiss (Cambridge: Cambridge University Press, 1970), 41–53.

13. Jean-Antoine-Nicolas de Caritat, marquie de Condorcet, *Sketch for a Historical Picture of the Progress of the Human Mind*, trans. June Barraclough (London: Weidenfeld and Nicolson, 1955).

14. Thomas Jefferson to William Green Mumford, June 18, 1799, 1063–66.

15. Jefferson, *Notes on the State of Virginia*, 284–85; Jefferson, "A Bill for Establishing Religious Freedom," 346–48; Thomas Jefferson to Moses Robinson, March 23, 1801, 1087–88.

16. Thomas Jefferson to Moses Robinson, March 23, 1801, 1087–88; Thomas Jefferson to William Short, October 31, 1819, 1431; Thomas Jefferson to John Adams, April 11, 1823, 1469.

17. Jefferson believed that New Englanders would only come over to his Republican party once New England had disestablished the church and overthrew "the dominion of the clergy." Thomas Jefferson to Moses Robinson, March 23, 1801, 1087–88; Thomas Jefferson to Benjamin Rush, September 23, 1800, 1080–82; Appleby, "What Is Still American?" 293. Jefferson's wall metaphor is the subject of an ongoing debate over what he meant by the separation of church and state. See Johann N. Neem, "Beyond the Wall: Reinterpreting Jefferson's Danbury Address," *Journal of the Early Republic* 27, 1 (spring 2007): 139–54; James H. Hutson, "Thomas Jefferson's Letter to the Danbury Baptists: A Controversy Rejoined," *William and Mary Quarterly*, 3rd ser., 56, 4 (October 1999): 775–90; Daniel L. Dreisbach, *Thomas Jefferson and the Wall of Separation between Church and State* (New York: New York University Press, 2002), 95–106; Daniel L. Dreisbach, "'Sowing Useful Truths and Principles': The Danbury Baptists, Thomas Jefferson, and the 'Wall of Separation,'" *Journal of Church and State* 39, 3 (summer 1997): 455–501, esp. 491–95.

18. On the idea of necessity in nineteenth-century historiography, see Allan Megill, *Karl Marx: The Burden of Reason (Why Marx Rejected Politics and the Market)* (Lanham, Md.: Rowman and Littlefield, 2002).

19. On Jefferson and classical republicanism, see Gordon S. Wood, *The Creation of the American Republic, 1776–1787* (Chapel Hill: University of North Carolina Press, 1969), 3–90, and "Conspiracy and the Paranoid Style: Causality and Deceit in the Eighteenth Century," *William and Mary Quarterly* 39, 3 (July 1982): 401–41; Drew R. McCoy, *The Elusive Republic: Political Economy in Jeffersonian America* (Chapel Hill: University of North Carolina Press, 1980); Lance Banning, *The Jeffersonian Persuasion:*

Evolution of a Party Ideology (Ithaca, N.Y.: Cornell University Press, 1978); Caroline Robbins, *The Eighteenth-Century Commonwealthman: Studies in the Transmission, Development and Circumstance of English Liberal Thought from the Restoration of Charles II until the War with the Thirteen Colonies* (Cambridge, Mass.: Harvard University Press, 1959).

20. Thomas Jefferson to Priestley, January 27, 1800, 1073; Thomas Jefferson to Roger C. Weightman, June 24, 1826, 1516–17. See also Thomas Jefferson to Priestley, March 21, 1801, 1085–87; Thomas Jefferson to Elbridge Gerry, January 26, 1799, 1057; Thomas Jefferson, Report for the Commissioners for the University of Virginia, August 4, 1818, 461–62.

21. McCoy, *Elusive Republic*, 13–47; Bernard Sheehan, *Seeds of Extinction: Jeffersonian Philanthropy and the American Indian* (Chapel Hill: University of North Carolina Press, 1973); Adam Ferguson, *An Essay on the History of Civil Society* (1767), ed. Fania Oz-Salzberger (Cambridge: Cambridge University Press, 1995). See also Marvin B. Becker, *The Emergence of Civil Society in the Eighteenth Century: A Privileged Moment in the History of England, Scotland, and France* (Bloomington: Indiana University Press, 1994).

22. Thomas Jefferson to William Ludlow, September 6, 1824, 1496–97.

23. Thomas Jefferson, "Second Inaugural Address," March 4, 1805, 520; my analysis here relies on Onuf, *Jefferson's Empire*, 18–52; Ari Helo and Peter S. Onuf, "Jefferson, Morality, and the Problem of Slavery," *William and Mary Quarterly* 60, 3 (July 2003): 583–614. On Jefferson and the Indians, see also Anthony F. C. Wallace, *Jefferson and the Indians: The Tragic Fate of the First Americans* (Cambridge, Mass.: Harvard University Press, 1999); Sheehan, *Seeds of Extinction*.

24. Jefferson, *Notes on the State of Virginia*, 273–74.

25. Thomas Jefferson to Joseph Priestley, March 21, 1801, 1085–87; Thomas Jefferson to John Dickinson, March 6, 1801, 1084–85; Thomas Jefferson, "First Inaugural Address," March 4, 1801, 493–96. See Onuf, *Jefferson's Empire*, 80–108.

26. Jefferson, *Notes on the State of Virginia*, 290–91.

27. Ibid., 273–74; Thomas Jefferson to Joseph Priestley, March 21, 1801, 1084; Thomas Jefferson to Littleton Waller Tazewell, January 5, 1805, 1150. For Jefferson and education in the early republic, see Richard D. Brown, *The Strength of a People: The Idea of an Informed Citizenry in America, 1650–1870* (Chapel Hill: University of North Carolina Press, 1996), 74–77; Carl F. Kaestle, *Pillars of the Republic: Common Schools and American Society, 1780–1860* (New York: Hill and Wang, 1983); Lawrence Cremin, *American Education: The National Experience, 1783–1876* (New York: Harper and Row, 1980), 107–21. On Jefferson and William and Mary, see Jürgen Herbst, *From Crisis to Crisis: American College Government, 1636–1819* (Cambridge, Mass.: Harvard University Press, 1982), 184–85; Bruce A. Campbell, "Law and Experience in the Early Republic: The Evolution of the Dartmouth College Doctrine, 1780–1819" (Ph.D. diss., Michigan State University, 1973), 114–22.

28. Thomas Jefferson, "Epitaph," 1826, 706–7; Jefferson, "Report for the Commissioners for the University of Virginia," 461–62, 467; Thomas Jefferson to Thomas Cooper, November 2, 1822, 1465.

29. Thomas Jefferson to Benjamin Waterhouse, June 26, 1822, 1459; Thomas Jefferson to Thomas Cooper, November 2, 1822, 1463–64.

30. Noll, *America's God*; Butler, *Awash in a Sea of Faith*; Hatch, *Democratization of American Christianity*.

31. Lyman Beecher, *Autobiography of Lyman Beecher*, ed. Barbara Cross, 2 vols. (Cambridge, Mass.: Harvard University Press, 1961) 1:252–53 (emphasis in original).

32. Lyman Beecher, *A Plea for the West* (1835; reprint, New York: Arno Press, 1977).

33. Beecher, *Autobiography of Lyman Beecher*, 1:253. On the religious cosmology of reformers, see Robert H. Abzug, *Cosmos Crumbling: American Reform and the Religious Imagination* (New York: Oxford University Press, 1994); John L. Thomas, "Romantic Reform in America, 1815–1865," *American Quarterly* 17, 4 (winter 1965): 656–81. On the spread of voluntary associations see Clifford S. Griffin, *Their Brothers' Keepers: Moral Stewardship in the United States, 1800–1865* (New Brunswick, N.J.: Rutgers University Press, 1960); Charles Foster, *An Errand of Mercy: The Evangelical United Front, 1790–1825* (Chapel Hill: University of North Carolina Press, 1960); Paul S. Boyer, *Urban Masses and Moral Order in America, 1820–1920* (Cambridge, Mass.: Harvard University Press, 1978); Johann N. Neem, "The Elusive Common Good: Religion and Civil Society in Massachusetts, 1780–1833," *Journal of the Early Republic* 24, 3 (fall 2004): 381–417; Johann N. Neem, *Creating a Nation of Joiners: Democracy and Civil Society in Early National Massachusetts* (Cambridge, Mass.: Harvard University Press, forthcoming 2008), esp. chap. 4.

3

The Romantic Era: Emerson's Churches of One

Matthew Mutter

One of the defining gestures among writers of the Romantic era is the prophetic stance. William Blake fraternized with Isaiah and Ezekiel in *The Marriage of Heaven and Hell*. William Wordsworth described his "poetic numbers," at the beginning of his great poem, *The Prelude*, as a "prophecy." Percy Bysshe Shelley, in poems like *Queen Mab* and *Prometheus Unbound*, unfurled apocalyptic visions as richly symbolical and elaborately condemnatory as the classic biblical texts. These writers and others constantly produced visions of change in which politics, social institutions, and the self would be spiritually renovated. Some of these prophesies were virulently atheistical; some were vigorously religious. Most were in some sense both. Shelley, the most explicitly atheistic poet of his age, nonetheless wrote disparagingly, in his sonnet "England in 1819," of "Religion Christless, Godless—a book sealed." And Samuel Taylor Coleridge, the Romantic who remained closest to Christian orthodoxy, complained, in "Fears in Solitude," that "the very name of God / Sounds like a juggler's charm." The atheist accuses religion of being godless, while the Christian is disgusted with the name of God. Such are the complexities of the Romantic poet-prophets.

This new rhetoric was made possible by a transformation of the meaning of prophecy itself. As the anthropologist Talal Asad has argued, for Romantic thinkers like Herder, Eichhorn, and Coleridge, "prophets were not men who sought to predict the future but creative poets who expressed a vision of their community's past—the past both as a renewal of the present and as a promise for the future."[1] We have already seen in this book that this model of prophecy was similar to that of the American Puritans. While they would not have understood prophecy as a form of poetry, they, too, sought to renew the future through a vision of an inspired past. The American Romantics, however, rejected the idea that a sacred origin should be a touchstone for contemporary action. Ralph Waldo Emerson insisted that "what was done in a remote age" has no "deeper sense" than what is done today.[2] In other ways, however, the spirit that Emerson, Margaret Fuller, Henry David Thoreau, and Walt Whitman inherited from the British Romantics was thoroughly entangled in America's Puritan heritage. While the British Romantic experience was shaped by resistance to an increasingly rigid industrialism and class structure and by disillusionment in the French Revolution, American Romanticism was marked by events that were already successfully contrarian: the inaugural radicalism of the Puritan social project and a less painful national revolution. America still had its injustices, but for these writers, it needed not an apocalyptic structural overhaul but a reorientation of vision. Emerson, for example, imagined himself a "bard of the Holy Ghost"—his image for the ideal minister in his controversial Harvard Divinity School address of 1838. But his religious language bore more on perception and the imagination than on the concrete social and political life of his day.

Emerson's prophesies were nevertheless unsettling. Henry James, reflecting on Emerson in 1888, wrote: "They [Emerson's contemporaries] were so provincial as to think brilliancy came ill recommended, and they were shocked at his ceasing to care for the prayer and the sermon. They might have perceived that he *was* the prayer and the sermon: not in the least a secularizer, but in his own subtle insinuating way a sanctifier." Emerson's reception thus turned, as James's commentary suggests, on whether his prophesies were seen as godless or not. Fifty years after Emerson's Divinity School address, James could not imagine a "condition of opinion" that would not welcome Emerson as a man of "superior piety."[3] This incredulity suggests that in James's circles, Emerson's prophetic aims had been realized.

What was that "condition of opinion"? To recover it, one must remember that the Puritans had blurred their own boundaries. At the heart of their theology lay a conviction that the sacred should not be relegated to special times, places, or events, for the whole of the everyday, secular realm was an arena of God's presence and salvation. As Charles Taylor has written, "By denying any special form of life as a privileged locus of the sacred, they were denying the very distinction between sacred and profane and hence affirming their interpenetration."[4] The sacred was not discarded; on the contrary, it absorbed areas formerly considered secular. This absorption, however, made the two categories more difficult to distinguish. By the era of the founding, the diffusion of the sacred across secular life had made religious sources, for a thinker like Thomas Jefferson, invisible. Jefferson had not abandoned belief in God, but he thought that the secular realm was sufficient unto itself. All that was indispensable about traditional faiths like Christianity—the universal and self-evident "moral sense" that had been clothed in mythic garb—could be retained, he thought, in an environment from which the cultic apparatus would gradually be expunged.

What Jefferson did not expect was that his approach, which could be broadly defined as a rationalist, empiricist Unitarianism, would in the years soon after his death begin to appear arid to a whole generation of young New England intellectuals. As chapter 2 has noted, he thought that all the young men he saw around him in the United States would die Unitarians. In fact, many of them died transcendentalists, under the tutelage of Emerson. These thinkers did not want, as did Jefferson, to abandon the function of the cultic establishment, but rather, like their Puritan forebears, to internalize it, so as to retain its role in preserving the sacred. Jefferson and the rationalist Unitarians had lost, in their rationalism, the visionary, mystical dimensions of religious life. Emerson and his circles sought to revitalize those dimensions while implicitly endorsing the process of institutional secularization that Jefferson thought central to the health of the country. In no way did they think that such *secularization*—for our purposes here, meaning the decline of religious authority in public life—necessarily led to *secularism*, the decline of religious consciousness. One could say they believed just the opposite: secularization, they hoped, would lead to a resurgence of authentic religious feeling. Thus Emerson came to write: "God builds his temple in the heart on the ruins of churches and religions."[5]

But was such secularization really taking place? What do we make of the great projects of religiously motivated social reform that dominated Emerson's age? Historians now insist that far from being implicitly secular, these projects presupposed an entire religious cosmology that served as a reference point for the remaking or sacralization of the whole world.[6] Yet in his early "Lecture on the Times" (1841), Emerson suggests that the explicitly "religious" work of churches has been replaced by a more neutral social work of "philanthropy." He speaks there of a "great army," the "martyrs" of reform, that now "occupy the ground which Calvinism occupied in the last age, and compose the visible church of the existing generation." These "successors" of Luther, Fox and Wesley are "the new voices in the wilderness crying 'Repent.'"[7] Emerson employs these elevated tropes of religion—martyrdom and ascetic prophecy—

to create a disjunction between the aspirations of this language and what it is describing. He wants his listeners to feel that the use of these parallels to represent the "noble" but spiritually bland projects of philanthropy is slightly ridiculous. Indeed, he classifies these persons as "actors," a term acknowledging the strenuous action characteristic of their work while simultaneously undermining the authenticity of their spirituality. They are mere performers: there is a gap between what they do and who they are. They therefore compose only the "visible," not the true, invisible church. (Emerson further radicalizes that familiar Reformation distinction. His use of "visible" does not mean "discernable"; his preferred synonym is "vulgar.")

There is a paradox in Emerson's evaluation of the public religious life around him. On the one hand, he admits that the philanthropists, by bringing religious ideas to bear on all aspects of social life, are actually continuing the Puritan work of consecrating the secular. They have invited "religion," he says, "to eat and drink and sleep with us." On the other hand, he rebuffs their work as "profane." The ostensibly sacred force of philanthropy masked deeper secularity, he thought, because it was animated by an anxious retreat from spiritual crisis. Near the end of the lecture, Emerson provides a diagnosis of what he calls "a new disease," the "torment" of "Unbelief" that haunts his cultural moment. His "forefathers" organized their lives around different terrors: the "fear of Sin" and of "Judgment."[8] They met those terrors head-on, but his generation, he claims, deliberately avoids the terror of unbelief by throwing themselves into the machinations of social life. Reform serves as a "paper blockade" that prevents the spirit from recognizing the crisis it is actually in. Reformers thus meet the threat of secularism—the advance of "Unbelief"—by doing secular work. By bringing religion to the world they have become worldly. Their logic, he says, has become purely instrumental; they are willing to use whatever "means" necessary to achieve their supposedly religious ends. But to say this is to say that they lack spirituality altogether, according to Emerson's definition of it: "The true meaning of *spiritual* is *real*; the law which executes itself, which works without means."[9]

Emerson very much shared the Puritan ideal of integrating the sacred and the secular. When he asks (in "Nature") "What is a farm but a mute gospel?" the two have become almost identical.[10] But this was a problem of perception and feeling rather than of action, which is inevitably a problem of means. In trying to confront this crisis of the spirit, then, Emerson tended to leave the secular realm of "means"—which he redefined as anything "outward," anything relying on "men, on multitudes, on circumstances, on money, on party"—to its own devices.[11] He wanted to purify the spiritual life, the inward life of feeling and imagination. Indeed, it might be said—to use two terms often used in opposition today—that Emerson was one of the first Americans to emphasize the language of the "spiritual" over the "religious" and the privatized conception of religion that accompanies this emphasis.[12] Yet the power and endurance of Emersonian spirituality in American culture suggests that the privatization of religion does not represent a short delay in the process of complete secularization.[13]

This is why Henry James said that Emerson did not discard the sermon and prayer but became the sermon and prayer, turning them into modes of subjective existence. The secret of the sermon, as he said in his Divinity School address, is an ability "to convert life into truth," not, as one might expect, truth into life.[14] The vocabulary of the prayer and sermon is not expunged but transposed. Emerson, like Whitman and Thoreau, instinctively expresses himself in religious language. However heterodox their own religious thought, "atheistic" remains for these writers a term of opprobrium. In "Song of Myself," Whitman groups adjectives in this way: "Frivolous, sullen, moping, angry, affected, dishearten'd, atheistical, / I know every one of you."[15] In contemporary Europe, when a secular, atheistic thinker like August Comte used phrases like "the religion of humanity," it was easy to see that what he meant by "religion" was nothing like what had gone under that name in previous millennia; his was a desire to inject into the organizational structure and social function of religion a new kind of scientific devotion.[16] For Emerson, in America, the opposite was true: he wanted to retain certain aspects of traditional religious language and feeling while discarding the organizational structure and social function. The language of his Divinity School address, though it appeared to many as the height of irreligion, is certainly not that of a traditional European secularist:

> From the views I have already expressed, you will infer the sad
> conviction, which I share, I believe, with numbers, of the universal
> decay and now almost death of faith in society. The soul is not
> preached. The church seems to totter to its fall, almost all life extinct.
> On this occasion, any complaisance would be criminal, which told
> you, whose hope and commission it is to preach the faith of Christ,
> that the faith of Christ is preached.[17]

Emerson here is a prophet of godlessness, preaching against the decay of faith in the tradition of the Puritan jeremiad.[18] But what James calls Emerson's "subtle insinuating way" is evident here. What he means by "the faith of Christ" is generally not what those "numbers"—among whom he counts himself—would likely mean. Every word that appears familiar ("soul," "faith," "Christ") has undergone a transvaluation. By "soul," Emerson means a principle of boundless selfhood with immediate access to the secrets of God and the universe—which, indeed, is largely indistinguishable from these secrets—and any "faith" is oriented toward this principle rather than toward a creed. It is easy to slide unawares over the fact that Emerson speaks of "the faith *of* Christ" rather than "the faith *in* Christ." The faith of Christ is, for Emerson, what we *share* with Christ: an affirmation of the soul's access to what Emerson calls the "moral sentiment." (Echoes of Jefferson's "moral sense" are audible here.) Its ground is a cosmic web of symbols in which every "fact" discloses its spiritual significance and moral interrelations. Increasingly throughout his career, the moral sentiment becomes for Emerson the foundation of all true religion, which could be described, in turn, as faith in that sentiment.[19]

Emerson's Contemporaries

Emerson liked to write about "representative men," and though his idiosyncrasy and individualism complicate his relation to his age, in a limited way we can see him as a representative intellectual, of his and coming generations, with regard to secularization. Emerson left the Unitarian church after just a few years as a minister, and he was not the only one to do so. While prominent transcendentalists such as Theodore Parker remained ministers, George Ripley left the church and went on to found Brook Farm, Christopher Cranch left to become a poet and painter, and John S. Dwight to become a music critic. Others urged an exodus from institutional religion in voices even more strident than Emerson's. Thoreau, who met and befriended Emerson in 1837, used language that exceeded Emerson's in its scornful prediction of the imminent disappearance of such institutions. Not only did he prefer the sound of "cowbells" to "church bells" on Sunday, but he insisted that the church was always the ugliest building in a given town, because

> it is the one in which human nature stoops the lowest and is most disgraced. Certainly, such temples as these shall ere long cease to deform the landscape. There are few things more disheartening and disgusting than when you are walking the streets of a strange village on the Sabbath, to hear a preacher shouting like a boatswain in a gale of wind, and thus harshly profaning the quiet atmosphere of the day.[20]

Whitman, also a younger "disciple" of Emerson, prophesied progress beyond those structures of religious authority as well. In the preface to the 1855 edition of *Leaves of Grass*, he wrote: "Soon there will be no more priests. Their work is done. They may wait awhile . . . perhaps a generation or two . . . dropping off by degrees. A superior breed shall take their place. . . . [T]he gangs of kosmos and prophets en masse shall take their place. A new order shall arise and they shall be the priests of man, and every man his own priest."[21] It is not clear what these "gangs" will look like, but they probably will not be listening to sermons.

Like Emerson, Whitman and Thoreau imagined a shift from external to internal religious authority. Emerson, however, recognized that a certain amount of institution building was "natural" in human life, whereas Whitman and Thoreau were more confident in an imminent dissolution of "the temples." But while Thoreau would likely have watched the collapse of public religion with a quiet smile, Whitman desired a "new order," and his language sounds more like Luther than Jefferson. Indeed, the radical Protestant sensibility is unmistakable; the Reformation precept of the so-called priesthood of all believers is further radicalized to serve Whitman's vision. Many early readers of Whitman saw him as the founder of a new religion, and he himself insisted late in life that *Leaves of Grass* was "the most religious among books."[22] The collection has a liturgical quality. It operates as a kind of open canon in the way it absorbs revisions and additions under a single banner, and it even makes internal appeals to its own biblical character. The poems become the material equivalent to what the bread and wine of the Eucharist are to Jesus' ascended body: "When you read these I that was visible am become invisible, / Now it is you, compact, visible, realizing my poems, / seeking me." Earlier in "Song of Myself" Whitman imagines his poem as a sacrament: "This is the meal equally set, this the meat for natural hunger, / It is for the wicked just the same as the righteous."[23] Whitman's prophetic, anticlerical religiosity is replete with such translated sacraments. Ultimately this distinguishes him from Emerson, for whom ritual, sacrament, and all other forms of religion are always a constraint.

Secular Tendencies in Emerson's Career

From the time that Emerson was a young man, he stood in a sort of double relationship to secularization, in an antagonistic stance toward both orthodox Calvinism and Unitarianism, which was an instance of already secularized Calvinism. Unitarian thinkers were sure that the principle of reason was being disseminated through society and enlightening the dark spots of residual religious enthusiasm. But as Perry Miller noted, Emerson suspected that Unitarian rationalism was making the country safe for unbridled commercialism and becoming indistinguishable from everyday social ambition. He questioned the secular aspect of Unitarianism even before he became a divinity student.

He wrote critically, in a letter to a friend, of the atmosphere of the Boston churches: "An exemplary Christian of today, and even a Minister, is content to be just such a man as was a good Roman in the days of Cicero." Dutiful national identity—and the connection to imperial commerce in "good Roman" should not be overlooked—was replacing spiritual identity; there was no longer a discernibly Christian content to the ideals of virtue. Although he was dissatisfied with orthodoxy, he thought that the Presbyterianism and Calvinism still found in areas like the American South had at least the virtue of making Christianity "a more real & tangible system" that could make headway with "the ignorance of men."[24] The transcendentalism of which he would become the most visible representative—but that never defined his thought—was an attempt to reenchant Unitarianism while still accepting many of its basic critiques of Christian orthodoxy.

Later in life, as an unpredictable, unstructured evangelicalism was gathering strength, it seemed to Emerson no more capable than Unitarianism of filling the cultural vacuum left by the disintegration of Puritanism and Calvinist orthodoxy. In a letter to James Cabot in 1859, he chastised his friend for sending him a book of meditations by the evangelist George Müller:

> I sometimes think that you and your coevals missed much that I &
> mine found: for Calvinism was still robust & effective on life &
> character in all the people who surrounded my childhood, & gave
> a deep religious tinge to manners and conversation. I doubt the race
> is now extinct, & certainly no sentiment has taken its place on the
> new generation—none as pervasive & controlling. But they were a
> high tragic school, & found much of their own belief in the grander
> traits of the Greek mythology,—Nemesis, the Fates, & the Eumeni-
> des, and, I am sure, would have raised an eyebrow at this pistareen
> Providence of . . . George Müller.[25]

By 1859, transcendentalism as a viable belief system and movement had, for the most part, come and gone. It certainly had not become the "pervasive and controlling" social presence Calvinism had once been. The older Emerson was ambivalent toward the decline of a former regime of strong social norms, one he described as "robust" and "effective" even if unsettling in its severity. The lack of structure in the new religious atmosphere made room for a spirituality as rigorously idiosyncratic as Emerson's but also made room for one as sentimental as Müller's. In a growing atmosphere of market-like religious opportunity, there was no certainty as to which of these religious styles a given public would adopt.

If Emerson was asking questions about the public future of traditional religion as a student, his ministry itself became an example of the general trends of secularization in America. Ordained at age twenty-six, Emerson received a post at Boston's Second Unitarian Church. After only a few years, however, his doubts about the singularity of Christian revelation and the efficacy of traditional rituals—precipitated, among other things, by his reading of the German "higher criticism" of the Bible, which used new methods of textual scholarship to distinguish between what was "historical" and what was "mythological"— became troubling enough to provoke him to leave his post. In 1832, he gave his final sermon, centered on his objection to the ritual of the Lord's Supper. The sermon ostensibly puts the responsibility for his resignation in his congregation's hands. He cannot, he says, continue in good conscience to administer the ritual. If his congregation decides they do not need it, he will stay. If they choose it, he will leave. They chose against him, and he resigned.

The sermon is interesting as more than just the occasion of this vocational drama. It is an early example of Emerson's preference for an abstract, universalized spirituality over an understanding of religion as the totality of social life in religious perspective. His objection to social rituals like the Eucharist was that they are constrained by the historical and the particular. Everything *local* is rejected: "But the Passover was local too and does not concern us; and its bread and wine were typical and do not help us to understand the love which they signified." Emerson speculates that Saint Paul most likely instituted the supper to appease immature Jewish converts, who were "yet unable to comprehend the spiritual character of Christianity." Judaism was a "religion of forms," whereas Jesus was quick to "spiritualize every occurrence."[26] In his late essay "Character" (the second of that title), Emerson acknowledges that forms so charged with feeling are worthy of respect but insists that they do a fundamental violence to religious life:

> One sees with some pain the disuse of rites so charged with humanity and aspiration. But it by no means follows, because those offices are much disused, that the men and women are irreligious; certainly not that they have less integrity or sentiment, but only, let us hope, that they see that they can omit the form without loss of real ground; perhaps that they find some violence, some cramping of their freedom of thought, in the constant recurrence of the form.[27]

Emerson's last work as a pastor, then, was to seek the liberation of Christianity from its Jewish origins. He did so because he doubted that it could be "practiced" through the performance of rituals or the sharing of symbols. Religion could not be public without form, but for Emerson, form was only the viscous residue of the spirit's encounter with time. The truly religious must extricate themselves from its static nature.

Emerson's Sociology

Though he was gifted with insight, Emerson's peripheral vision was flawed. Though his Bostonian circles cannot be taken as representative of America as a whole, he treated them as if they were entirely typical. The future of religion in American public life would have been seen differently outside of Emerson's highly educated, financially prosperous circles of social elites, a small section of a large and growing country. Several contemporary reviewers suggested as much. In a review of *The Conduct of Life* in 1861, Noah Porter questioned whether Emerson had enough information to speak accurately about "the state of religion," and wondered if Emerson's scope of observation did not "extend farther than 'his study' in Concord, or his 'club,' in Boston,—even though it seems to him to invest the universe."[28] Here Emerson foreshadows many later intellectuals who have taken their peers for a representative sample.

In a late address at an organizational meeting of a group called the Free Religious Association (1867), Emerson alludes to (but does not cite) "statistics" showing that, at least in American cities, the large majority of the population was no longer going to church.[29] However, the historian Nathan Hatch has noted, pace Emerson, that organized American religion was not declining but rapidly expanding in the middle of the nineteenth century. Between 1775 and 1845, for instance, the number of ministers per capita had tripled, from one per fifteen hundred people in 1775 to one per five hundred people in 1845. Emerson writes almost as if the Second Great Awakening had not happened at all. Perhaps this was due to the fact that his experience was largely limited to the Unitarian and Congregationalist churches, which had twice the clergy of any other American church in 1775, but only one-tenth the clergy of Methodism alone by 1845.[30] Or perhaps the fluidity and putative chaos of these religious organizations negated, for Emerson, their claims to real social presence. In his essay "Worship," published in 1860, he complains: "Nothing can exceed the anarchy that has followed in our skies. 'Tis a whole population of gentlemen and ladies out in search of religion. 'Tis as flat anarchy in our ecclesiastic realms, as that which existed in Massachusetts, in the Revolution."[31] Hatch writes that religious life in midcentury America was indeed characterized by a kind of chaos, but one of great democratic power. It was dissenting, republican, and radical, and it formed polymorphous institutions that "shared with Jeffersonian republicans an overt rejection of the past as a repository of wisdom."[32] It is surprising, then, that Emerson found this state of continuous religious revolution unappealing, for he, too, was suspicious of the wisdom of the past and always insisted that religious life took place in the present tense.

Yet he assumed that this "anarchy in our ecclesiastic realms" was a sign of organized religion's imminent collapse rather than a sign of vitality.

Public Religion and Personal Worship

Emerson's essay "Worship" is worth examining in detail, because it discloses the emphases and contradictions in his account of the past and future social meanings of religion. "What greater calamity can fall upon a nation," he had asked in the prophetic idiom many years before, "than the loss of worship?"[33] This essay redefines the terms of the earlier question. It is a sort of natural history of religion, juxtaposed with an account of a very different species of "true" religion. "Men naturally make a state, or a church, as caterpillars a web," he writes at the beginning of the essay, and "a man bears beliefs, as a tree does apples."[34] This guiding analogy shows how Emerson tends to reduce culture to nature, and at the same time preserves a higher concept of "Nature" that transcends both categories. Here cultural religious behavior (belief or church building) is not really self-determining, because all of its particular manifestations derive from an almost biological imperative. On the one hand, his language implies that we are inveterately social animals, a sentiment somewhat at odds with his characteristic stance. On the other hand, his argument implies that because this cultural work is a product of natural necessity, and therefore mindless as the work of trees or caterpillars, there is little reason to trust our souls to it. From a merely cultural perspective, church building and belief can be no more "true" than spinning a web is "true." This is why both institutions and creeds are ultimately unreliable.

Thus, the purported decline of public religion diminishes as a concern for the older Emerson, because the problem is only apparent. "I and my neighbors," he writes, "have been bred in the notion, that, unless we came soon to some good church—Calvinism, or Behmenism, or Romanism, or Mormonism—there would be a universal thaw and dissolution." But this is a mistake, he says. The "decline" of ecclesial influence "need give us no uneasiness."[35] His audience should not confuse the decline of institutions associated with these names with the decline of religion's "public nature." He continues: "The builder of heaven has not so ill-constructed his creature as that the religion, that is, the public nature, should fall out: the public and private element, like north and south, like inside and outside, like centrifugal and centripetal, adhere to every soul, and cannot be subdued, except the soul is dissipated." The persistence of religion's "public nature" for Emerson may mean its abstract life in American print culture, a new dimension of the public sphere that, as Michael Warner has argued, was critical in the development of American republicanism.[36] Emerson certainly made great use of impersonal forms of discourse such as the lecture and the essay as replacements for the sermon. But he would so particularize *local* religious institutions that they become indistinguishable from the individual herself: "How many people are there in Boston?" he asks in another late essay. "Two hundred thousand. Then there are so many sects. I go for churches of one. Break no springs, make no cripples."[37] And because Emerson believed that the self was in need of constant revision, even these churches might undergo schisms on a day to day basis.

Indeed, Emerson proceeds to suggest that the community and cultural dimensions of religion inherently opposed authentic religious feeling:

> But the whole state of man is a state of culture; and its flowering and completion may be described as Religion, or Worship. There is always some religion, some hope and fear extended into the invisible— from the blind boding which nails a horseshoe to the mast or the threshold, up to the song of the Elders in the Apocalypse. But the religion cannot rise above the state of the votary. Heaven always bears some proportion to earth. The god of the cannibals will be a cannibal, of the crusaders a crusader, and of the merchants a merchant.[38]

Here Emerson moves remarkably close to the account of religion and culture that Ludwig Feuerbach, among other philosophers, and the early anthropologists were articulating in Europe at roughly the same time. In this account, "religion" can be thought of as an anthropomorphic projection of finite cultural values onto an infinite object. Religion is culture worshiping itself, as Durkheim would later argue. As such, it can't escape its own contingency and moral narcissism. The gods of a people will look like larger versions of the kind of persons that people values: the gods of cannibals will also be cannibals. Emerson, who had little patience for mercantilism, crusading benevolence societies, or anthropophagy, is clearly severing links between culture and "true" religion altogether. In this light, the description of religion as the "flowering and completion" of culture is almost ironic, because such religion will be unable to transcend the local limits Emerson found so unappealing.

Unsurprisingly, Emerson recommends the "souls out of time" who are "rather related to the system of the world, than to their particular age and locality." These souls "announce absolute truths."[39] They are, by very definition, outside of culture, representatives of Religion rather than the religions. The articulation of this Religion is constantly changing, like the poetic imagination; it needs no canonical image or form. Emerson had already distinguished the poet from the mystic, who ossifies a single theological image and mistakes it for the Real. The poet, however, possesses the truly religious imagination, because he knows the quality that is "to flow and not to freeze." When temporary spiritual insight and its condensation in a linguistic or symbolic form (like a creed) are made universal and permanent, when the symbol is made "too stark and solid," we are at the origin of "all religious error."[40] Symbols, images, and practices are quickly exhausted. They must return their essential origin: "the moral sentiment," the spiritual principle animating all things, "the judge and measure of every expression" of religion.[41]

Religion, Nationhood, and Conflict

Emerson conceded—perhaps even nostalgically—that religion not only "comforted nations" but "*made* nations." He recognized that the American identity had significant origins in the Puritan social model, and acknowledged that the Puritans had found in the classic Christian creeds resources for "their longings for civil freedom."[42] What he retained of this intimate relationship between religion and nationhood was an abstract belief in Providence and national destiny, such as he articulated during a speech just a few days after Lincoln's death in 1865. "There is a serene Providence which rules the fate of nations," he claims, in which everything is sacrificed that "resists the moral laws of the world."[43] If post-Christians like Emerson expected a dark future for the institutional church, they harbored, nonetheless, a clearly *religious* affirmation of the country's institutions as a whole.

Emerson's address "The Progress of Culture" (1867) exudes confidence in the nation's continuing moral improvement, which will see "the fusion of races and religions," women's rights, and free immigration, all of which are inaugurated by a vague providential sweep.[44] Others, like Lincoln and Whitman, shared these sentiments—sometimes called America's civil religion—concerning God's mystical endorsement of the country's future. For Lincoln, the Union was "the last, best hope of earth," and God, who had "never yet forsaken this favored land," would ensure its success.[45] Though Whitman was shaken by the war in many ways, in *Democratic Vistas* (1871) he writes with confidence that democracy is to the "field" of social and institutional life what Christ was to "the moral-spiritual field" of the individual's soul. American democracy is, and is becoming, that "fusion of races and religions" of Emerson's imagining. Whitman writes that "at the core of democracy, finally, is the religious element. All the religions, old and new, are there. Nor may the scheme step forth, clothed in resplendent beauty and command, till these, bearing the best, the last fruit, the spiritual, shall fully appear."[46] The "religious element," not this or that particular religious identity or institution, will guide the nation's progress, as the individual religions bear their final fruit in their own death as they dissolve into the medley of the "spiritual."

The relationships among the war, secularization, and civil religion, however, are complex. Louis Menand has argued that the American pragmatist philosophers came to reject absolutism in the realms of morality and knowledge in part because of their experiences in the war, which was waged on behalf of such absolutisms. In the South, meanwhile, the defeat engendered what has been called the Religion of the Lost Cause, which had its own saints (Lee, Jackson) and theological dramas of betrayal and crucifixion.[47] And if American civil religion was vindicated by the Union victory, others suspected that the war had undermined America's religious self-understanding. This very suspicion seemed, paradoxically, to open a space for a more traditional theological discourse. As chapter 4 argues, by the end of the war, Lincoln's theology had become more cautious, tragic, and Calvinistic—characterized by those very principles, in other words, that for Emerson marked off high old theology from the "pistareen Providence" of George Müller. In his Second Inaugural Address, Lincoln doubted that the language of God's purpose or justice could be easily appropriated by either "side," even if the Union had to continue with "firmness in the right" as God gave them "to see the right." His one unswerving conviction was that God was just, but whether human intention or will had any role in instantiating that justice was uncertain.[48]

Herman Melville's writing about the war makes this picture even more complex. His collection of Civil War poems, *Battle Pieces*, suggests how, paradoxically, the war seemed at once a secularizing force and a demonstration of Christianity's fundamental principle of original sin. In "The House-Top," the speaker beholds the wasteland the war has produced and hears the "muffled sound" of "the Atheist roar of riot." The poem ends:

> Wise Draco comes, deep in the midnight roll
> Of black artillery; he comes, though late;
> In code corroborating Calvin's creed
> And cynic tyrannies of honest kings;
> He comes, nor parlies; and the Town, redeemed,
> Gives thanks devout; nor, being thankful, heeds
> The grimy slur on the Republic's faith implied,
> Which holds that Man is naturally good,
> And—more—is Nature's Roman, never to be scourged.[49]

There is a deep ambiguity of sentiment here. War brings with it a kind of atheism; the question is whether this atheism is a consequence of the unbelief produced by war's chaos and the self-righteous religious language of both sides or war *itself* is a product of an implicit and horrid atheism. It seems as though the war has brought a frightful but just rejection of the republic's civic, secular "faith" that "Man is naturally good." The war actually corroborated "Calvin's creed." The poem suggests that Draco might be in the service of either Calvinism or atheism, but what is certain is that he removes the pseudosecular middle—the civil religion that tried to preserve the sense of providential progress while pretending that God's redemption of a sinful world had become an obsolete concept.

The prose conclusion to *Battle-Pieces* commends the specific principles of Christian charity during Reconstruction and admonishes a "sacred uncertainty"[50] about the future of the nation rather than a smug confidence in God's favor. This suggests that for all of Melville's religious doubt, classic Christian principles, to his mind, had better survived the aftermath of the war than a secular faith in progress and perfectibility. The uneasy combination of acute skepticism and classical Calvinist sentiment linked him more closely with the mind of Lincoln at the end of the war than with the mind of Emerson.[51]

Emerson's Final Prophecy

For Emerson, however, a war could not truly affect religion more than any other historical circumstance. The "identity of history," he had written in his early essay on that subject, is "intrinsic," and we have access to that identity through our spiritual minds.[52] The fate of religions is the surface manifestations of the unified Spirit—sometimes called the "Over-soul" or the "One"—permeating history and the phenomenal world, and only that Spirit, which we intuit through the moral sentiment, is fully real. So the threat of secularization in "a transition period, when the old faiths . . . have spent their force," can never really be a threat for Emerson, because religion is for him an aesthetic work, a spiritual task of seeing the unity *behind* history.[53] The temporal coordinates of classic American prophecy—the covenant or inspired origin of the past, the possible fidelity or faithlessness in the future—are for him obsolete, for everything we need is before us in a perfect present; we just need to reorient our vision. The feeling is close to Whitman's in "Song of Myself":

> But I do not talk of the beginning or the end.
> There was never any more inception than there is now,

> Nor any more youth or age than there is now;
> And will never be any more perfection than there is now,
> Nor any more heaven or hell than there is now.[54]

No historical vacillation can improve or impair the vision of that perfection. An authentic "cultural crisis" involving religion would occur only if Nature—and thus we ourselves—disappeared. So Emerson writes:

> In spite of our imbecility and terrors, and "universal decay of religion," &c. &c., the moral sense reappears to-day with the same morning newness that has been from of old the fountain of beauty and strength. You say, there is no religion now. 'Tis like saying in rainy weather, there is no sun, when at that moment we are witnessing one of his superlative effects.[55]

The sun is what makes our vision possible. If we understand that this ground of vision is always present, it changes that vision into a form of witness. What we see is always a "superlative effect." Religion's public decline, then, is like the rain that waters the seed of Spirit itself to prepare it for a new emergence.

"Worship" closes on this prophetic imagination of future health. After largely dismantling culture's pretension to disseminate true religion, he returns to a language studded with intimations of the future, almost irresistibly:

> There will be a new church founded on moral science, at first cold and naked, a babe in a manger again, the algebra and mathematics of ethical law, the church of men to come, without shawms, or psaltery, or sackbut; but will have heaven and earth for its beams and rafters; science for symbol and illustration; it will fast enough gather beauty, music, picture, poetry. Was never stoicism so stern and exigent as this shall be. It shall send man home to his central solitude, shame these social, supplicating manners, and make him know that much of the time he must have himself to his friend. He shall expect no cooperation, he shall walk with no companion. The nameless Thought, the nameless Power, the superpersonal Heart—he shall repose alone on that. He needs only his own verdict.[56]

This is Emerson's final, most austere prophecy.

It is hard to say that it came to pass, but it is also hard to know what would count as evidence of its instantiation, other than the appearance, on the American scene, of an individual spiritual genius or two equal to Emerson's rigorous interiority. William James (discussed later) is perhaps a congregant in this church; he, too, imagined that religion is, as the philosopher Alfred North

Whitehead said, what an individual does with his solitariness. Yet this conception of religion as a mode of individual authenticity has undoubtedly had a major influence on American culture. The historian Leigh Schmidt has not only traced the recent "seeker" culture of spirituality back to Emerson and his generation but also has uncovered an uninterrupted history of eclectic, mystical, "liberal" spirituality since that generation. Figures such as Sarah Farmer, Rufus Jones, Thomas R. Kelley, and Max Ehrmann produced flourishing spiritual communities and literatures throughout the late nineteenth and twentieth centuries. Those liberal traditions, moreover, found in Emerson a foundational model for a sophisticated appreciation of non-Western religions.[57] Aesthetic, solitary spirituality has also consistently reemerged in the world of American literature. For Emily Dickinson, at least in certain moods, "The Brain is just the weight of God." Wallace Stevens explicitly identified the imagination with a demythologized religious consciousness, through a method more severe than even Matthew Arnold might have anticipated: "We say that God and the imagination are one." One finds Emerson's religious influence as well in Hart Crane, whose poetic Columbus, that primal figure of American identity, proclaims in a prayer to the "incognizable Word of Eden" that "Utter to loneliness the sail is true."[58]

Contrary to Emerson's expectation of their decline, however, the social forms of religion have continued to multiply, and they have often been characterized by unbridled, creative mythmaking. Emerson's last prophecy shows how his religious sensibility became less and less mythological and more and more scientific and mathematical. He is not worshiping science as an ideal, but constantly purging everything obscuring the deepest, most formless structures and laws of the moral sentiment's presence in Nature. So understood, American religion has often conformed more to Whitman's vision of the coming "gangs of kosmos" than to Emerson's companionless ascetics. Like Whitman, Americans have worshiped almost everything. Emerson, by the end of his life, worshiped almost nothing.

In our own time, Harold Bloom has defended Emersonian religion, which he associates with Gnosticism, as the "American Religion" par excellence. By this he means that in American religion, no matter how ostensibly conservative, the self is conceived as an uncreated spark of the Godhead and is therefore unconstrained by any immanent boundary. American religion has no "content," he argues, because, as in Emerson, it is a series of fluctuating and interchangeable tropes. Yet in Bloom's account, this national faith exists alongside, rather than in opposition to, our "secular origin."[59] For him, social and political secularism and Emersonian religion are completely compatible. If Bloom's account is true, we see not only how pervasive such a spirituality remains in the United States but also how limited its perspective, for it continues to find the political and social ambitions of religion peculiar and extraneous rather than understanding them as intrinsic tendencies. Religious descendants of Emerson will always tend to regard events such as the Scopes trial (discussed later), for instance, with a sense of surprise, for what does the uncreated spirit care about its material origins? These religious descendants will also likely have difficulty understanding the motivating force behind Islamic jihad (discussed in chapter 11). The glaring miscalculations of secularization theory, however (also discussed in several proceeding chapters), are something they might have anticipated, because Emersonian religion is generally undismayed by the processes of modernization that have sometimes led to secularism. Material disturbances actually accentuate Emersonian religion's native fluidity and capacity for spiritual transvaluation. Science, technology, urbanization, war—this kind of religion absorbs these pressures because its imagination is nimble. This very fluidity may, indeed, be a clue to why America's modernization has not made America, despite a multitude of prophesies, less religious.

NOTES

1. Talal Asad, *Formations of the Secular: Christianity, Islam, Modernity* (Stanford: Stanford University Press, 2003), 44. For an extensive analysis of the prophetic dimension of European Romanticism, see Ian Balfour, *The Rhetoric of Romantic Prophecy* (Stanford: Stanford University Press, 2002).

2. *Emerson: Essays and Poems*, ed. Joel Porte and Harold Bloom (New York: Library of America, 1996), 239. Note that other figures of the age did retain the structure of the covenant model so important to the Puritans. For Abraham Lincoln, the Declaration of Independence was the "sacred origin" against which all contemporary political backsliding was measured. His speeches consistently remind his listeners of the sentiments of the Declaration and admonish renewal in light of them.

3. Lyon N. Richardson, ed., *Henry James: Representative Selections* (New York: American Book, 1941), 119. For excellent accounts of these controversies and Emerson's general social context, see Mary Kupiec Cayton, *Emerson's Emergence* (Chapel Hill: University of North Carolina Press, 1989), and Lawrence Buell, *Emerson* (Cambridge, Mass.: Harvard University Press, 2003).

4. Charles Taylor, *Sources of the Self: The Making of the Modern Identity* (Cambridge, Mass.: Harvard University Press, 1989), 217.

5. *Emerson: Essays and Poems*, 882.

6. See in particular Robert Azbug's excellent *Cosmos Crumbling: American Reform and the Religious Imagination* (New York: Oxford University Press, 1994).

7. *Emerson: Essays and Poems*, 158, 160.

8. Ibid., 165.

9. Ibid., 888.

10. Ibid., 29; it has been argued that the "blurring of the differences," or the "tendency to attribute to everything a sacred sense," contributes unwittingly to the secularizing process. Lesek Kolakowski has claimed that "to universalize the sacred is to destroy it: to say that everything is sacred is tantamount to saying that nothing is, for the two qualities, sacred and profane, can be understood only in contrast to one another; every description is a form of negation; the attributes of a totality are inapprehensible." *Modernity on Endless Trial* (Chicago: University of Chicago Press, 1989), 68.

11. *Emerson: Essays and Poems*, 162.

12. On this distinction in contemporary American culture and for a historical survey of the idea, see Robert C. Fuller, *Spiritual but Not Religious: Understanding Unchurched America* (New York: Oxford University Press, 2001).

13. In his remarkable book *The Disenchantment of the World*, the French social theorist Marcel Gauchet has argued that the relation between religious privatization and secularization is still uncertain: "Though the age of religion as a structuring force is over, it would be naive to think we have finished with religion as a culture. But can we imagine that in the long run the disappearance of the 'infrastructure' would not have any effect on the 'superstructure'? Should not the disappearance of the basic social function of the religious provoke a slow but inexorable fading or erosion of the very possibility of a belief? It is tempting to think so. But here we come up against another problem which clearly complicates the issue: that of the subjective function preserved—or acquired—by religious experience when its social function is obliterated." Trans. Oscar Burge (Princeton: Princeton University Press, 1999), 102–3.

14. *Emerson: Essays and Poems*, 85.

15. *Whitman: Poetry and Prose*, ed. Justin Kaplan (New York: Library of America, 1996), 78.

16. For more on Comte, see chapter 5 here.

17. *Emerson: Essays and Poems*, 83.

18. See chapter 1 here. Also see Sacvan Bercovitch, *The American Jeremiad* (Madison: University of Wisconsin Press, 1978).

19. On Jefferson and the "moral sense," see chapter 2 here.

20. Henry David Thoreau, *A Week on the Concord and Merrimack Rivers* (Princeton: Princeton University Press, 1983), 76.

21. *Whitman: Poetry and Prose*, 24.

22. Quoted in Horace Traubel, *With Walt Whitman in Camden* (Boston: Small, Maynard, 1906), 1:372.

23. *Whitman: Poetry and Prose*, 287, 205. For a full-scale examination of Walt Whitman and religion, see David Kuebrich, *Minor Prophecy: Walt Whitman's New American Religion* (Bloomington: Indiana University Press, 1989).

24. Quoted in Perry Miller, "Jonathan Edwards to Emerson," *New England Quarterly* 13, 4 (1940): 611. For a good intellectual biography of Emerson that examines the early years as a divinity student and minister, see Robert Richardson, *Emerson: The Mind on Fire* (Berkeley: University of California Press, 1995).

25. Quoted in Miller, "Jonathan Edwards to Emerson," 613–14.

26. *Emerson: Essays and Poems*, 959, 960.

27. *The Spiritual Emerson: Essential Writings by Ralph Waldo Emerson*, ed. David M. Robinson (Boston: Beacon, 2003), 252.

28. *Emerson and Thoreau: The Contemporary Reviews*, ed. Joel Myerson (New York: Cambridge University Press, 1992), 300.

29. Ralph Waldo Emerson, *Miscellanies* (New York: AMS Press, 1968), 478.

30. Nathan Hatch, *The Democratization of American Christianity* (New Haven: Yale University Press, 1989), 4, 5. For a surprising account of how evangelical Christianity was not original with the southern United States but gained dominance there over a nominal Christian culture during the course of the nineteenth century (and thus representing a sacralizing rather than secularizing trend) see Christine Heyrman, *Southern Cross: The Beginning of the Bible Belt* (New York: Knopf, 1997).

31. *Emerson: Essays and Poems*, 882.

32. Hatch, *Democratization of American Christianity*, 10.

33. *Emerson: Essays and Poems*, 882.

34. Ibid.

35. Ibid.

36. See Michael Warner, *The Letters of the Republic: Publication and the Public Sphere in Eighteenth-Century America* (Cambridge, Mass.: Harvard University Press, 1990).

37. From "The Essential Principles of Religion," in *The Spiritual Emerson*, 240.

38. *Emerson: Essays and Poems*, 883.

39. Ibid., 883.

40. Ibid., 463–64.

41. "Character," in *The Spiritual Emerson*, 250.

42. *Emerson: Essays and Poems*, 87. See Sacvan Bercovitch's classic study *The Puritan Origins of the American Self* (New Haven: Yale University Press, 1977).

43. Quoted in Mark Noll, *America's God: From Jonathan Edwards to Abraham Lincoln* (Oxford: Oxford University Press, 2002), 433.

44. Emerson, *Letters and Social Aims* (New York: AMS Press, 1968), 207.

45. Lincoln, *Speeches and Writings, 1859–1865* (New York: Library of America, 1989), 223, 415.

46. *Whitman: Poetry and Prose*, 971, 973.

47. On both the southern church and the black church, see Charles Reagan Wilson, "Religion and the Results of the American Civil War," in Randall M. Miller, Harry S. Stout, and Wilson, eds., *Religion and the American Civil War* (New York: Oxford University Press, 1998), 360–82. For Menand's account of the effects of the Civil War on thinkers like Oliver Wendell Holmes Jr. and William James, see *The Metaphysical Club* (New York: Farrar, Straus, and Giroux, 2001).

48. Lincoln, *Speeches and Writings, 1859–1865*, 687. On this shift in Lincoln's thinking see Noll, *America's God*, 426–38. For a full-scale account of Lincoln's religion arguing that his religious thought and sensibility was "romantic" or "poetic" in ways that bring him formally closer to Emerson, see Stewart Winger, *Lincoln, Religion, and Romantic Cultural Politics* (DeKalb: Northern Illinois University Press, 2002).

49. Herman Melville, *Tales, Poems and Other Writings*, ed. John Bryant (New York: Modern Library, 2001), 346.

50. Ibid., 367.

51. It should be noted that Melville's thinking evolved on this issue. In a famous passage from his early novel *White-Jacket*, the protagonist identifies America with both Israel and the Messiah and refers to America's "future" as "The Bible of the Free." Of course, the fact that these are the words of the narrator, who is also a character, makes the identification of the sentiment with Melville himself slightly more complex. See *White-Jacket* (Evanston, Ill.: Northwestern University Press, 1970), 150–51.

52. *Emerson: Essays and Poems*, 242.

53. Ibid., 884.

54. *Whitman: Poetry and Prose*, 28.

55. *Emerson: Essays and Poems*, 887.

56. Ibid., 902.

57. For an excellent summary of Emerson's interest in Asian religion and an examination of him as a progenitor of the discipline of "comparative religion," see Buell, *Emerson*, 169–98.

58. Leigh Eric Schmidt, *Restless Souls: The Making of American Spirituality* (New York: HarperCollins, 2005). *The Poems of Emily Dickinson* (Cambridge, Mass.: Harvard University Press, 1999), 598; Wallace Stevens, *The Collected Poems* (New York: Vintage, 1982), 524. The *Complete Poems of Hart Crane* (New York: Liveright, 2001), 49. For accounts of how Emerson's individualism has impacted American culture (not necessarily in terms of religion), see Charles E. Mitchell, *Individualism and Its Discontents: Appropriations of Emerson 1880–1950* (Amherst, Mass: University of Massachusetts Press, 1997), and Christopher Newfield, *The Emerson Effect: Individualism and Submission in America* (Chicago: University of Chicago Press, 1996).

59. Harold Bloom, *The American Religion* (New York: Simon and Schuster, 1992), 258, 271.

4

The Civil War: Redeemer President and Warrior Prophet: Abraham Lincoln, William T. Sherman, and Evangelical Protestantism

Wayne Wei-siang Hsieh

For better or for worse, there has been no more messianic a figure in American history than Abraham Lincoln. It was Lincoln's biblical declaration "a house divided against itself cannot stand" that foretold the coming Civil War in 1858; his presidency that presided over that war; and his violent martyrdom that led to his apotheosis in the North as the "Redeemer President."[1] But at the center of this maelstrom of prophecy and redemption stood a man who subscribed to Deist heterodoxy in his youth, who searched for the divine will as president in a manner that would have made most of his contemporary mainstream clergymen profoundly uncomfortable, and who died an unchurched man more gripped by the inscrutability of God's will than were the vast majority of his contemporaries. In the end, the North's transformation of Lincoln into a conventional Christ figure represented in microcosm the resilience of broader evangelical culture in Civil War America.

If Northerners assimilated Lincoln into that broader evangelical culture, Major General William T. Sherman remained an outsider. Sherman won wide fame leading an army, but his brilliant, mercurial, and contrarian personality always set him far apart from the

American mainstream. Lincoln's more unorthodox religious views still had strong resonance with many of what this study calls the scripts of American religious culture (see the introduction for discussion of these); Sherman's deification of the American Union and sometimes outright opposition to evangelical benevolence made him something of a warrior heretic. Indeed, despite Lincoln's obviously sectional appeal, his larger participation in the broad scripts of American religious culture gave him common ground with his Confederate adversaries. Jefferson Davis, his counterpart in the South, relied even more heavily than Lincoln on Fast Day proclamations and invocations of the jeremiad, while General Robert E. Lee became the South's own postwar Christ figure. At the war's end, Lincoln could use the jeremiad script to call for a sectional reconciliation grounded in part on mutual, bisectional guilt over slavery and common purgation in war. While Sherman stood outside these broad scripts, we cannot ignore the man Harriet Beecher Stowe called, more aptly than she realized, the "war-prophet."[2] Indeed, without Sherman's capture of Atlanta, Lincoln might never have been reelected, and his apotheosis after his assassination an irrelevant might-have-been. If the doubting Lincoln's somewhat ironic absorption into his age's American religious culture represented the resilience and adaptability of the evangelical persuasion, the crucial role of the fiery and flame-haired Sherman reminds us of the disruptions and distortions that persuasion suffered from the unwelcome intrusion of the God of Battles.

Nevertheless, Sherman's repudiation of republican, evangelical, and Enlightenment Christianity foreshadowed postwar American intellectuals' departure from evangelicalism, and thus represented the possibility that the war would lead to a broader religious declension. Evangelicals, North and South, proved capable of answering the challenge, however, and the broad outlines of popular evangelical culture survived the war intact. The story of this survival is unintelligible without recourse to the role evangelicals' prophesies of godlessness played in it. The long-standing jeremiad script served them as a potent tool to explain the war's sufferings and dislocations, while vindicating in the end their respective sections' special covenanted relationship with God. Even the defeated Confederacy could still point to Israel's earlier tribulations as precedent for its own divine righteousness amid temporal defeat. To use another perspective, as the historian Mark Noll has commented, "Despite the conflict's horrific character and the way it touched personally many of America's greatest religious thinkers, the conflict seems to have pushed theologians down the roads on which they were already traveling rather than compelling them to go in new, creative directions." Despite claims by writers such as George Frederickson, the changes in American religious life that occurred

toward the end of the nineteenth century resulted not from the direct consequences of the Civil War but from the social, economic, and demographic
changes of the Gilded Age and the Progressive Era.[3]

What then was this evangelical culture that proved so adaptable and resilient, even in the face of the country's greatest war? In Noll's words,

> the evangelical Protestantism that dominated public life at mid-
> century had gained its place because it successfully clothed the Chris-
> tian faith in the preeminent ideological dress of the new Republic. In
> particular, it had vivified, ennobled, and lent transcendent value to
> republican political assumptions, democratic convictions about social
> organization, scientific reasoning pitched to common sense, and belief
> in the unique, providential destiny of the United States.[4]

While the established churches of the Old World and of the American colonial
period manifested a close connection between secular and religious hierarchy,
contemporary observers such as Tocqueville recognized that the evangelical
denominations of the nineteenth century reflected, buttressed, influenced, and
furthered the antihierarchical Jacksonian political order of antebellum America. The evangelical denominations subscribed to a theology that emphasized
the ability of human individuals to accept God's grace and redemption and thus
benefited from the voluntary and democratic nature of their denominations.

As a consequence, at the eve of the Civil War, evangelical Protestantism
could claim at least the respect (as manifested by regular participation in
church life) of two-thirds to four-fifths of Americans. The evangelicals thus
represented the religious mood of the period, but they also drew much of their
authority from long-standing continuities in American religious history. After
all, evangelicals saw themselves as the Protestant champions who would redeem, amid the social chaos and tumult of Jacksonian America, the unruly
American populace and prevent religious decline.[5] Furthermore, as a religious
community, the evangelicals drew from historical sources separate to some
degree from the peculiarities of the American experience and anchored in
several millennia of religious practice. This created a constellation of ideas that
had a resilience and adaptability frequently underrated by both the critics and
defenders of revealed religion, which helps explain the survival of American
religious practice despite recurrent prophesies of godlessness.

Not only did evangelicalism survive the war, it also helped sustain both
contending sections' war efforts. The shared heritage of the jeremiad script
allowed both sections to conceive of their causes as divinely sanctioned, and to
cope effectively with the reverses both suffered during the long course of the
war. The jeremiad's explanation of setbacks as divine chastisements that, if

properly received by a virtuous and pious people, would help lead to a final triumph helped sustain both sections' wartime morale throughout a prolonged conflict, both in and out of the armies.[6] However, this script also paradoxically made postwar reconciliation and resignation in the defeated Confederacy more likely, by allowing white Southerners to see their temporal defeat as simply another chastisement that would only in the end vindicate their special relationship with God, much as the ancient Israelites had suffered calamitous political defeats in their own history. Evangelical Christianity and the associated jeremiad script thus proved to be a cultural force so pervasive and adaptable that it could sustain itself in the face of drastic political and social change.

Lincoln's Doctrine of Necessity

Abraham Lincoln himself had emerged out of the milieu of the evangelical mission to Christianize the unruly frontier. His parents, Thomas and Nancy Lincoln, had both been members of the intensely revivalist Separate Baptists in Kentucky, and both were present for the great revivals in Kentucky at the turn of the century. Abraham, however, grew into something of a scoffer, and in his youth, he parodied Baptist sermons, to his father's displeasure. In 1831, Lincoln moved to New Salem, Illinois, where he became something of a freethinking skeptic. He may even have written an essay arguing against Christ's divinity and biblical inspiration.[7] His views became well enough known that when he ran for Congress in 1846 against Peter Cartwright, the famous Methodist circuit rider, he published a handbill defending himself against the charge of apostasy.

Lincoln acknowledged that he was "not a member of any Christian Church" but claimed that he "never denied the truth of the scriptures" and had "never spoken with intentional disrespect of religion in general, or of any denomination of Christians in particular." More interestingly, he also commented: "In early life I was inclined to believe in what I understand is called the 'Doctrine of Necessity'—that is, that the human mind is impelled to action, or held in rest by some power, over which the mind itself has no control." Although Lincoln himself points out that this statement is not necessarily incompatible with orthodox Christianity, his "Doctrine of Necessity" was very different from any orthodox conception of Providence.[8]

The historian Allan C. Guelzo has traced in part this Doctrine of Necessity to Lincoln's reading of Benthamite thought; the natural laws of the Doctrine of Necessity correspond well to Lincoln's explorations of utilitarianism and his particular brand of Whig political belief. Lincoln thus had no patience for radical and perfectionist reform movements, such as abolition, but he could make common cause with moderate reform movements, such as the gradualist advocates of temperance. Missionary work, tract societies, and other similar efforts, in addition to temperance, all composed a larger bisectional evangelical effort to reform American society and prepare it for the coming millennium, or the thousand-year golden age at the end of the world. Lincoln also believed in progressive reform, but in a more secular and rational form than what the evangelicals envisioned. Indeed, the only Springfield church Lincoln even vaguely affiliated himself with (though even here he never became a member) was an old-school Presbyterian congregation led by James Smith, a formerly freethinking Scotsman known for his rationalist defenses of Christianity. In sum, the younger Lincoln subscribed to a gradual, orderly, rational, and for the most part secular conception of progress.[9]

Lincoln, like most Americans who saw their country as having a covenanted relationship with God, conceived of the United States as having a special place in history. In his first major speech, the Lyceum Address of 1838, Lincoln revealed his view of America's exceptional position in the long continuum of historical progress. He called the United States "the fondest hope, of the lovers of freedom, throughout the world." However, the speech is for the most part a secular piece of work in which religion is given a subordinate place to politics. Lincoln exhorted his auditors to let a "reverence for the laws . . . become the *political religion* of the nation; and let the old and the young, the rich and the poor, the grave and the gay, of all sexes and tongues, and colors and conditions, sacrifice unceasingly upon its altars." However, even this vaguely religious tenor was lost when Lincoln changed his argument and claimed that "cold, calculating, unimpassioned reason, must furnish all the materials for our future support and defense."[10]

Lincoln's appropriation of many of the scripts of American religious belief, despite his own lack of that belief—as defined by contemporary evangelical norms—illuminates the particular power of those scripts. Indeed, Lincoln also adopted a secularized version of the jeremiad script after the deeply divisive Kansas-Nebraska Act of 1854 repealed the Missouri Compromise's long-standing restrictions on the territorial growth of slavery. Lincoln believed that the new legislation reflected a dangerous state of declension in the nation's attitudes toward human bondage. While in Lincoln's view "the framers of the Constitution intended and expected the ultimate extinction of that institution [slavery]," their descendants had allowed themselves to be corrupted by it when they should have been fighting for the Revolution's principles of liberty and equality. Lincoln contrasted an old "faith" based on the Declaration of Independence's principles of human equality with a new "faith" based on popular sovereignty, the Kansas-Nebraska Act, and slavery's territorial expansion. Every jeremiad included a call to reformation, and Lincoln's political jeremiads were no exception: "Our republican robe is soiled, and trailed in the dust. Let us repurify it. Let us turn and wash it white, in the spirit, if not the blood, of the Revolution."[11] Little did he know how much new blood would soon be available for the washing.

Providence and the Coming Civil War

Early in the war, little changed in Lincoln's notions of a Whiggish and naturalistic progress. Shortly before his inauguration, he declared that he hoped to be "an humble instrument in the hands of the Almighty, and of this, his almost chosen people," to preserve the legacy of the Founding Fathers, including the Deistic Jefferson, which "held out a great promise to all the people of the world to all time to come." But unfortunately for Lincoln, the troubled and bloody course of the war made a mockery of his belief in a mechanistic Providence and irresistible Whiggish progress.[12] Northern and Southern evangelicals' conception of Providence, channeled through the jeremiad script, proved far more adaptable and effective at dealing with the vicissitudes of war than did Lincoln's original Doctrine of Necessity. A personalized conception of a God who intervened directly in human affairs proved a far more plausible explanation for the war's ebb and flow than Lincoln's orderly, rational, and mechanistic notions of progress. The jeremiad script became a potent tool for evangelical clergymen in both North and South to explain the harsh vicissitudes of war.

This particular script explained wartime setbacks as just punishments for national sins, especially ones involving inadequate religious belief, while at the same time holding out the certainty of eventual redemption, if only the people hastened to reform their ways. Suffering thus became a natural and necessary part of the self-sacrificial process needed to align a polity with God's will.

Examples of this abound. After the Union defeat at First Bull Run in July 1861, the Northern minister Horace Bushnell declared that "there must be tears in the houses, as well as blood in the fields; the fathers and mothers, the wives and the dear children, coming into the woe, to fight in hard bewailings. . . . In these and all such terrible throes, the true loyalty is born." And after all those sufferings, "the victory, when it comes, will even be a kind of religious crowning of our nationality." Or, as a Confederate religious journal toward the end of the war tried to explain the litany of military disasters, while yet still seeing final victory over the horizon: "We forgot the source of our strength. God in anger withdrew his support. . . . Our cause will be strengthened and our liberty secured as soon as we deserve it." The Protestant clergy of the North thus believed that they knew God's purposes reasonably well: God was purifying America with fire and sword to cleanse the country of sin and restore its place at the forefront of history in anticipation of the Christian millennium. While they prayed and hoped for a Union defeat, their Confederate counterparts also saw their struggles as a form of divine cleansing, which in turn would also lead to an independent Confederacy at the forefront of history, but one with the biblical institution of slavery intact. For all their political differences, both sides' evangelicals had roughly comparable religious views of Providence and history.[13]

Lincoln stands as a contrast to this consensus. As the war churned on, he acquired a new sense of Providence as something that took an active role in human history—a view different from both his own youthful ideas and those of his contemporaries, North and South. Early intimations of this were not long in coming. As early as the first Sunday after the aforementioned Union defeat, Orville Hickman Browning, senator from Illinois, suggested that God would not bless the Union cause until the North struck at slavery. Lincoln mused in his retort: "Browning, suppose God is against us in our view on the subject of slavery in this country, and our method of dealing with it?" When a delegation of Quakers met Lincoln in late June 1862 and expressed their "earnest desire that he might, under divine guidance, be led to free the slaves and thus save the nation from destruction," Lincoln replied that "God's way of accomplishing the end which the memorialists have in view may be different from theirs."[14]

Emancipation

The Union's military setbacks caused Lincoln to develop a more personalized conception of Providence, one that might question a more aggressive military strategy coupled with emancipation. He had discussed the idea of an Emancipation Proclamation with secretary of war Edwin M. Stanton as early as May 1862. Many Union clergymen at the time considered the war's length to be an act on the part of Providence against slavery, and Lincoln himself came to a similar conclusion, at least in terms of policy. He presented to his cabinet on July 22 a draft version of what was later to become the Emancipation Proclamation, but secretary of state William Seward convinced him that to issue such a proclamation after so many military frustrations would "be viewed as the last measure of an exhausted government, a cry for help." Lincoln decided to wait for a victory and use that as the occasion to promulgate his Emancipation Proclamation.

Unfortunately, no victory came. Lee defeated Pope at Second Bull Run on August 29, 1862, and events on the battlefield stymied Lincoln's new political and military measures.[15] Lincoln then found himself with no alternative but to restore Major General George B. McClellan to command of the primary eastern army in order to repel Lee's invasion of Maryland. With the restoration of McClellan, the living embodiment of a war policy that eschewed emancipation, Lincoln questioned whether or not Providence truly wished him to free the slaves. In response to the defeat at Second Bull Run, he had penned a personal note his secretaries called "A Meditation on the Divine Will," in which he mused: "The will of God prevails" and "in the present civil war it is quite possible that God's purpose is something different from the purpose of either party." Furthermore, "By his mere quiet power, on the minds of the now contestants, He could have either *saved* or *destroyed* the Union without a human contest. Yet the contest began. And having begun He could give the final victory to either side any day. Yet the contest proceeds."[16] Lincoln now worried that he had misread God's signals, that "God's purpose [was] something different from the purpose of either party." Perhaps God, as Lincoln speculated to Browning, did not want to free the slaves. Perhaps Lincoln's new emancipation policy was a mistake.

These brooding thoughts not only frustrated Lincoln personally but also distanced him from his compatriots. On September 13, 1862, only nine days before the publication of the Preliminary Emancipation Proclamation, Lincoln received a delegation of Northern clergymen bearing a memorial calling for a general decree of emancipation. Lincoln sardonically remarked, "I am approached with the most opposite opinions and advice, and that by religious men, who are equally certain that they represent the Divine will. I am sure that either the one or the other class is mistaken in that belief, and perhaps in some respects both." After repudiating these clergymen's claims that they knew the will of God, Lincoln referred obliquely to his own dilemma:

> I hope it will not be irreverent for me to say that if it is probable that
> God would reveal his will to others, on a point so connected with my
> duty, it might be supposed he would reveal it directly to me; for . . . it
> is my earnest desire to know the will of Providence in this matter.
> *And if I can learn what it is I will do it!* These are not, however, the days
> of miracles, and I suppose it will be granted that I am not to expect a
> direct revelation.

The clergymen, prudent men that they were, agreed that direct revelations were no longer possible, but defended their advice on the grounds that "as according to his own [Lincoln's] remark, Providence wrought by means and not miraculously, it might be, God would use the suggestions and arguments of other minds to secure that result."[17]

Although Lincoln told the clergymen that in the absence of revelations, he "must study the plain physical facts of the case, ascertain what is possible and learn what appears to be wise and right," in actuality he had already resorted to a "covenant" of his own with God, something much closer to a direct revelation than any of those mainstream clergymen would have liked. Lincoln laid out the terms of this covenant when he informed his cabinet on September 22 that he was finally issuing a preliminary Emancipation Proclamation. The secretary of the navy, Gideon Welles, explained that Lincoln "made a vow, a covenant, that if God gave us the victory in the approaching battle, he would consider it an indication of Divine will, and that it was his duty to move forward in the cause of emancipation."[18] Lincoln's contradictory statements to the Chicago delegation reveal the misgivings he had in attempting to divine God's will through such direct and personal means.

Lincoln himself acknowledged that "it might be thought strange . . . that he [Lincoln] had in this way submitted the disposal of matters when the way was not clear to his mind what he should do." Chase noticed that Lincoln's voice was "hesitating a little" right before he said that he had made a "promise" to his Maker. Although Lincoln worried about the possible presumption of his personal covenant with God, he seems to have felt that he must act in some way to learn God's will. In Chase's account, Lincoln proclaimed, "I must do the best I can, and bear the responsibility of taking the course which I feel I ought to take."[19]

Historians may never fully understand the motivations behind Lincoln's covenant making. Allen C. Guelzo, the leading historian of the issue, attributes it to his supposedly Calvinist upbringing, but this argument has its weaknesses. Lincoln's parents had had strong associations with the Separate Baptists, more Arminian than the Regular Baptists. Furthermore, while Lincoln's behavior was not without precedent in American history, extending back to the Puritan John Winthrop, the logical implication of Lincoln's covenant was that human beings could in effect compel the Almighty to send clear political signals on specific questions of state.[20] While Winthrop accepted God casting the Puritans' colonizing party into the sea if they did not have God's favor, Lincoln's request for divine clarification included no such drastic recourse for the Almighty to punish the president for any potential hubris. On the other hand, Lincoln did genuinely hope to do God's actual will, as opposed to what either he or his contemporaries perceived God's will to be; in this way, the covenant's anxious attempt to discover God's will points forward to the inscrutable Providence of Lincoln's Second Inaugural Address. In the end, Lincoln's demand that the Almighty resolve his providential uncertainty remains one of the more curious moments in American history.

The ambiguous nature of Antietam as a military victory, followed by two outright catastrophes for the Union in Virginia at Fredericksburg in December and Chancellorsville the following May, showed Lincoln that God might not wish to give him such an easy decision. Indeed, although the Emancipation Proclamation served as a crucial turning point in the war and a key part of the eventual Union strategy for victory, as late as the summer of 1864 Lincoln expected a defeat in that year's elections due to the bloody stalemate of that spring's Overland campaign. Lincoln himself may have realized the problems with his covenant making; he never seems to have tried such a thing again, and the divine inscrutability at the center of his Second Inaugural Address hardly reflects the same sensibility. But instead of adopting his evangelical contemporaries' jeremiad-driven conception of Providence to explain the war's woes as divine purgation on the road to paradise, Lincoln moved onto an altogether different path.

The Second Inaugural Address

Delivered on March 4, 1865, barely six weeks before his death and with victory in sight, the Second Inaugural Address represents the final state of Lincoln's religious development. Lincoln himself said: "I expect the latter [the Second Inaugural] to wear as well as—perhaps better than—any thing I have produced." Lincoln opened nondescriptly enough with a paragraph saying that he would not address specific questions of policy. He then attempted to speak to both sections, North and South, in an attempt to reunify a country whose divisions, ironically enough, had been exacerbated by a common jeremiad tradition. Instead of focusing on the triumph of a Northern people chosen by God, Lincoln instead emphasized the idea that both North and South had not wanted war: "All dreaded it—all sought to avert it." He made it clear that the South was the aggressor: "Both parties deprecated war; but one of them would *make* war rather than let the nation survive; and the other would *accept* war rather than let it perish." But he ended the paragraph with the laconic "and the war came," which more than anything else emphasized the irrelevance of human intentions.

The unimportance or impotence of those intentions, on the part of North and South alike, emerged more clearly in the third paragraph, which addressed slavery. "All knew that this [slave] interest was, somehow, the cause of the war," but "neither [side] anticipated that the *cause* of the conflict might cease with, or even before, the conflict itself should cease. Each looked for an easier triumph, and a result less fundamental and astounding." Lincoln, of course, included himself in these statements. He had entered the war pledged to a free-soil platform but committed to nothing further on the question of emancipation. A year and a half into the conflict, he finally moved on the issue, but only after he had made a covenant with the Almighty, an act that, before the war, he could never have predicted he would resort to. That experiment with discerning the divine will seemed to miscarry, as the war dragged on long after Antietam. Indeed, "the Almighty has His own purposes."

Lincoln then echoed the jeremiad script when he blamed both the North and the South for the sin of "American Slavery," eschewing pleas for God's mercy with a humbled acquiescence to the inscrutability, yet justice, of God's Providence.

> Fondly do we hope—fervently do we pray—that this mighty scourge of war may speedily pass away. Yet, if God wills that it continue, until all the wealth piled by the bond-man's two hundred and fifty years of unrequited toil shall be sunk, and until every drop of blood drawn with the lash, shall be paid by another drawn with the sword, as was said three thousand years ago, so still it must be said "the judgments of the Lord, are true and righteous altogether" [Psalm 19:9].

Lincoln's ascription of mutual guilt attempted to reunify both contending sections into one nation answerable to one God, as opposed to the two contending chosen peoples of the now concluding war. This one nation as a whole deserved chastisement, with its common sin of slavery. Departing further from the Northern clergy's jeremiads during the war, Lincoln also deliberately made no reference to his Northern contemporaries' hopes that the war's blood sacrifice would cleanse America of its sins and prepare the nation for its destined role at the forefront of the imminent millennium. Instead, he ended his address with a less sectional appeal to Christian charity: "With malice toward none; with charity for all . . . to bind up the nation's wounds." Even here, though, Lincoln emphasized the role of Providence's independent purposes, emphasizing that the tasks of reconciliation should be done humbly, "with firmness in the right, as *God gives us to see the right*" (emphasis added).[21] For Lincoln, only God decided how much Americans could possibly understand of God's plan for the future.

Lincoln's distinctive message became overshadowed, to some degree, by his postassassination apotheosis as the redeemer president whose blood helped expiate America for the sin of slavery. Evangelical clergymen studiously ignored the unconventional elements of Lincoln's religious thought: his scoffing youth, his failure to join any church, his flirtation with direct revelation in the fall of 1862, and a final conception of a Providence far more inscrutable and ambiguous than that of most of his contemporaries. Lincoln himself had recognized the gulf between himself and his contemporaries. Commenting on the Second Inaugural Address, he claimed that it was "not immediately popular. Men are not flattered by being shown that there has been a difference of purposes between the Almighty and them. To deny it, however, in this case, is to deny that there is a God governing the world."[22]

Nevertheless, the God of the Second Inaugural Address drew Lincoln far closer to his Christian contemporaries than the Doctrine of Necessity of his youth, even if it had a more strongly Calvinist tinge than was usually the case in such an Arminian age. In fact, in theological terms, Lincoln's conception of Providence actually had more in common with the broad scope of histori-cal Christian doctrine than with the distinctive Arminianism of nineteenth-century American evangelicalism. While the likes of Auguste Comte's Amer-ican followers saw the forces of progress as leading to the decline of organized religion, the revolutionary effects of the Civil War led to an orthodox turn in Lincoln's own religious thinking. In a time of crisis, for Lincoln, the rich cultural heritage of the King James Bible and Protestant history proved more potent than the utilitarianism of Jeremy Bentham, or the scientific deter-minism of Enlightenment materialism.

Sherman: Godless "War-Prophet"

While Lincoln and his contemporaries would have seen Providence as the guiding hand behind the victory that made the Second Inaugural Address possible, a more cynical observer would point instead to generals like William T. Sherman. Sherman's dismissive attitude toward contemporary evangelicals can be seen in his long-running feud with ministers trying to bring the gospel to his army; he declared once that "200 pounds of powder or oats are worth more to the U.S. than that amount of bottled piety." Sherman's outright hostility to evangelicalism personified larger American fears of godlessness, especially in connection to its military institutions. For example, O. O. Ho-ward, the so-called Christian General who later went on to head the Freed-man's Bureau, earned no popularity points among his fellow cadets for openly favoring prayer meetings and temperance during his enrollment at West Point. The men he commanded as a Civil War corps commander also fre-quently chafed under the influence of his sincere and overt piety. Indeed, early in the war, many Virginia ministers also fretted over the effects military life would have on impressionable young men, stripped of the positive religious influence of home and community.[23]

Furthermore, Sherman, like Lincoln, in his own early life had done and said things that could provoke evangelicals' fears of an infidel America. Sherman's prewar declaration to his Catholic wife that "good works rather than faith [were] the basis of true religion, both as revealed in scripture and taught by the experience of all ages and common sense," did not stand too far apart from Jefferson's rationalist Deism. However, Sherman was no atheist, and his religious views evolved during the war. But while Lincoln wandered in an eccentric fashion back to a conception of Providence that was compatible with Christian orthodoxy, Sherman's journey put him further out on the religious fringe. For this "war-prophet" the Union was in effect God, and the Confederacy a form of rebellion akin to Satan's defiance of the Almighty. While evangelicals' appeal to nationhood still stood grounded in the larger Christian story of divine Providence and redemption, Sherman conceived of the Union and God as virtually inseparable. According to Sherman, the war was simply the Almighty's means of vindicating the legitimate authority of the Union.[24] Because of this, while Lincoln's conception of Providence echoed Calvinist notions of God, the president could still end the Second Inaugural Address with an appeal to charity completely foreign to Sherman's identification of God with the Union.

Instead, in Sherman's view, "To make war, we must & will harden our hearts. Therefore when Preachers clamor, & the Sanitaries Wail dont give in, but Know that war, like the thunderbolt follows its laws, and turns not aside even if the beautiful, the virtuous and charitable stand in its path." War was the harsh force of nature—Sherman frequently likened it to a thunderstorm—that the Confederacy had brought on itself as punishment for secession. And most important, God himself used war as his instrument to restore order to a people riven by "prejudice and passion."[25]

Contrast that view with his contemporaries' visions. When Confederate general John Bell Hood protested Sherman's compulsory evacuation of Atlanta, he appealed to "God and humanity," "the civilized world," and "the laws of God and man." Such language represented the idiom of evangelical religion, shared ironically enough by North and South, even as they fiercely disputed who truly represented "God and humanity." Sherman set himself deliberately apart by repudiating that idiom in its entirety, telling Hood that

> in the name of common sense I ask you not to appeal to a just God in such a sacrilegious manner. You who in the midst of Peace and prosperity have plunged a nation into War, dark and cruel War.... If we must be Enemies let us be men, and fight it out as we propose to do, and not deal in such hypocritical appeals to God and humanity.[26]

With the natural force of war unleashed by Providence, there was no sense in appealing to the Almighty. While evangelicals, North and South, hoped to induce or provoke God to intercede in the war by atoning for their sins on fast days, Sherman only saw a Providence unleashing war to vindicate the authority of the Union. Even Lincoln's early views of "political religion" and Jefferson's Unitarian Deism did not go so far in their repudiation of conventional evangelical Christianity.

Conclusion: A Fighting Faith in War and Peace

Sherman's disciplining fury looked forward to the repudiation of humanitarian reform, so closely connected to evangelical ideals, by postwar intellectuals, while Lincoln looked back in the Second Inaugural Address to a God more like that of Augustine than that of his evangelical contemporaries. But neither Lincoln nor Sherman were in any way representative men. For most Americans, North and South, evangelicals found ways, in their own conception, at least, to defuse the threat Sherman's military values posed to American religious life and to deflect the critique Lincoln's theology entailed to Americans' understanding of God's governance of history. Both North and South undertook comprehensive programs to Christianize their armies through benevolent organizations akin to the missionary and tract-distribution efforts of the antebellum period, and evangelicals both North and South thought themselves successful in these efforts. For Northerners, the destruction of slavery and military victory manifested clear divine approval; in contrast, in the defeated South, defeat was only another sign of the Lost Cause's special relationship with God. Furthermore, in both sections, the evangelical trope of individual conversion and salvation remained alive and well.[27]

While these commonalities furthered both war efforts between 1861 and 1865, they also helped contribute to the postwar political rapprochement. While the jeremiad tradition reassured Southerners of their special covenanted relationship with God after the war, it also helped reconcile them to defeat by continuing to provide a providential mission. After all, the Old Testament showed that even God's chosen people had once sat by the waters of Babylon and wept. Even in defeat, former Confederates could still draw on the covenant and jeremiad traditions to see themselves as God's chosen people, with its own pair of Christ figures in Lee and Jackson. Former Confederates proved more than willing to use the methods of political terrorism to ensure the subject status of the freedpeople in their midst, but the vision of an independent Confederate nation-state never resurrected itself in any realistic fashion. Indeed, some former Confederates even saw defeat as just punishment from God for un-Christian abuses in the institution of slavery, although they never gave up defending slavery's inherent Christian legitimacy, if managed properly. One Confederate general, not known for his piety, saw the military and political dangers of the jeremiad tradition's focus on God's will, grumbling after the war:

> I think it was a serious incubus upon us that during the whole war
> our president & many of our generals really & actually believed
> that there *was* this mysterious Providence always hovering over the
> field & ready to interfere on one side or the other, & that prayers &
> piety might win its favor from day to day.[28]

This probably overstated the case, but the jeremiad tradition's emphasis on chastisement and Providence did seem to help reconcile Confederates to defeat.

For the North, the final destruction of slavery and the vindication of Federal authority (objectives not identical to a regime of racial equality) represented the essential and successful culmination of their own jeremiad script. Once it became clear that former Confederates could content themselves with a system of racial subjugation different from classic chattel slavery, and that they no longer hoped for actual political independence, white reconciliation between the two sections proceeded apace.[29]

Both North and South thus found satisfaction in God's verdict, and while their interpretations differed, the common script they used helped ameliorate the animosities the war produced. Indeed, Mark Noll and Harry S. Stout, two of the more prominent current historians of Civil War religion, have both overstated the violence-inspiring tendencies of the jeremiad script and ignored the degree to which it helped defuse postwar tensions. A generation of military historians have found as much restraint as wrath even in the war's conduct, applying even to Sherman's deliberately destructive march from Atlanta to the sea. In the broad sweep of military history, the American Civil War has no special claim to viciousness, if we use such broad measures as open violence against noncombatants, repudiation of ideas of quarter, and the overall butcher's bill; indeed, it is hard to imagine how some white Southerners would have been willing to fight in the Spanish-American War if the earlier conflict had been completely unrestrained. Such restraints had roots in the common culture shared by both North and South, including a jeremiad script that could explain Confederate defeat in palatable terms. In this sense, both sides' acceptance of the North's military victory as a divine judgment echoed Lincoln's reconciliationist transfiguration of the rhetorical form of the jeremiad, even if they ignored some of the specific details in Lincoln's frank admission of mutual guilt and divine inscrutability.[30]

Nevertheless, the war-prophet still hovered over the land, and not all Americans found the jeremiad tradition a sufficient explanation for the forces Sherman represented. New ideas about science, professionalism, and social discipline now raised their heads, challenging the humanitarian reformism of antebellum evangelicals. Perhaps Oliver Wendell Holmes Jr. went the farthest down this path toward an America evangelicals would have seen as godless, declaring, "In the midst of doubt, in the collapse of creeds, there is one thing I do not doubt . . . that the true faith is true and adorable which leads a soldier to throw away his life in obedience to a blindly accepted duty, in a cause which he little understands, in a plan of campaign of which he has no notion, under tactics of which he does see the use."[31] Some of us may blanch at such a fighting faith, but we misunderstand the Civil War era if we do not recognize the historical influence of different types of religious fervor on the war and its warriors.

NOTES

I thank the editors for their close and fruitful reading of earlier versions of this piece, and David Brion Davis, who directed my undergraduate senior essay on Lincoln and religion at Yale University, which is in some ways the genesis of much of this essay. Any errors or misinterpretations are, of course, my own responsibility.

1. Abraham Lincoln, *The Collected Works of Abraham Lincoln*, ed. Roy Basler, 9 vols. (New Brunswick, N.J.: Rutgers University Press, 1953), 2:461. On Lincoln as redeemer president, see Allen C. Guelzo, *Abraham Lincoln: Redeemer President* (Grand Rapids, Mich.: Eerdmans, 1999), 440–41.

2. On Jefferson Davis and the jeremiad script, see, for example, Harry S. Stout, *Upon the Altar of the Nation: A Moral History of the Civil War* (New York: Viking Penguin, 2006), 85–86, 212–14, 274–75. On Lee as Christ figure, see Charles Reagan Wilson, *Baptized in Blood: The Religion of the Lost Cause, 1865–1920* (Athens: University of Georgia Press, 1980), 122–23. On Lee as Christ figure, see Emory M. Thomas, *Robert E. Lee: A Biography* (New York: Norton, 1995), 416–17. For the "war-prophet," see Harriet Beecher Stowe, *Men of Our Times, or Leading Patriots of the Day, Being Narratives of the Lives and Deeds of Statesmen, Generals, and Orators* . . . (Hartford, Conn.: Hartford Publishing, 1868), 431.

3. On the postwar South's comparison of itself to Israel, see Wilson, *Baptized in Blood*, 71. On theological continuities, see Mark A. Noll, *The Civil War as a Theological Crisis* (Chapel Hill: University of North Carolina Press, 2006), 16. Noll does believe the war shattered the long-term significance of scriptural authority in American political life (see 161). On the Civil War fundamentally changing American religious and intellectual culture, see George M. Fredrickson, *The Inner Civil War: Northern Intellectuals and the Crisis of the Union* (New York: Harper and Row, 1965), 198–201.

4. Noll, *Theological Crisis*, 18.

5. Ibid., 11. On the need to save the frontier from godlessness, see Perry Miller, *The Life of the Mind in America from the Revolution to the Civil War* (New York: Harcourt, Brace and World, 1965), 8.

6. Stout, *Upon the Altar of the Nation*, xvii–xxii.

7. Lincoln's maternal grandmother, Lucy Shipley Hanks, was known for her religiosity, and three of her sons became clergymen. See Louis A. Warren, *Lincoln's Youth: Indiana Years, Seven to Twenty-One, 1806–1830* (Indianapolis: Lakeside Press, 1959), 6–7; on the Lincolns and Separate Baptists, see 13, 114. On the intensely revivalist character of the Separate Baptists, see John B. Boles, *The Great Revival, 1787–1805* (Lexington: University Press of Kentucky, 1972), 3–4. Also see Douglas L. Wilson and Rodney O. Davis, eds., *Herndon's Informants: Letters, Interviews, and Statements about Abraham Lincoln* (Urbana: University of Illinois Press, 1998), 615. On Lincoln's youth, see Guelzo, *Abraham Lincoln*, 36–38, 50–51; David Herbert Donald, *Lincoln* (London: Jonathan Cape, 1995), 33, 49.

8. Lincoln, *Collected Works*, 1:382.

9. Guelzo, *Abraham Lincoln*, 117–21, 149–50, 153–54. On millennialism and evangeical reform in the North, see James H. Moorhead, *American Apocalypse: Yankee Protestants and the Civil War, 1860–1869* (New Haven: Yale University Press, 1978), 9–14. On the substantial participation of the southern evangelical churches in evangelical benevolence movements, see Beth Barton Schweiger, *The Gospel Working Up: Progress and the Pulpit in Nineteenth-Century Virginia* (New York: Oxford University Press, 2000), 87, who downplays postmillennial motivations in the southern churches (also see 196). For a contrary viewpoint, see Elwyn Thomas Colbenson, "Millennial Thought among Southern Evangelicals, 1830–1885" (Ph.D. diss., Georgia State University, 1980), 7, and Jack Maddex Jr., "Proslavery Millennialism: Social Eschatology in Antebellum Southern Calvinism," *American Quarterly* 31, 1 (spring 1979): 46–47.

10. Lincoln, *Collected Works*, 1:112, 115.

11. Ibid., 2:492, 2:275–76.

12. Ibid., 4:236; Guelzo, *Abraham Lincoln*, 326.

13. Horace Bushnell, *Reverses Needed: A Discourse Delivered on the Sunday after the Disaster of Bull Run, in the North Church, Hartford* (Hartford, Conn.: L. E. Hunt, 1861), 23, 25. Confederate quotation in Stout, *Upon the Altar of the Nation*, 408. For Northern millennialism and the war, see Moorhead, *American Apocalypse*, 43. On slavery and the Confederate millennium, see Maddex, "Proslavery Millennialism," 57–58. On the jeremiad in general, see Stout, *Upon the Altar of the Nation*, 38, 47.

14. Michael Burlingame, ed., *An Oral History of Abraham Lincoln: John G. Nicolay's Interviews and Essays* (Carbondale: Southern Illinois University Press, 1996), 5; Lincoln, *Collected Works*, 5:279. Also see Guelzo, *Abraham Lincoln*, 325. In his remarks to the Quakers, Lincoln also referred to the possibility that "he might be an instrument in God's hands of accomplishing a great work." Note that this is from a newspaper account and is not established as an exact quotation of Lincoln.

15. On the political narrative regarding emancipation, see Donald, *Lincoln*, 360–66, 371; quotation from 366. On the war's length as a providential sign, see Moorhead, *American Apocalypse*, 99–100.

16. Lincoln, *Collected Works*, 5:403–4.

17. Ibid., 5:419–20, 422.

18. Ibid., 5:420; *Diary of Gideon Welles: Secretary of the Navy under Lincoln and Johnson*, ed. Howard K. Beale, 3 vols. (New York: Norton, 1960), 1:143. My chronology of the covenant making is as follows. Lincoln told his cabinet on September 22 that he had made his covenant "when the rebel army was at Frederick," Salmon Chase, *The Salmon Chase Papers*, ed. John Niven (Kent, Ohio: Kent State University Press, 1993), 1:394. Lincoln received a telegram from McClellan that Lee's main army had been at Frederick on September 10, which means that Lincoln must have made his covenant no later than this date, three days before he made his contradictory statements to the Chicago clergymen on September 13, George B. McClellan to Abraham Lincoln, telegram, September 10, 1862, Abraham Lincoln Papers, Library of Congress, reel 141, no. 18339 (microfilm copy in Yale University library). It should be acknowledged that in Chase's diary, Lincoln's covenant making seems much less bold, and is a personal vow made to God to issue the proclamation after Confederate defeat, as opposed to a demand for divine guidance. That being said, the oddity of the account in Welles seems reliable, both because of its greater detail and the general reliability of Welles's diary; and to read Lincoln's promise in the way it is portrayed in Chase's account would indicate that Lincoln had been completely confident of a Union victory in Maryland. Considering Lincoln's rocky relationship with McClellan, and his frequently despondent attitude toward the war with regard to Union arms, Chase's account seems unreliable. It thus seems likely that Chase at least unconsciously smoothed over the boldness of Lincoln's appeal to God, especially since he favored this policy direction far more than did the conservative Welles. On the general reliability of Welles's diary, see *Diary of Gideon Welles*, xviii–xxii.

19. *Diary of Gideon Welles*, 143; *Salmon Chase Papers*, 394.

20. Guelzo, *Abraham Lincoln*, 327. On the general Arminianizing trend in this period, even among nominally Calvinist groups, see Boles, *Great Revival*, 138. There is even evidence from Herndon's informants that Thomas Lincoln was a Free Will Baptist in Indiana (Wilson and Davis, *Herndon's Informants*, 97). Furthermore, a Methodist minister married Thomas Lincoln and his second wife, Sally Bush (Warren, *Lincoln's Youth*, 61). There is also evidence that Thomas Lincoln died as a Campbellite, a denomination that was anything but Calvinist (Wilson and Davis, *Herndon's Informants*, 97, 693; on the Campbellites, see Boles, *Great Revival*, 153–58). The Pigeon Creek Church in Indiana, which Thomas Lincoln joined when his son was fourteen, was indeed Calvinist in its formal creed and doctrine (Warren, *Lincoln's Youth*, 113), but we should not read too much significance into this. On Winthrop, see Perry Miller and Thomas H. Johnson, eds., *The Puritans*, rev. ed. (New York: Harper and Row, 1963), 1:198.

21. Lincoln, *Collected Works*, 8:332–33, 356.

22. Ibid., 8:356. On Lincoln's appropriation, see Stout, *Upon the Altar of the Nation*, 449–50; Guelzo, *Abraham Lincoln*, 439–47.

23. *Sherman's Civil War: Selected Correspondence of William T. Sherman, 1860–1865*, ed. Brooks D. Simpson and Jean V. Berlin (Chapel Hill: University of North

Carolina Press, 1999), 619–20. On Howard, see William S. McFeely, *Yankee Step-father: General O. O. Howard and the Freedmen* (New Haven: Yale University Press, 1968), 33; Bruce Catton, *The Army of the Potomac: Glory Road* (New York: Doubleday, 1952), 175. On irreligion in the antebellum United States army, see Edward M. Coffman, *The Old Army: A Portrait of the American Army in Peacetime, 1784–1898* (New York: Oxford University Press, 1986), 78, 178–79. On fears of Confederate degradation, see Wayne Wei-siang Hsieh, "Christian Love and Martial Violence: Baptists and War—Danger and Opportunity," in Peter Wallenstein and Bertram Wyatt-Brown, eds., *Virginia's Civil War* (Charlottesville: University of Virginia Press, 2005), 87–100.

24. Sherman quoted in Stephen E. Bower, "The Theology of the Battlefield: William Tecumseh Sherman and the U.S. Civil War," *Journal of Military of History* 64, 4 (October 2000): 1006; see also 1015, 1017.

25. *Sherman's Civil War*, 624; Bower, *Theology of the Battlefield*, 1024–25, Sherman quoted 1027.

26. William Tecumseh Sherman, *Memoirs of General W. T. Sherman* (New York: Library of America, 1990), 593, 595; *Sherman's Civil War*, 706.

27. On efforts to Christianize the armies, see Stout, *Upon the Altar of the Nation*, 288–92, 391–92. On the decline of humanitarianism, see Fredrickson, *Inner Civil War*, 198. Alice Fahs has found in her study of Civil War literary culture that the sentimentality so strongly associated with evangelicalism remained alive and well in both Northern and Southern popular literature, despite the war's suffering and dis-locations. See Alice Fahs, *The Imagined Civil War: Popular Literature of the North and South, 1861–1865* (Chapel Hill: University of North Carolina Press, 2001), 93–94, 118–19. Drew Faust has also done work that emphasizes the survivability of evan-gelical notions of peaceful and sentimental death, even in the face of the war's trying circumstances. See Drew Gilpin Faust, "The Civil War Soldier and the Art of Dying," *Journal of Southern History* 67, 1 (February 2001): 37. For a more negative view of evangelicalism's resilience in the face of war, see Anne C. Rose, *Victorian America and the Civil War* (New York: Cambridge University Press, 1992), 63–64.

28. On Confederate defeat as God's punishment on his chosen people for slavery's abuses, see Eugene D. Genovese, *A Consuming Fire: The Fall of the Con-federacy in the Mind of the White Christian South* (Athens: University of Georgia Press, 1998), 67–71. On the wartime application of the jeremiad to slavery reform, see Drew Gilpin Faust, *The Creation of Confederate Nationalism: Ideology and Identity in the Civil War South* (Baton Rouge: Louisiana State University Press, 1988), 76–79. On the comparison of Jackson to Christ, see Stout, *Upon the Altar of the Nation*, 228–29. For grumbling about excessive religiosity, see Edward Porter Alexander, *Fighting for the Confederacy: The Personal Recollections of General Edward Porter Alexander*, ed. Gary W. Gallagher (Chapel Hill: University of North Carolina Press, 1989), 59.

29. For the stand work on postwar reconciliation, see David W. Blight, *Race and Reunion: The Civil War in American Memory* (Cambridge, Mass.: Harvard University Press, Belknap Press, 2001).

30. See, for example, Mark Grimsley, *The Hard Hand of War: Union Military Policy toward Civilians, 1861–1865* (Cambridge: Cambridge University Press, 1995),

and Joseph T. Glatthaar, *The March to the Sea and Beyond: Sherman's Troops in the Savannah and Carolinas Campaigns* (New York: New York University Press, 1985). For a contrary perspective, see Charles Royster, *The Destructive War: William Tecumseh Sherman, Stonewall Jackson, and the Americans* (New York: Knopf, 1991), and Michael Fellman, *Inside War: The Guerrilla Conflict in Missouri during the American Civil War* (New York: Oxford University Press, 1989). This interpretation obviously departs from Stout and, to a lesser extent, Noll, who have expressed profound disappointment with what they see as a lack of theological gravitas in American evangelicals' reactions to the war, buttressing, in their view, violent forms of patriotism that ignored questions of racial and social inequality (Stout, *Upon the Altar of the Nation*, xvi–xxii; Noll, *Theological Crisis*, 92–94, 159–61).

31. *The Essential Holmes: Selections from the Letters, Speeches, Judicial Opinions, and Other Writings of Oliver Wendell Holmes, Jr.*, ed. Richard A. Posner (Chicago: University of Chicago Press, 1992), 89. For some literary examples of individuals who remained dissatisfied with the jeremiad tradition, see Noll's treatment of Dickinson and Melville in Mark A. Noll, *America's God: From Jonathan Edwards to Abraham Lincoln* (New York: Oxford University Press, 2002), 435–36.

5

After the Civil War: Auguste Comte's Theory of History Crosses the Atlantic

Andrew Witmer

In 1856, a French philosopher with aspirations to world power wrote a letter to one of his followers in the United States. With typical grandiosity, Auguste Comte (1798–1857) predicted that the tiny community of his American disciples would eventually grow powerful enough to establish an independent state. No one ever accused Comte of false modesty. He believed that the demise of belief in God and the spread of his own ideas were phases in the inevitable progress of humanity. The dramatic inaccuracy of his predictions concerning his American followers should not prevent us from seeing that many of Comte's ideas were seriously discussed in the United States, or that his central prophesies about religion were later widely accepted.[1]

While nineteenth-century Americans possessed several home-grown narratives about the religious future of the United States that welcomed the spread of godlessness, Comte's imported narrative was the most controversial and enduring. Beginning in the 1830s, American intellectuals debated the arguments of this audacious Frenchman who grounded his positivist philosophy in a theory of history predicting the end of theism and the triumph of naturalistic science and humanistic religion. These were not popular ideas. During the antebellum period, reformers such as William Lloyd Garrison and Lucretia Mott excoriated churches and clergy who threw the weight of organized religion behind social injustice, but only a few Americans openly rejected belief in God.[2] Debates over positivism peaked in the United States between the 1860s and 1880s. Most Americans, even those who modified their views significantly after encountering Comte's ideas, dismissed his predictions that belief in God would vanish. His theories, however, won over a small group of important thinkers, clothed Enlightenment attacks on traditional religion in the garb of scientific neutrality and historical inevitability, spurred on the academic secularizers who sought to reduce religion's public influence, and emerged during the middle decades of the twentieth century as a commonplace of modern sociology.

Comte's Prophesies

Auguste Comte believed fervently in a godless future. In the opening pages of his six-volume *Cours de philosophie positive*, published between 1830 and 1842, he elucidated his "law of human development," sometimes called the "law of three stages." This law, which formed the cornerstone of his progressive theory of history and became the most widely noted aspect of his thought, held that every human being and every branch of human knowledge passed through three stages of development. Everyone who reflected on his own intellectual growth, Comte claimed, realized that he "was a theologian in his childhood, a metaphysician in his youth, and a natural philosopher in his manhood."[3] Similarly, humankind had first come to know and describe the world in the theological stage of world history, during which people understood events in supernatural terms. This stage began in the dim recesses of prehistory with fetishism, progressed to polytheism, and reached its zenith in the monotheism of the medieval Roman Catholic Church (Comte viewed Protestantism as corrosive, divisive, and dangerous), an institution that for a time bequeathed social and intellectual unity to the West. During the second, metaphysical stage, Enlightenment thinkers substituted impersonal, abstract forces for divine providence. Comte credited this stage with shattering ecclesiastical tyranny and setting men free to explore the world, but he argued that its work was entirely critical, and that it had been unable to erect a new edifice amid the ruins of the theological systems it destroyed. The third stage promised to usher in a new era of unified knowledge and social concord. Comte associated this stage with the development of his positive, or scientific, philosophy, which rested on reasoning and observation, sought to discover and elucidate natural laws, and rigorously avoided appeals to supernatural causes or abstract forces.[4]

In the history of Western thought, theories of progressive historical development were nothing new. As earlier chapters have shown, such theories, including those of Kant, Condorcet, Ferguson, Jefferson, and Comte's teacher Henri de Saint-Simon, were abundant and well known during the eighteenth and nineteenth centuries. Comte's contribution to this body of theory was twofold. He elaborated a scientific *law* of human progress (he possessed none of Jefferson's fears about the possibility of historical regression) and linked progress to the death of belief in God more openly and systematically than any of his contemporaries. Yet Comte was not irreligious. In common with many other nineteenth-century apostles of science, he advocated a morally charged alternative to traditional faith, one that pursued scientific understanding and progress with religious fervor.[5] He hoped to use science to improve social conditions, and later in life he developed an antisupernatural religion that promoted ethical living and venerated humanity in place of God.

For Comte, the social, political, and moral crises of nineteenth-century Europe were signs of a deeper conflict between the theological, metaphysical, and positive systems. He was confident that these clashes would not continue forever. He declared that "all considerations whatever point to the Positive Philosophy as the one destined to prevail."[6] Over the following decades, Comte believed, positivism would gradually usurp the social, political, and intellectual authority of theology and metaphysics, and "leave to them only an historical existence."[7]

In speaking of the universal advent of the positive philosophy, Comte referred to the "necessary tendency of the human mind to substitute for the philosophical method which suited its infancy that which is appropriate to its maturity," and "the inevitable tendency of the human mind toward an exclusive positive philosophy, throughout the whole range of the intellectual system."[8] For Comte, the progressive development of individual intellect was an inherent quality of the human brain; as human beings matured, they inevitably substituted naturalistic, positivistic explanations for outmoded supernatural and metaphysical accounts of the world.

Comte also argued that the triumph of positivism was a law of history. He claimed that positivism had first achieved prominence during the age of Bacon, Descartes, and Galileo, when "the spirit of the positive philosophy rose up in opposition to that of the superstitions and scholastic systems which had hitherto obscured the true character of all science."[9] Positivism had subsequently made such enormous gains, while theology and metaphysics had declined so markedly, that "no rational mind" could doubt its ultimate victory.[10] Of course, the shift toward positivism occurred at varying speeds in different branches of knowledge. It was complete in astronomy but only beginning in the new field of sociology (a term invented by Comte, one of the discipline's founders). Comte believed that his application of positivist methods to the study of society would make the triumph of positivism "much more rapid and easy."[11]

We can put Comte's predictions in the form of a spiritual weather forecast: pleasantly godless, with a strong chance of lingering religious ritual. Positivists were officially agnostic regarding the existence of God, but their position on the question differed only nominally from atheism, however much some of them resisted the association. By setting strict limits on what could be known, and how, Comte effectively rendered a supernatural God unknowable. The Unitarian minister James Walker saw this clearly, observing that religion and metaphysics were destined to die if positivism won the day, "not by being denied and confuted, but by being ignored; not by the answer given to religious questions, but by the fact that the time is coming when no religious questions will be asked."[12] This vision of the future was highly congenial to Comte, who longed for science to fumigate the idle musings of theologians and philosophers, grounding all thought in careful observation of the world and the laws that governed it. His view that natural laws directed all phenomena rendered belief in the supernatural absurd.[13] Even if there was a God, there was no way to gain knowledge of him.

This did not mean, however, that Comte opposed all forms of religion. To the contrary, he believed that human beings possessed a deep religious drive, and he developed a new religion, which he labeled the Religion of Humanity, to direct this impulse along positivist lines.[14] The rituals of this new religion, sometimes referred to as the Second System (in distinction from the First System, associated with the *Cours de philosophie positive*), earned Comte a great deal of ridicule, though many Western intellectuals took its ethics and ideals of service to humanity seriously.[15] The Comtean church worshiped humanity rather than a supernatural God. It possessed a sacramental system; a liturgical calendar commemorating leaders in religion, art, science, and government (including William Penn and Thomas Jefferson); and a clergy headed by Comte.[16] Comte was addressed by church members as the High Priest of Humanity, Very Reverend Father, and First Supreme Pontiff of Humanity, and benefited financially from a Pontifical Fund established in 1848 for his priestly support.[17] The new religion's material culture featured a flag, green ribbons worn on the left arm, and statuettes of Humanity, resembling the image of the Virgin Mary, to be worn around the neck. To many observers, the Church of Humanity resembled the Roman Catholic Church stripped of its supernaturalism.[18] Though most intellectuals distinguished between the rigorous scientism of the First System and the sectarian religiosity of the Second System, Comte insisted on the unity of the two schemes. Both combined atheism, scientism, humanism, and social ethics. It was a combination that appealed deeply to some and repelled many others.

Comte's Readers

Few readers anywhere accepted everything Comte wrote. His work was largely ignored in Germany, and even the communities of religious positivists that sprang up in France and England during the second half of the nineteenth century frequently disagreed over how much of Comte's teachings to embrace. These communities never exceeded a few hundred members and attracted a total of only about two thousand adherents. In England, members included literary critic Frederic Harrison and novelist George Eliot, both of whom embraced the Religion of Humanity even as they continued to draw on other thinkers critical of traditional Christianity. During the 1850s, Eliot published an English translation of *The Essence of Christianity*, a widely read book by German philosopher Ludwig Feuerbach that echoed some of Comte's most important ideas in its depiction of God as nothing more than the projection of human qualities and needs.

In addition to cultivating positivists, Comte influenced academics. In France, his most important contributions were to the history of science, and his ideas were dispersed through the writings of Emile Littre. A young university student named Emile Durkheim, later a towering figure in the sociology of religion, studied his work during the 1880s. In England, John Stuart Mill, George Lewes, and Harriet Martineau embraced aspects of his thought, though all three rejected his religious system. Comte's work was widely debated by nineteenth-century British religious intellectuals, earning positivism notoriety in the years after his death in 1857.[19]

In the United States, interest in Comte peaked during the decades following the Civil War, as the pace of social, economic, and technological change quickened and religious leaders worried about the "crisis in religion" and the "war" between religion and science. Their fears were not groundless, though they were often misplaced. While most scientists were Christians with no desire to harm religion and most ministers esteemed the scientific disciplines, science competed successfully with religion for public admiration, fascination, and authority during the nineteenth century.[20] Some scientists and scientific popularizers, moreover, such as the men behind *Popular Science Monthly* and *Scientific American*, really did work hard from the 1870s onward to discredit the Baconian approach to science, which was hospitable to religious claims, and replace it with a purely secular approach.[21] Most Americans still believed in God but, ceded cultural authority to scientists and other secular experts as the nation applied its technological might to the effort to spread Western Christianity and culture around the globe. Growing numbers of Americans rejected belief in God altogether; just as important, freethinkers, including Robert Ingersoll, used periodicals and the lecture circuit during the last quarter of the nineteenth century to spread their arguments for unbelief much more widely than ever before.[22]

In this setting, Comte's work, which prophesied the end of Christianity and the triumph of scientific religion, posed a serious challenge to the religious establishment. Even American religious thinkers who were willing to rework and assimilate nearly every other supposed danger to religious faith viewed positivism as a starker and more fundamental challenge. Comte thus became a lightning rod for criticism and a potent symbol of the challenges facing religious faith in the West. Reactions to Comte varied widely, from positivist evangelist Henry Edger and the handful of Americans who embraced Comte's Second System to theological liberals and "judicious conservatives" who, often unintentionally, modified their religious views in light of positivism to theological conservatives who energetically attacked Comte's ideas and any others that could be tarred with the label of positivism.[23] The majority of Comte's nineteenth-century American readers rejected his predictions that faith in God would disappear, and even the early American sociologists who accepted Comte's claims and derived significant inspiration from him in their campaign to define their field in secular scientific terms were often slow to acknowledge his influence. Only during the twentieth century, through the work of European social theorists who were themselves mostly unconscious disciples of Comte, did Comte's prophesies of godlessness achieve the status of unquestioned sociological orthodoxy in the United States.

American Positivists

English immigrant Henry Edger, who corresponded regularly with Comte and viewed himself as a positivist missionary to the New World, never succeeded in winning more than a few Long Island converts to the Religion of Humanity. He did, however, influence a small circle of New York City positivists that during the late 1860s and 1870s drew adherents from the comfortable middle class, especially journalists and editors.[24] While the degree of their adherence to the Second System varied, members of this fellowship accepted the broad outlines of Comte's theory of history. Henry Evans, secretary of the New York Positivist Society, argued in an address on positivism that the "old cargoes of Theology and Metaphysics must be thrown overboard, and the decks thoroughly washed."[25] In an 1871 speech to the society, John Elderkin claimed that the "old interpretation of nature and the assumptions of theology are altogether too shallow for the broad and deep intelligence of the modern mind," and recommended that humanity look to positivism as "the old theology fails before the light of science."[26]

The most prolific of the New York positivists was David Croly, a news-paperman who wrote a book and numerous articles on positivism. Croly believed that traditional religion was outmoded, unscientific, a powerful brake on human endeavor and progress, and a "disease, of which mankind is slowly but surely getting cured."[27] He claimed that "there can be no reconciliation between modern science and the old theologies now taught in our churches," and argued that orthodox religion had been decisively undermined by modern science, which had "taken all past conceptions of Deity, has put them in a crucible, and after the gases have been driven off and the dross burned out in the fire of criticism, all the pure metal which has been found remaining is Humanity,—nothing more."[28]

Thaddeus Wakeman, a radical writer whose work reflected positivist influences, grew increasingly hostile to theism during the 1880s and 1890s. Writing in a leading national journal in 1884, Wakeman declared "Theology is the past tense; Science is king" and criticized the custom of prayer as "simply evidence of man's weakness and needs, and of the childish views he once entertained of the world and of God. As far as the needs remain, science will supply them under intelligent human effort."[29]

American positivists eagerly anticipated the demise of orthodox Christianity, which they believed had played its historical role in elevating humanity from savagery and should now be shoved as forcefully as possible off the world stage. Already, orthodox Christianity was on the ropes and reeling under its opponents' heavy pounding, for as "science is constantly destroying all the intellectual conceptions upon which the prevailing theologies rest, the old priestly body is losing its influence."[30] Along with Christian belief would go its God and its claims to understand the supernatural. If Christianity left some of its liturgy and costumery behind when it stumbled into the wings, positivists would happily use them to fit out their new leading men—the scientists, philosophers, and artists who would rule in the future.[31] This new priesthood's authority would be widely accepted by a public overawed by its scientific expertise.

Science and Religion Rumble

This notion of a bruising battle between science and traditional religion that would end in victory for science was perhaps the most influential intellectual legacy of Auguste Comte and his American followers. It established a false dichotomy between science and religion that, as subsequent chapters will show, was effectively deployed by later enemies of traditional religion such as Robert Ingersoll, Clarence Darrow, and countless supposedly neutral social scientists. No one did more to promote this view than the American scientist and historian John William Draper. Though not a strict positivist, Draper was deeply influenced by Comte's progressive theory of history and notion of the oppositional relationship between science and religion. In his widely read *History of the Conflict between Religion and Science* (1874) and other books, Draper, according to historian Donald Fleming, constructed a "myth of the reifications Science and Religion wrestling together for dominance," along with a pantheon of scientific martyrs such as Copernicus, Galileo, German higher critics of the Pentateuch, and nineteenth-century evolutionists.[32]

While Draper was especially hostile to Roman Catholics, his terms for reconciliation between science and religion were unacceptable to most American Protestants. He required believers to refrain from assertions of dogma on scientific matters, demanding unilateral disarmament in the alleged conflict between repressive, politically powerful Christianity and the liberating forces of science.[33] He asked:

> As to the issue of the coming conflict, can any one doubt? Whatever is resting on fiction and fraud will be overthrown. Institutions that organize impostures and spread delusions must show what right they have to exist. Faith must render an account of herself to Reason. Mysteries must give place to facts. Religion must relinquish that imperious, that domineering position which she has so long maintained against Science.[34]

Among other things, the positivist vision of science systematically destroying belief in God strongly influenced American debates over the evolutionary theories of Charles Darwin. While theological conservatives denied any antipathy toward science rightly understood, they were as quick as their positivist counterparts to assert the irreconcilability of Comtean science—which they viewed as atheistic materialism—and theism. As historian Charles Cashdollar has shown, American responses to Darwin were frequently colored by associations, real and imagined, with Comte. Theological conservatives accommodated certain strains of evolutionary theory (which had not yet become exclusively linked with the idea of natural selection) but fiercely resisted anything with a positivist connection.[35] Darwin's reception in the United States suffered from his ties with alleged positivists such as Herbert Spencer and

Thomas Huxley.[36] For many, the Comte connection signaled that Darwin, too, was an atheist. Conservative theologian Robert L. Dabney, for example, claimed that Darwin and Comte thrust the human soul toward a "gulf of the blackness of darkness . . . a gulf without immortality, without a God, without a faith."[37]

Darwin's association with Comte was a powerful weapon in the hands of the clergy and the conservative press, for as long as Darwin was connected with Comte, his ideas were suspect. Only when the two were disconnected could Darwinism be reconciled with theology.[38] Some followers of Comte and Darwin denied the association, but David Croly embraced it, claiming that Darwin had shown that the "harmonies of the universe can be satisfactorily accounted for without the interposition of any creative will or First Cause whatever."[39] A conservative journal made precisely the same point when it described Comte and Darwin as apostles of a "scientific scepticism" that denied "the Deity all share in the supervision and control of his works" and attempted to "efface all those proofs of design from which his existence even as a Creator can be deduced."[40] Predictably, the alleged connections between Comte and Darwin were most often highlighted by conservative Methodists, Lutherans, Presbyterians, and Baptists.[41] The confusion of Darwin with Comte was unique to the United States and helps explain the fierce battle, also unique to the United States, waged between religious conservatives and apostles of the new scientific worldview in the century and a half since.

Liberal Protestants and Comte

Not all American Protestants were so suspicious of Comte. In fact, there are interesting similarities between the story Comte constructed about science and religion and the perspective liberal Protestants in the United States adopted, a perspective more fully described in chapter 7. In a series of lectures and articles culminating in his two-volume *History of the Warfare of Science with Theology in Christendom* (1896), Andrew Dickson White, cofounder and first president of Cornell University, distinguished himself from John William Draper by arguing that the crucial conflict was between science and dogmatic theology rather than science and religion. In a sentence that sounds as if it could have been taken directly from Comte, White framed the relationship as "a conflict between two epochs in the evolution of human thought—the theological and the scientific." This conflict, according to White, would continue to drain the strength of "Dogmatic Theology based on biblical texts and ancient modes of thought," even as it allowed true religion (the recognition of a higher power and the love of God and neighbor) to flourish. White filled his articles and books with tales of the triumphs of science over dogmatism, and he claimed that as clergymen would "cease to struggle against scientific methods and conclusions" and labor "in the field left to them," their work would become more noble and more beautiful.[42]

White's views on science and religion offer a fair representation of the general liberal Protestant response to Comte. Liberal Protestants were typically eager to reshape their theology through engagement with modern thought, including the writings of Comte and other positivists, but unwilling to embrace Comte's predictions about the death of theism, as shown by White's distinction between religion and dogmatic theology.[43] For liberals, Comte was useful insofar as his theories helped to undermine the biblical literalism and supernaturalism of conservative Protestants, but he was badly mistaken in predicting that science would inevitably weaken belief in God. Liberals believed that science and theism would together make the world a better place. Only in later generations did a handful of liberal theologians—including Harvey Cox, whose work is discussed in chapter 9—embrace secularization and the demise of what they called the "gods of traditional religions" as elements of religious and social progress.

Conservative Protestants and Comte

Nineteenth-century liberals shared their reluctance to embrace Comte's prophesies of theistic decline with a second group of Protestant intellectuals whom Charles Cashdollar calls "judicious conservatives." This group, which included James McCosh, a leading Scottish theologian who served as president of Princeton University, and Noah Porter, president of Yale University, were less eager to adapt their theology to harmonize with Comte, but nevertheless altered their beliefs in significant ways as they engaged with modern philosophy.[44] Still, judicious conservatives rejected Comte's prophesies of godlessness, aligning themselves on this point with their more theologically conservative brethren, such as Charles Hodge of Princeton Seminary and southern theologian Robert L. Dabney.

Conservative criticisms of Comte's predictions concerning the death of God usually took one of three forms: discrediting Comte's views by emphasizing his ties with other dangerous thinkers; critiquing his ideas about the relationship between science and religion; and disagreeing with the accuracy of his historical account. While most conservative writers took the threat of positivism seriously, their own relentlessly optimistic view of history assured them that God would ultimately prevail against his enemies. Theirs was an ascendant view of a gradual march toward the triumph of Christianity.

The tendency to link Comte with other European thinkers and schools of thought was the product of historical circumstance as well as a deliberate strategy for undermining Comte. Few American conservatives in fact read Comte; most learned about positivism exclusively from secondary sources, especially the work of British philosopher John Stuart Mill.[45] There was thus an obvious reason for associating Comte with British empiricism, though Mill had carefully defined his differences with the Frenchman. In addition, Comte described his work as the culmination of a proud philosophical tradition stretching back to Bacon, Descartes, and Galileo.[46] For equally polemical purposes, his critics expanded positivism into an amorphous term under which they lumped a range of suspect views. Comte's conservative detractors most frequently criticized his ideas as part of a trend toward atheism. Lyman Atwater, for example, a Princeton professor, excoriated positivism as an example of "unblushing Atheism" that "purposely ungods the universe," while James McCosh described Comte as "an open and rabid atheist."[47]

A second set of criticisms reveals conservatives' reluctance to admit the existence of any necessary conflict between theism and science (when science was rightly understood). Far from accepting the supposed antagonism, a writer in the Biblical Repertory and Princeton Review argued that science could proceed only on the basis of the uniformity of nature, a belief grounded in biblical revelation.[48] A related argument held that scientists failed to comprehend the full meaning of their discoveries unless guided by the principles of revealed religion. Erastus O. Haven, president of Northwestern University, viewed Comte and his fellow theorizers as "mere collectors of facts" with "no desire to know what facts mean."[49] Critics of the notion that science and religion were necessarily antagonistic also pointed out that even modern science rested on certain articles of faith. A writer named William Hague charged scientists with smuggling unwarranted assumptions into their much-hyped naturalism, mockingly referring to the "Theological School of Scientific Naturalism" and the "Theological Naturalistic School."[50]

The third leading form of criticism tackled Comte's three-stage theory of history directly, claiming that it was simply untrue. In an article published shortly after Comte's death, Charles Shields denied that all individuals moved through theology and metaphysics to positivism, as Comte postulated. He also denied that these three stages had unfolded progressively through history. Actually, Shields contended, theology and metaphysics had never been stronger, and the putative conflict between the three stages had "not as yet resulted in the extinction of any one of the series."[51] This indicated to Shields that the stages did not inevitably oppose one another, in fact had developed amicably and could now be found "harmoniously coexisting in the most advanced nations, and in the most accomplished minds."[52]

Many other conservative writers criticized Comte's theory of history. Haven called the theory a half truth, arguing that while Comte believed in progress through three stages of mental development, the three stages actually coexisted in mature adults.[53] James McCosh pointed out that "there is as much, and as intense, religious feeling in our country at this present time as there ever was in any country since man appeared on earth."[54] Theologian Theodor Christlieb argued that the relationship between science and theology was constantly improving in America, claiming that the two would eventually collaborate to demonstrate God's glory.[55]

While conservative intellectuals vigorously combated Comte, few seemed overly worried about the future. Charles Hodge noted that since there were only a handful of positivists while "nine hundred and ninety-nine millions of the thousand millions of our race still believe in God, it is a rather violent assumption that mankind have reached the stage of positivism."[56] Robert L. Dabney was more alarmed than most, but even he was convinced of Christianity's ultimate triumph. He warned listeners to his 1871 sermon "A Caution against Anti-Christian Science" that "if things go on as they do now, the church will have a generation of infidel sons."[57] The threat that made Dabney's sensitive hackles rise was scientific naturalism, especially positivism. According to Dabney, naturalism had long existed in one form or another. Now, however, the sciences spewed forth discoveries and claims at a faster pace, ranging from arguments for an ancient earth and a localized flood to the assertion that man had developed from lower forms of life. For Dabney there were only two options: resist naturalistic science or surrender Scripture as an infallible source of truth. And yet, even in the midst of these worries, Dabney could boldly declare, "I am not afraid to predict an assured final triumph for the Bible in this warfare." In his view, there would always be "forces to overwhelm unbelief with defeat."[58]

Almost without exception, American Protestants countered Comte's prophesies with their own deeply held belief that God himself was guiding America into a brighter future. The exceptionalism and mission of the Puritans were renewed in criticisms of Comte's predictions. The Congregationalist professor of theology Samuel Harris claimed in an 1870 lecture, for example, that only Christianity provided the grounds for a progressive civilization. He criticized the "unprogressive and stagnant" future society prophesied by Comte, a society with no individual rights and a despotic priesthood of the intellectually gifted.[59] Harris contrasted this dystopia with his own millennial hope for the "transformation of human society into a kingdom of God, in which men will realize the highest possibilities of their being, and the reign of justice and love will be extended over all the earth." He was persuaded that this glorious future would be ushered in through "Christian progress."[60]

For a variety of social and political reasons, most nineteenth-century Americans shared Harris's rejection of Comte's prophesies of godlessness. Comte wrote in postrevolutionary France, where he was influenced by the reactionary policies of the government and the Roman Catholic Church. The Church's efforts to expand its control over education and intellectual life in France likely increased Comte's tendency to view tensions between religion and science in the starkest terms. Such ideas were less likely to have traction in the American context. American intellectuals wrote in a society in which Christianity exerted a powerful but constitutionally limited influence, posing no formal threat to free scientific inquiry. The majority of American Protestants viewed scientific advances and the spread of Christianity as compatible and mutually supporting projects. While they configured the relationship between science and religion in many different ways, most Americans shared Comte's optimistic view of history while vigorously rejecting his vision of a godless future.

Comte and American Sociology

An important exception to this widespread rejection of Comte's prophesies were the men who during the late nineteenth and early twentieth centuries defined the new field of American academic sociology. Lester Frank Ward, an important early figure in sociology, wholly embraced Comte's three-stage theory of history.[61] Even before Ward encountered Comte's writings, he had rejected his conservative Christian upbringing and come to view the "religious crisis" of the nineteenth century as a fight between "bigots" and "the rational element," deriding Christian beliefs as "the modified superstitions of barbarous ages, the natural offspring of man's primitive ignorance."[62] In his foundational and field-defining work *Dynamic Sociology* (1883), Ward repeatedly and even lavishly endorsed Comte's theory of history, claiming that Comte's "knowledge of the general trend of society and human thought is certainly wonderful."[63]

Like Ward, nearly all of America's early academic sociologists, from William Graham Sumner and Albion Small to Edward A. Ross and Franklin Giddings, were personally hostile to traditional religion.[64] This antagonism, combined with their desire to professionalize sociology and restrict its practice to guild-certified experts, fueled their efforts to define sociology as a strictly secular science. Though they were opposed by religious reformers who wished to place sociology in the service of the social gospel, the academic sociologists prevailed.[65] In their contempt for traditional religion and confidence in the triumph of secular science, along with many other positivistic views embedded in the seminal sociological textbooks they authored between the 1880s and the 1920s, these zealous "apostles of secularization" clearly reflected the influence of Auguste Comte, who, with Herbert Spencer, was foundational to their thought.[66]

Still, academic sociologists were often reluctant to acknowledge their debt to Comte. In some cases, this was because they felt the need to be more guarded about their secularizing aims than association with the crusading and polarizing Comte allowed, but it was also due to the fact that Comte's brand of grand historical theorizing had become unfashionable by the 1890s. As the young discipline of sociology turned toward more (allegedly) neutral, empirical studies of narrowly defined social problems, scholars like Albion Small, founder of the *American Journal of Sociology*, downplayed Comte's importance for American sociology.[67]

In spite of such denials, Comte continued to exert an important, though usually indirect, influence on American sociology throughout the twentieth century. When American sociologists embraced European theoretical perspectives assuming the inevitable demise of belief in God, they did so under the influence of theorists who in some cases had absorbed their secularizing views from Comte. With few exceptions, the most important European sociologists adopted some version of the secularization thesis.[68] Max Weber and Emile Durkheim, both of whom were indebted to Comte for their views, were widely read and widely influential in the United States.[69] By the 1950s, the Comtean prophecy of theistic obsolescence, of the inevitable triumph of naturalistic science, had again penetrated the mainstream of American social science, this time entwining itself with fears of totalitarianism and theories of modernization (in ways to be explored in later chapters). It was a belief that had already informed significant social scientific work and encouraged crusaders' efforts to spread the authority of secular science into areas of public life formerly dominated by religion. Now it blossomed into a fully articulated theory of secularization that held sway in the American academy for decades.

NOTES

1. The letter is in Richmond Laurin Hawkins, *Positivism in the United States (1853–1861)* (Cambridge, Mass.: Harvard University Press, 1938), 181.

2. Susan Jacoby, *Freethinkers: A History of American Secularism* (New York: Holt, 2004), chap. 3.

3. *The Positive Philosophy of Auguste Comte*, trans. and ed. Harriet Martineau (New York: Calvin Blanchard, 1858), 27. This was the edition most Americans read.

4. Ibid., 25–27. I have also drawn on Charles D. Cashdollar, *The Transformation of Theology, 1830–1890: Positivism and Protestant Thought in Britain and America* (Princeton: Princeton University Press, 1989), 9–11, for this summary.

5. For an illuminating discussion of the competing moral horizons of science and religion during the nineteenth century, see Charles Taylor, *Sources of the Self: The Making of the Modern Identity* (Cambridge, Mass.: Harvard University Press, 1989), chap. 22.

6. *Positive Philosophy of Auguste Comte*, 36.

7. Ibid., 30.

8. Ibid., 764 and 531.

9. Ibid., 29.

10. Ibid., 29.

11. Ibid., 817.

12. Quoted in Richmond Laurin Hawkins, *Auguste Comte and the United States (1816–1853)* (Cambridge, Mass.: Harvard University Press, 1936), 17. The quotation is from a September 1849 article in the *Christian Examiner*.

13. *Positive Philosophy of Auguste Comte*, 28.

14. Comte elaborated his new religious and political systems in *Catechisme positiviste* (1852) and in his four-volume *Systeme de politique positive* (1851–54).

15. It is worth noting in this connection that Comte coined the term "altruism." His social ethics prompted self-criticism on the part of some of his religious contemporaries.

16. Gillis J. Harp, " 'The Church of Humanity': New York's Worshiping Positivists," *Church History* 60, 4 (December 1991): 509–11; Hawkins, *Auguste Comte and the United States*, 13.

17. Hawkins, *Positivism in the United States*, 132–33, 138, 140, 145.

18. Thomas Huxley famously derided Comte's philosophy as "Catholicism *minus* Christianity"; quoted in Cashdollar, *Transformation of Theology*, 165.

19. W. M. Simon, *European Positivism in the Nineteenth Century: An Essay in Intellectual History* (Ithaca, N.Y.: Cornell University Press, 1963); Gladys Bryson, "Early English Positivists and the Religion of Humanity," *American Sociological Review* 1, 3 (June 1936): 343–62; Cashdollar, *Transformation of Theology*.

20. James Turner, *Without God, without Creed: The Origins of Unbelief in America* (Baltimore: Johns Hopkins University Press, 1985), 124–25. The growing authority of science in realms formerly dominated by religion is evident in the rise of the major research university late in the nineteenth century. See George Marsden, *The Soul of the American University: From Protestant Establishment to Established Unbelief* (New York: Oxford University Press, 1996).

21. Eva Marie Garroutte, "The Postivist Attack on Baconian Science and Religious Knowledge in the 1870s," in Christian Smith, ed., *The Secular Revolution: Power, Interests, and Conflict in the Secularization of American Public Life* (Berkeley: University of California Press, 2003).

22. Jacoby, *Freethinkers*, chap. 6.

23. The term "judicious conservative" is from Cashdollar, *Transformation of Theology*, and is explained later.

24. Harp, "Church of Humanity,'" 508–23.

25. Henry Evans, "Positivism," in C. G. David [David G. Croly], *A Positivist Primer: Being a Series of Familiar Conversations on the Religion of Humanity* (New York: David Wesley, 1871), app. A, 117.

26. John Elderkin, "Positivism and Contemporary Immorality," in David, *Positivist Primer*, app. B, 122–23.

27. David, *Positivist Primer*, 20. Harp identifies Croly as the author of this book in "'Church of Humanity,'" 519; "C. G. David" was a pseudonym.

28. Ibid., 6–7.

29. "Science and Prayer," *North American Review* 137 (July 1883): 193, 201, quoted in Gillis J. Harp, *Positivist Republic: Auguste Comte and the Reconstruction of American Liberalism, 1865–1920* (University Park: Pennsylvania State University Press, 1995), 74; for a discussion of Wakeman, see chap. 4.

30. Ibid., 34.

31. David, *Positivist Primer*, 33–35.

32. Donald Fleming, *John William Draper and the Religion of Science* (New York: Octagon Books, 1972), 128–29.

33. John William Draper, *History of the Conflict between Religion and Science* (New York: Appleton, 1897), v–vii.

34. Ibid., 367.

35. Ronald L. Numbers has shown that by the late 1870s most American scientists had embraced evolution but not natural selection, a doctrine that remained marginalized in America for much of the nineteenth century. The separability of evolution and natural selection created ample intellectual space for the reconciliation of evolution and Christianity. See Ronald L. Numbers, *Darwinism Comes to America* (Cambridge, Mass.: Harvard University Press, 1998), chap. 1.

36. Cashdollar, *Transformation of Theology*, 184–85. Charles Hodge of Princeton Theological Seminary cited Herbert Spencer in order to show that Darwin's theories militated against divine activity in Creation. See Charles Hodge, *What Is Darwinism?* (New York: Scribner, Armstrong, 1874).

37. Quoted in Cashdollar, *Transformation of Theology*, 188.

38. Ibid., 187. James McCosh was a prominent conservative theologian who distinguished between Comte and Darwin and proved willing to embrace aspects of Darwin's theories.

39. David, *Positivist Primer*, 9.

40. *Biblical Repertory and Princeton Review* 42, 1 (January 1870): 58–59.

41. Cashdollar, *Transformation of Theology*, 188.

42. Andrew Dickson White, *A History of the Warfare of Science with Theology in Christendom* (New York: Appleton, 1903), all quotations from the introduction. White participated in at least one meeting of the Nineteenth Century Club, a positivist salon organized during the 1880s. See Harp, *Positivist Republic*, 68–70.

43. Cashdollar, *Transformation of Theology*, chap. 10.

44. Ibid., chap. 9. Princeton University was known until 1896 as the College of New Jersey.

45. Charles D. Cashdollar, "Auguste Comte and the American Reformed Theologians," *Journal of the History of Ideas* 39, 1 (January–March 1978): 62–65. Even those American Reformed theologians who read Comte for themselves tended to use the 1853 abridged translation by Harriet Martineau; few read him in the original French.

46. *Positive Philosophy of Auguste Comte*, 29.

47. Lyman Atwater, article 3, *Biblical Repertory and Princeton Review* 28, 1 (January 1856): 61–62; James McCosh, *Christianity and Positivism: A Series of Lectures to the Times on Natural Theology and Apologetics* (New York: Robert Carter and Brothers, 1871), 168.

48. "The Logical Relations of Religion and Natural Science," *Biblical Repertory and Princeton Review* 32, 4 (October 1860): 577–608.

49. E. O. Haven, "Soul: A Positive Entity," in Rev. James McCosh et al., eds., *Questions of Modern Thought: Lectures on the Bible and Infidelity* (Philadelphia: Ziegler and McCurdy, 1871), 2.

50. William Hague, "The Self-Witnessing Character of the New Testament Christianity," in ibid., 17–18.

51. Charles Woodruff Shields, "The Positive Philosophy of Auguste Comte," *Biblical Repertory and Princeton Review* 30, 1 (January 1858): 10–11.

52. Ibid., 16.

53. Haven, "Soul," 7–8.

54. James McCosh, *Examination of Mr. J. S. Mill's Philosophy* (1866), quoted in Cashdollar, *Transformation of Theology*, 355.

55. Theodor Christlieb, *The Best Methods of Counteracting Modern Infidelity* (New York: Harper and Brothers, 1874), 70.

56. Charles Hodge, *Systematic Theology* (Grand Rapids, Mich.: Eerdmans, 1975) (orig. pub. 1872), 257.

57. Robert Lewis Dabney, "A Caution against Anti-Christian Science: A Sermon on Colossians, II, 8" (Richmond, Va.: J. E. Goode, 1871), 7.

58. Ibid., 19.

59. Samuel Harris, "The Christian Doctrine of Human Progress Contrasted with the Naturalistic," in *Christianity and Skepticism: Boston Lectures 1870* (Boston: Congregational Sabbath-School and Publishing Society, 1870), 26.

60. Ibid., 14.

61. See Harp, *Positivist Republic*, 135–36.

62. Quoted in ibid., 123.

63. Quoted in ibid., 135–36.

64. Jeffrey K. Hadden, "Toward Desacralizing Secularization Theory," *Social Forces* 65, 3 (March 1987): 589–94; Christian Smith, "Secularizing American Higher Education: The Case of Early American Sociology," in Christian Smith, ed., *The Secular Revolution: Power, Interests, and Conflict in the Secularization of American Public Life* (Berkeley: University of California Press: 2003).

65. Smith, "Secularizing American Higher Education," 105–14.

66. Ibid., 114–53.

67. Harp, *Positivist Republic*, 168–72. See "A Comtean Centenary," *American Journal of Sociology* 27, 4 (January 1922): 510–13. Harp attributes this piece to Small.

68. José Casanova, *Public Religions in the Modern World* (Chicago: University of Chicago Press, 1994), 17.

69. See Philip Gorski, "The Return of the Repressed: Religion and the Political Unconscious of Historical Sociology," in Julia Adams, Elisabeth S. Clemens, and Ann Shola Orloff, eds., *Remaking Modernity: Politics, History, and Sociology* (Durham, N.C.: Duke University Press, 2005), 172–75. Gorski argues that Durkheim and Weber broke only partially with Comte, retaining his assumptions about the decline of traditional religion and bequeathing this vision to the sociology of religion. Gorski argues that sociologists of religion are still partially trapped in a positivist framework that views secularization teleologically, as a developmental trend; he calls for a new "post-positivist sociology of religion."

6

The Gilded Age and Progressive Era: Mastery, Modern Doubt, and the Costs of Progress

Christopher McKnight Nichols

"The 'tramp' comes with the locomotive, and almshouses and prisons are as surely the marks of 'material progress' as are costly dwellings, rich warehouses, and magnificent churches." These words from *Progress and Poverty*, published by Henry George in 1879, struck a best-selling chord. Modern society, it seemed to many of his readers, was rife with suffering. Yet, George argued, suffering was not inevitable. "The laws of the universe," he wrote, "do not deny the natural aspirations of the human heart." Deeply religious, George was the father of the single tax idea and was widely influential, even among secular reform thinkers. He infused his work with a sense of righteous indignation that there was no necessity to the march either of progress or of poverty. Man, said George, must turn to God for strength. However, man must then use his God-given strength to bring about much-needed change. As one scholar later observed, "The struggle of good with evil was to Henry George the process that reduces economics and religion to common terms."[1]

By the end of the nineteenth century, religiously based reform perspectives such as George's collided with scientific and secular predictions about progress. They particularly contrasted with the views of the outspoken lecturer Robert Green Ingersoll, widely known as the Great Agnostic and an exponent of so-called freethinking atheism. He deemed religion to be at odds with the advance of progress. Poverty could be solved by science, not faith, he said. And like George, Ingersoll had a large and sympathetic audience for his views. The struggle between these two views deeply shaped American thought, both in terms of society and politics as well as the nature and future of religion in America.

Yet there was also a third major strand of thinking on this topic that can be seen in Harvard philosopher and psychologist William James's attempts to study religious experience rigorously and to reconcile authentic religious beliefs with science. Each of these intellectual communities understood George's famous remark in their own ways as they struggled to make sense of what the realities of industrial America might mean for the nation's moral and religious future. They shared a common question: if the tramp comes with progress, can God?

From Hell to Hell's Kitchen

Progressive ideas were not necessarily or exclusively premised on faith in science; they were particularly persuasive among the Christian ranks of the Social Gospel movement. This group generally agreed that personal salvation and faith alone would not make society better and could not address the problems of a modernizing, industrial America. Instead, they asserted that reform must be done by man for man. However, most of them did not believe that religion and scientific advancement were at odds. One of their most persistent metaphors of progress was that of "building the Kingdom of God on earth." A prominent proponent of such social reforms was Charles Sheldon. In 1897 he published *In His Steps*, which was wildly popular, selling nearly 15 million copies—the most successful piece of fiction in the era. The book, in which a successful young minister leaves his comfortable position to tend to the needy, posed a fascinating and enduring question: "What Would Jesus Do?"[2]

Building on this maxim, George A. Campbell Jr., the editor of *The Christian Oracle*, a small-circulation magazine, surveyed the changing society around him and believed it revealed a progression toward a more moral, more Christian future. In 1900 he renamed his publication the *Christian Century*. "We believe that the coming century is to witness greater triumphs in Christianity than any previous century has ever witnessed," Campbell wrote, from his offices in Chicago. "And that it is to be more truly Christian than any of its predecessors." Religious progressives like Campbell envisioned a century defined by mainline Protestantism—Presbyterian, Lutheran, Episcopalian, Methodist, and his own church, the Disciples of Christ.[3]

At the turn of the twentieth century, and not just in the United States, William Gladstone surveyed the state of the jeremiad form. Writing in 1898, he noted that hell had been "relegated . . . to the far-off corners of the Christian mind . . . there to sleep in deep shadow as a thing needless in our enlightened and progressive age." The Puritans' motivating meditations on hell's terrors— what Edwards once called the "smoke of your torment"—no longer appeared effective in generating socioreligious change. Without hell and with heaven as motivation, the turn of the twentieth century brought fresh ideas that trans- formed long-standing predictions of American godlessness. A useful metaphor for this change is the shift in attention from a concern with going to hell in the afterlife to Social Gospelers working to alleviate the dire poverty and crime in Hell's Kitchen, New York. [4]

Others in the progressive cause shared a growing scientific skepticism about supernatural tenets of Christianity; what Jesus might do was not as important as what practical reforms would do to help create the meaningful changes in economic and political structures and in living conditions that they believed were critical to a better American future. In considering the future role of religion in society, the question for many secular progressives was what function religious belief would serve in motivating and propelling any given reform process. In addition, they wondered if the civic republicanism they affirmed required shared values other than the common civic beliefs that were required for secular improvement. As industrialization rapidly expanded, social justice for the poor, for women, for workers, and for the alleviation of social ills emerged as a powerful call to arms to many who came to think of themselves as "progressives."

The progressive journalist Walter Lippmann produced one of the most influential formulations of this view in his book *Drift and Mastery* (1914). "Religions," he maintained, "have placed human action in a large and friendly setting. They have enabled men to play their little role by making it essential to the drama of eternity."[5] But that was not enough, he asserted. Americans nee- ded to employ "the scientific method" in a process he termed "mastery"; but it must not be a "passionless" absorption in facts. Science was driven by curiosity, he wrote. Emotion and scientific organization, therefore, could be reconciled and need not be diametrically opposed. Moreover, in charting a course for the future, Lippmann believed that progressives should reject the "gloomy sanctity" of the past. He asked: "Can we not free ourselves in the light of its great varie- ty?"[6] Lippmann's concerted scientific "uses" of the past—his "mastery" for enhancing the present for the future—therefore seemed antithetical to more religious, providentialist forms of thinking.

William James raised similar concerns, asking what makes religion useful? Such a question was characteristic of the era from the 1870s through the 1910s. During these years, the nation roared through a rapid industrialization that sparked debates over whether religion could help mankind become better. Widespread skeptical thinking about how to change society and improve it for the future flourished. Many absolutes in American society—from belief in God to reliance on laissez-faire capitalism—were subjected to critical assessment by thinkers, writers, and activists, including George, Sheldon, James, and scores of others. Religion, however challenged, remained an important feature of everyday life for most Americans in these years. This was as true for intellectuals, although they did not always recognize it, as for those more common women and men buffeted by tides of uncertainty. Yet most Americans also shared the sense that the unmasking effects of new scientific and industrial advances undermined sureness of personal conviction. Late Victorians had a term for the growing anomie: "modern doubt."

Ideas about "progress" and "progressivism" became catchall concepts for the new reformers. These progressives shared certain distinguishing ideals, while often differing on policies and positions. Of course they believed in "progress," but they differed over its precise meaning, even among themselves. What united most progressives was what might best be characterized as activism. That is, they argued that social ills would not take care of themselves; the evils of society—most evident in the cities awash in penury and prostitution—were getting worse. It was wrong to sit by passively, they said. As progressive Herbert Croly put it, the future would "not take care of itself"; it would "have to be planned and constructed, rather than fulfilled of its own momentum."[7] Progressive reforms in the present, therefore, were a means. They were directed toward achieving idealistic ends in the future: namely, a more efficient, just, moral, and harmonious society. On the other hand, conservatives of both secular and religious persuasions tended to believe that time, nature, and God would bring about favorable progress.

One key progressive belief was a core faith in the perfectibility of humanity and human institutions, particularly by the application of the "scientific method." They assumed that through scientific management and hard work, masses of people could be energized to bring about genuine social progress. Americans could, they said, work together to diminish poverty and injustice. To do so, they argued, the positive powers of government and civil society should be deployed to achieve these ends. "Investigate, educate, and legislate" encapsulated in a single motto many progressive reformers' convictions. Three of the most important strands of this movement exhibit the tensions and shifting balance among ideas about progress, religion, and science, and resulting predictions about America's religious future. These three stands of thought were the populist-secular, the progressive intellectual, and the Christian (cast in terms of the Social Gospel).

The populist-secular group was exemplified by Robert Ingersoll, anticipating Lippmann's later arguments. Ingersoll, the Great Agnostic, was one of the preeminent orators of the period. On the national lecture circuit, he spoke to citizens across the country. He advocated a secular philosophy of "free-thinking" that adapted the rhetoric of Enlightenment rationalism in an effort to debunk religious supernaturalism. While his ideas did not find wide approval, Ingersoll was widely heard. His prophesies blended the older jeremiad form with a heightened emphasis on atheistical science and Enlightenment rationality. In many ways, Ingersoll's beliefs anticipated those of later thinkers such as Bertrand Russell and Richard Rorty.

The second group, from the ranks of progressive intellectuals, were represented in part by the powerful style of thinking about religion that William James developed. A distinguished philosopher and psychologist who wrote largely for an academic audience, James was a radical empiricist who made religious experience a central subject of his scientific studies. He tried to legitimize faith for an era of increasing secular and scientific progress. Pragmatism in James's life became his methodological means to illuminate how religious experience was beneficial to humankind and thus to America's future social health.

The third group was a diverse group of Christian ministers and thinkers who advocated mastery along Christian lines, frequently using explicitly religious idioms to support their varied causes. George, Sheldon, Campbell, and particularly Walter Rauschenbusch thought this mastery could be achieved by combining an explicit ascensionist aim to create a more religious future with the reform tools of modern progressivism. As one scholar has noted, progressives frequently noted the "pervasiveness of Calvinist influences" in their youths, and while rebelling to some extent, they often channeled these ideas into their reform efforts.[8] While we will not focus on them much here, Social Gospel reform ideas were widely influential, and they remain a strong presence to day, most notably in the form of private-public initiatives such as faith-based social reform.

The massive social and cultural changes of the late nineteenth and early twentieth centuries produced a sharply rising skepticism about many topics that previously were not open to debate. The growing acceptance of Darwinian evolution sparked ideas about eugenics and the role of inheritance in the development of individuals and races. These concepts spread broadly, carried along by a stronger faith in the scientific method of mastery that Lippmann strongly advocated. Potent reform notions shaped a wide-ranging cluster of ideas and movements grouped under the rubric *progressive*. It is little wonder that such freethinking extended to challenging the precepts of religious faith of all varieties. Progressives of various stripes raised the stakes to ask where to steer the nation and promote the future moral values of its people.

Others were less sanguine.

Escalating Social Change: An Indication of Coming Godlessness?

Henry Adams had grave misgivings about the fast pace of social change in the twentieth century. He believed that humankind was racing toward a chaotic future. In private, Adams remarked that evolution was not a record of human progress but the story of man's increasing "unfitness" to live comfortably in the world. "In the scale of evolution," he said, "one vertebrate was as good as another." Reason, which since the Enlightenment had formed the basis of a humanistic confidence in man, separated human beings from vital, instinctual sources of behavior. Adams therefore doubted even the possibility of any "moral evolution" in a time when "coal-power alone asserted evolution—of power—and only by violence could be forced to assert selection of type." Among all the species in the world, Adams pointed out that only mankind had the capacity to remain mired in self-doubt.[9]

Dwight Moody, the world-famous revivalist, divided all of history into time periods known as "dispensations." Yet he sounded much like Adams. He argued that the social tumult of the latter half of the nineteenth century heralded apocalypse in the twentieth century. Jesus would come at any moment, he thought. America, therefore, might well be doomed. Faithful Christians should do as much good as they could in their lifetimes, yet Moody was gloomy about the future of the earth. "I view this world as a wrecked vessel," he said. "The Lord has given me a lifeboat and said, 'Moody, save all you can.' "[10] Many historians have described responses such as those of Moody and Adams as part of a prevalent antimodern sentiment. These arguments tended to be characterized by nostalgia for days gone by, a search for a return to the seemingly idealistic communitarian ethic of the village and town life of the past. Such characteristically antimodern laments were evident in the editorial pages, popular songs, and literature as well as pulpits and schools of the late nineteenth century.[11]

At the level of the wider public, Mark Twain voiced a representative attitude about religion. Organized religion and the clergy seemed to have very little "use" in everyday life, Twain observed. A less "religious" future would be " 'jus fine" for many of the central characters in his popular novels and short stories.

Huckleberry Finn struck this wry note, saying: "[The minister] never charged nothing for his preaching, and it was worth it, too."[12]

On the opposite side, Social Gospel preachers, including Washington Gladden and Walter Rauschenbusch, and writers, including Charles Sheldon, advocated the application of shared Protestant values. Rauschenbusch, a Protestant theologian and quasi-socialist from Rochester, New York, interestingly inverted the Spencerian logic of social Darwinism. Rauschenbusch's Social Gospel aimed toward a brighter future than the dim conditions of the present appeared to portend. He encouraged the masses of Protestant brothers and sisters to deploy Christian principles for the humanitarian evolution of the "social fabric." Social Darwinism itself, with a dependence on beliefs in "survival of the fittest" and "social structures [that would] arise out of social functions," was not sufficient to create order and benefit mankind, Rauschenbusch said; so good works must be emphasized.

Placing all of these developments in context was a challenge for those living at the time. As Lippmann aptly put it: "We are unsettled to the very roots of our being . . . . There are no precedents to guide us, no wisdom that wasn't made for a simpler age."[13] Jeremiads of a secular sort exhorted people to attend to man's injustice and social needs, rather than divinely revealed truths, to overcome this unsettled feeling and to enact progressive reforms like those Lippmann advocated. Perhaps best summed up by the title to Herbert Croly's 1909 book, the *Promise of American Life*, this optimistic cast to the nation's future depended on the enactment of meaningful change to fulfill that promise, lest failure lead to the nation's decline.

Ingersoll's "Atheistical" Jeremiad

In many ways, American society seemed to be moving away from dogmatic Christianity. Informed in part by Comtean positivism and the evolutionary biological perspectives that were widely gaining acceptance, elite Americans in particular saw an inevitable march of naturalistic science superseding their parents' beliefs. One scholar of American culture has described this apparent secularization as uniquely obvious to contemporary observers. It "exacerbated the problem of personal moral responsibility and contributed significantly to the sense of unreality underlying the crisis of cultural authority."[14] For many of these Americans, religious decline and the ascent of scientific rationalism portended an atheistical future, with the potential to rend the very fabric of American society.

By the 1880s, progressive-minded agnostics began to test these observations. Individualism and skepticism, combined in what was known as "freethought," were daunting opponents to the continuance of dogmatic forms of religious belief into the future, it seemed. Freethinking—a philosophical system that first emerged in Europe in the 1600s and took hold in America in the years following the Civil War—was, from roughly 1875 through 1914, an increasingly influential mode of judging religion (and other beliefs) on the basis of reason and evidence from the natural world rather than of tradition, authority, or revealed truths.

It is no coincidence that this movement came to prominence in the wake of the Civil War, which challenged Americans' long-standing beliefs. Some referred to the war as a national "baptism by blood" that had made the nation providentially better; others found organized religion lacking in the necessary explanations for the evils they had witnessed and the personal and social catastrophes the conflict had caused.

The most notable exponent of freethought, Robert Green Ingersoll, mostly forgotten today, was in his time as widely known as Andrew Carnegie, Mark Twain, and William Randolph Hearst. A lawyer from Illinois, former Union army colonel, and respected orator, Ingersoll gave the presidential nomination speech for James G. Blaine at the Republican national convention in 1876. But after that political high point, his outspoken antireligious views made him untenable as a candidate for elected office. Even so, he remained a personal friend and confidant to three presidents.

Ingersoll's predictions were bold. His attacks were witty and blasphemous. His most prominent prescription was for America to become entirely godless, particularly in the public square. "We have retired the gods from politics," he said. "We have found that man is the only source of political power, and that the governed should govern."[15] He proposed that secular humanism could do a better job of encouraging social cohesion and progress than faith could in the modern industrial era. For him, America was uniquely possessed of the ideals and institutions it needed to become more prosperous and more democratic, but it was held back from fulfilling its potential by generally religious and antiquated beliefs. He proclaimed:

> In my judgment, the days of the supernatural are numbered. The dogma of inspiration must be abandoned. As man advances—as his intellect enlarges,—as his knowledge increases,—as his ideals become nobler, the bibles and creeds will lose their authority, the miraculous will be classed with the impossible, and the idea of special providence will be discarded.[16]

Newspapers such as the *Truth Seeker*, which was founded in 1875, then rapidly became the nation's best-known freethought organ, and along with an array of speakers, such as the suffragist Elizabeth Cady Stanton, author of *The Woman's Bible*, helped agnostic proponents of freethought disseminate their ideas.[17]

Scientific advances and the ascent of new ways of debunking old beliefs formed the core of these agnostic critiques and the sometimes Comtean progressive-minded assault on organized religious thought. "Creeds cannot remain permanent in a world in which knowledge increases," Ingersoll said. "Science and superstition cannot peaceably occupy the same brain. This is an age of investigation, of discovery and thought. Science destroys the dogmas that misled the mind and waste the energies of man." Ingersoll placed himself alongside the icons of American democracy, including Jefferson, and among the ranks of the Enlightenment rationalists, who he believed opposed all dogmatisms of faith in their pursuit of pure knowledge through investigation.[18]

Ingersoll cultivated what he saw as a rationalist, tolerant form of atheistical individualism. He urged his audiences to follow him in this pursuit. Secular thought and a relatively godless future democracy were congruent with the founding ideals of the nation, he repeatedly alleged. Nor did he feel that the secular underpinnings of the nation necessarily conflicted with personal faith for those who chose religious beliefs. Ingersoll, though, never believed that there was any innate need or use for religion, natural or otherwise. Citing examples of the depravity of societies that were explicitly religious, he held that society did not need biblical morals to be ethical.

In this we find an interesting reorientation of the Puritan jeremiad script. Whereas the social reform jeremiads (e.g., those of Samuel Hopkins in the 1770s) had built on the shared values of so-called true religion, Ingersoll's antispiritual rebuke of the current state of society was built on the shared values of what he called "true reason." He hailed progress in social reform and the scientific investigations that debunked atavistic forms of supernaturalism.[19]

Ingersoll's most popular lecture sounded this note; calling on his audience to hallow national ideals, he put a specific freethinking interpretation on the thinking of the founding generation. "The [founders] knew that to put God in the Constitution was to put man out," he exclaimed. "They knew that the recognition of a Deity would be seized upon by fanatics and zealots as a pretext for destroying the liberty of thought." Ingersoll followed along Comtean lines when he argued that the forces of religion in America often had obscured the nation's essentially secular foundations.

According to Ingersoll, the root problems of industrializing America stemmed from the lack of adherence to the country's democratic and secular ideals. He often chastened his audiences to recognize that the founders knew the terrible history of the church too well to place in her keeping, or in the keeping of her God, the sacred rights of man.... They intended that all should have the right to worship, or not to worship; that our laws should make no distinction on account of creed. They intended to found and frame a government for man, and for man alone.[20]

And what did such notions indicate for the future? Ingersoll concluded that the founders "wished to preserve the individuality of all; to prevent the few from governing the many, and the many from persecuting and destroying the few."[21]

Ingersoll's prophesies were not, of course, religious jeremiads. But they partook somewhat of the jeremiad form and were based on a sense of the nation's history. Ingersoll's positions also shared certain civic republican values embodied in the jeremiad tradition,. According to Ingersoll's reading of the founders' intentions, the right approach to civic betterment considers "the ends that can be accomplished; takes into consideration the limits of our faculties; fixes our attention on the affairs of the world, and erects beacons of warning on the dangerous shores." In short, America would be better without any theisms at all. He asserted: "The truth of any system of religion based on the supernatural cannot by any possibility be established—such a religion not being within the domain of evidence." Rather, Ingersoll concluded, "All our duties are here . . . all our obligations are to sentient beings." Science, according to Ingersoll, "is the enemy of fear and credulity."[22] In the 1880s and 1890s, Ingersoll saw evidence that his movement, and thus society at large, was leaving behind religious delusions as an increasing number of Protestants and theologians were attempting to find ways to reconcile evolution with Christianity. Henry Ward Beecher, whose ecclesiastical pedigree was unimpeachable, was the most celebrated convert to this camp. He affirmed earnestly that the doctrine of evolution, as he understood it, represented "the deciphering of God's thought as revealed in the structure of the world."[23]

Hardheaded skepticism and irrefutable science had moved to the fore. But where should a scientific America be headed, in Ingersoll's view? "We are not endeavoring to chain the future," he said, "but to free the present." He argued that philosophy lacks the "egotism of faith," and from this loss of such absolutes comes the strength of inquiry, liberty, and justice. His ambitious vision may have been overly optimistic about a future loss of religious belief, but it did not lack idealism. "We are laying the foundation of the grand temple of the future—not the temple of all the gods, but of all the people—wherein, with appropriate rites, will be celebrated the religion of Humanity."[24]

The message Ingersoll hoped to get out to the wider public was that superstition and faith were at odds with the logical reasoning at the heart of his secular, reforming humanism. So how should freethinking Americans bring about this desired less dogmatic and more just future? Ingersoll was clear in his prescription: "We are doing what little we can to hasten the coming of the day when society shall cease producing millionaires and mendicants—gorged indolence and famished industry—truth in rags, and superstition robbed and crowned." By focusing on human justice on earth rather than deferring to God's dictates, America could be renewed. Ingersoll's vision can be summed up by his assessment of the movement he represented: "We are looking for the time when the useful shall be the honorable; and when REASON, throned upon the world's brain, shall be the King of Kings and the God of Gods."[25]

Not many people were moved to reject religion outright by agnostic prophets like Ingersoll. However, many Americans were exposed to his ideas about freethought by attending his talks or reading sensational accounts about him in newspapers and magazines.[26] It was in the same years that many Americans joined the ranks of progressive social justice activists and made a strong case for continued and strengthened secularist approaches to public affairs, even if they did not agree that atheistic freethinking was the future of American belief.

Reason and William James's Metaphysics

Reason "enthroned" was the zeitgeist of this period; it was the essence of scientific management and formed the crucial analytic instrument for most progressives. It was also the primary philosophical tool William James employed. But unlike Ingersoll, James cautioned that when wielded as a solitary, empirical means of verifying truths and delving into the nature of religious experience, reason was flawed. Instead, James aimed to study religious experience in its totality, examining more than just science alone. He once wrote: "Religion is the great interest of my life."[27] Since his death, James has been repeatedly recognized as one of the greatest modern thinkers on religion.

Unlike many other intellectuals of his time, James wanted to study religion as an academic subject. He did not intend to examine it in the halls of seminaries or pews and pulpits. Diverging further from his contemporaries, James willingly embraced defining religion broadly in "pluralistic" terms, refusing to privilege Christianity over all others faiths. Personally, however, James was troubled by religion. He often remarked that he longed for true faith but could not find it in himself. [28] By the early 1900s, religious experience was not just an interest but also a major subject of study for James. In many of his writings on "willing" belief, he seemed almost desperate to show that some issues could not be judged by pure reason alone. Personally, though, he had a hard time with such a project. In 1904, he wrote that God was only "dimly" real to him and that he had "no living sense of commerce with a God." In later works, for example *The Varieties of Religious Experience,* and in his private letters, we see that James envied true believers. He wanted those fruits of certainty for himself. Yet he confidentially wrote that he despaired of his religious potential, feeling only a "mystical germ" within him when he heard others speak about the depth of their faith.

The study of religious experience also became a part of his revolutionary new pragmatic philosophy, which measured the value of an idea by means of the "conduct that the idea dictates." James maintained a fascinating connection between faith, philosophy, and practical reforms. "Pragmatism can be called religious," he lectured, but only "if you allow that religion can be pluralistic or merely melioristic in type."[29] From his youth, James took all religions seriously. He thought they formed an essential part of human belief systems and generally were a force for social good, but he also found much merit in skepticism. Where the minister Theodore T. Munger argued that disbelieving skepticism had advanced so far and fast through society that it "envelops all things in its puzzle,—God, immortality, the value of life, the rewards of virtue, and the operation of conscience. It puts quicksand under every step," James perceived a similar trend but hoped to abate the spreading quicksand of blinding skeptical disbelief.[30]

James and Munger were far from alone in exploring the importance of religious experience and its apparent diminution in the late nineteenth century. But James was virtually alone among those who sought to study religion rigorously as psychology and as philosophy. He brought a unique intellectual tool kit to bear on his subject. Addressing believers and unbelievers alike, James articulated a startling solution to the problematic modern relationship between doubt, authentic religious belief, and voluntarism. "Whether you will finally put up with that type of religion or not is a question that only you yourself can decide. Pragmatism has to postpone dogmatic answer, for we do not yet know certainly which type of religion is going to work best in the long run," he said in his 1907 lecture on pragmatism and religion. Pragmatism, James told a surprised audience, was a "religious way" of looking at the world. You see, he said, believing in pragmatism was a valuable test for ideas and practices, thereby a faith of a very real sort.[31]

James's pragmatic "faith" led him to probe the depths of his own philosophy. He thereby expanded the range of legitimate empirical inquiry to

include subjective experience. The test for any idea was related to its effec-
tiveness. The ability to satisfy the expectations a person placed on an idea (or
idea system), according to James, was the means to measure whether it met
expected outcomes. Thus, Jamesian pragmatism opened the doorway to many
individual types of religious experience.

Together with James, writer and professor C. S. Peirce had hosted periodic
meetings of what they "half-ironically, half-defiantly" called the Metaphysical
Club. Along with Oliver Wendell Holmes, the "great dissenter" and jurist, who
argued that "laws develop with society," and Josiah Royce, a Harvard philosopher and advocate of a practical philosophy that unified all of reality, these
thinkers sought to make sense of an uncertain universe. Scientific evaluation
of evidence in support of ideas, theories, and judgments was crucial to coming
to a pragmatic conclusion. James openly accepted not just the three major
monotheistic religions of Christianity, Judaism, and Islam but also Buddhism
and even forms of mysticism, animism, and belief in extrasensory perception
as valued, verifiable expressions of religious experience.[32]

Faith, according to James, was best understood as determined by a person's psychological "temperament," along with environment and personal
choice. He famously wrote in *Pragmatism*: "The true is the name for whatever
proves itself to be good in the way of belief, and good, too, for definite and
assignable reasons."[33] Dogmatic answers and practices were to be avoided.
Genuine religious experience, however, was to be embraced, no matter its
source. In 1897, James said, "Religion is the great interest of my life"; but what
did he mean by this?[34] As one of his most able biographers, Ralph Barton
Perry, noted, since "it would be unjust to hold a man strictly to a statement
made in an unguarded moment, let us say that religion was *one* of the great
interests of his life."[35] For James, the future of religious beliefs began in this
personal way, by accepting the existence of a plurality of valid faiths. No one
religion could be proven right. Belief in a supernatural other, for James, was
integral to the psychological health of most people. It also appeared to be
socially cohesive for most human societies. "Religion, whatever it is, is a man's
total reaction upon life," he said in 1902. He maintained that religious "reaction" was and probably always would continue to be elemental to human
existence, as well as an apt subject for scientific study.[36]

The Varieties: Legitimizing Faith for the Present and Future

James initiated the first major effort by American thinkers to connect psychology, religious faith, and philosophy. The result was his seminal and widely

influential *Varieties of Religious Experience* (1902). The work illuminates the world of late nineteenth-century thinking about how to treat religious experience, and the challenges of trying to reconcile faith and science. In an era of heated debate, James's work showed that simple constructions of "faith versus science" break down when we critically assess the combination of experience and belief.

Varieties was a defense of the religious outlook and represented a prediction that a multiplicity of faiths would continue to have personal as well as societal importance. James's religious thought never depicted a teleological march with a kingdom of God on earth, or an ultimate belief winning out over all others. Instead, he prophesied diversity and opposed what he termed "bigness" in beliefs as well as business, government, and other institutions.

Each individual, according to James, has the right to affirm religious propositions solely on the basis of emotional predilection—yet only under certain conditions. The choice confronting the individual must be inescapable, so that not choosing also represents a choice. He summed up this inexorable choosing:

> If radically tough, the hurly-burly of the sensible facts of nature will be enough for you, and you will need no religion at all. If radically tender, you will take up with the more monistic form of religion: the pluralistic form, with its reliance on possibilities that are not necessities, will not seem to afford you security enough.[37]

It is important to note that James did not write for the popular market. *Varieties* (which was based on his Gifford Lectures, which he gave in 1901 and 1902 at the University of Edinburgh) was intended for academics, yet it found a surprisingly large audience. James intended the work to be as a rebuttal to those elite thinkers, enraptured in their ivory towers, who were unduly impressed with reason. Their reliance on academic tools alone carried along an inhibiting dependence on science and scientific evidence. Yet James's writings clearly reveal that he was conflicted about the uses to which such faith might be put (e.g., barbaric wars of clashing religions, cultural repression). To study it as a behavioral and philosophic subject, however, was uniformly useful, he thought.[38]

To James, considering the relationship between religious faith, experience, and the scientific method, the alternatives must be "living."[39] By this he meant that appealing alternative options could only be those that might plausibly be genuine and embraced in the present. The decision must be "momentous" and complete. His studies of the value of excess and its role as essential to acts of saintliness demonstrated that active "willing" was paramount. But James was not ready make any precise predictions about whether this was a good thing or something to be replicated widely in society. Such decisions, he declared, require only sufficient practical grounds for acceptance but need not be entirely empirical, so long as they have high value to the person willing to believe.[40]

In contrast, Robert Ingersoll often argued that there was no place for atavistic religion as a conscious choice in the future modern America. Science and fact had to be respected, Ingersoll frequently remarked, at the expense of what could not be proven. Similarly, James discounted the pursuit of the moral "truth" of religion and doubted that any particular religious doctrine was "true." Only what could be shown to be effective should be prized. James went further by saying that most people need to have their faiths "broken up and ventilated" to rid them of psychospiritual doubt. He hoped faith would arise from conscious, reasoned choice rather than from forced or implanted dictates.

Willing Belief: James and Agnosticism

Six years before *Varieties*, in 1896, James published an essay entitled "The Will to Believe." This exploration of will offered one of his most powerful assessments of religion, with far-reaching implications for the future of faith in America. He found orthodox theism "monarchical," but saw problems in its antithesis as well. He attempted to negate agnosticism not just for himself, as a personal belief, but also as a philosophical system.

A close reading of "The Will to Believe" alongside *Varieties* reveals a useful distinction in how James viewed agnosticism and made predictions about its future. He considered agnosticism, if carefully reasoned, to be the best approach for the study of the natural world, because investigating the natural world required gathering as much truth as possible without deference to higher powers and with the ability to reject beliefs and assumptions as evidence dictated. But an agnostic approach would not be the most effective method of evaluating moral or religious questions, for precisely the converse reason. "I, therefore, for one, cannot see my way to accepting the agnostic rules for truth-seeking, or willfully agree to keep my willing nature out of the game," James declared. "I cannot do so for this plain reason, that *a rule of thinking which would absolutely prevent me from acknowledging certain kinds of truth if those kinds of truth were really there, would be an irrational rule*" (emphasis in original). James found the rising influence of agnostic empiricism lacking in meaning but not in utility. "If a man chooses to turn his back altogether on God and the future, no one can prevent him; no one can show beyond a reasonable doubt that he is mistaken."[41]

Clearly, according to James, choices must be made. More than merely a selection, though, he implied that some form of "choosing" of God or religious belief represented a meeting of mind and heart. This, he said, was only possible for those for whom it was a "live option." Apologetic in tone at times, he was not sure how or whether this path should be traveled at all. "We stand on a mountain pass in the midst of whirling snow and blinding mist, through which we get glimpses now and then of paths which may be deceptive," he wrote evocatively. He concluded—on his mountain pass—that willing religion was as dangerous as it could be rewarding. "If we stand still we shall be frozen to death. If we take the wrong road we shall be dashed to pieces. We do not certainly know whether there is any right one."[42]

James contended that human beings tend to believe spontaneously the elements that present themselves to their senses, unless previously held beliefs contradict these elements. In his assessment, faith came not just by "willing it" but also by discrediting contradictory beliefs (as can be said to be the case with the scientific method, which was then the rising paradigm for the social sciences). *Varieties*, in turn, later revealed James's broad definition of religious experience and demonstrated his direct approach to examining, rather than discounting, religious faith. In the scientific age lived in, fraught what Victorians lamented as "modern doubt," James could see many reasons why religion would be appealing. It had established explanations that provided a sense of existential certainty. It was a type of mastery for a complex, modern world.

But James rejected the conclusion that faith was merely an expedient to overcome existential angst. In "Will to Believe," he argued against the renowned British mathematician and philosopher W. K. Clifford's view that there always must be sufficient evidence to warrant anyone believing in anything. He wrote: "It is wrong always, everywhere, and for anyone, to believe anything upon insufficient evidence."[43] Clifford provocatively declared that it is actually immoral to believe something without proper substantiation. James responded by arguing that we do not need to determine whether God's existence can be proved for either the present or the future before organizing our lives morally around a tacit answer to that very question. Moral arguments cannot simply be settled with facts such as those Clifford called for. In addition, commonsensical critiques that were central to Ingersoll's disputations against belief in "Jonah inside the whale" or the notion of an "immaculate conception" did not appear to James to get at the essential power of religion. Instead, James contended that it is appropriate for our will to help move us to belief and to action. He asserted that one should "determine what difference" (if any) believing in God will make in one's life. Belief, rather than a measure of any true "reality," held its own value. At the heart of this dispute is what can be called a spiritual judgment: that is, assessing things of value, significance, and meaning. James perceived the possibility, even the instrumental usefulness, for people and, by extension, social groups, to move along a "faith ladder." Through a series of practical decisions of the will, a person might progress toward increasingly strong religious commitments.[44]

"Bent as we are on studying religion's existential conditions," James demurred, "we cannot possibly ignore these pathological aspects of the subject. We must describe and name them just as if they occurred in non-religious men." He was fully prepared to do both. He aimed to explore the existential side of religion, despite the fact he could not bring himself to believe.[45] But science could not be an ultimate refuge for him either. He chastised those who worshiped the false god of science as well. "Empiricism is not skepticism," he said. Thus, James rebutted those like Ingersoll who founded their skepticism in the advance of pure science. By the same token, James issued a sharp warning against believing that religion arises only from environmental conditions or acts of willful ignorance or is determined by physiological "states," for example, those that Freud and the early French psychoanalysts described.[46]

Walter Lippmann had several keen insights into the progressive nature of James's religious inquiries and their implications for the nation's moral and religious prospects. "In the long controversy with religious belief the true temper of the scientific mind was revealed," he wrote. According to Lippmann,

> William James . . . was accused of treason because he listened to mystics and indulged in psychical research. Wasn't he opening the gates to superstition and osbcurantism? It was an ignorant attack. For the attitude of William James toward "ghosts" was the very opposite of blind belief. He listened to evidence. No apostle of authority can find the least comfort in that. For the moment you test belief by experience you have destroyed the whole structure of authority . . . . But when truths are held because there is no evidence for them, their whole character is changed. They are no longer blind beliefs; they are subject to amendment when new evidence appears, and their danger is gone.[47]

Lippmann depicted James as a hero of the scientific study of belief. His inquiries represented a harbinger of things to come. "The Nineteenth Century undoubtedly meant a shattering of the traditional faiths," Lippmann wrote. "And yet no century has ever been so eager to understand the very idols it was breaking."[48] Looking forward, the progressive Lippmann expanded his understanding of the relationship between past and present. "The modern sense of what the past contains can give new realization of the fertility of existence," he concluded. For Lippmann, as for James,

> that is a rock upon which to build. Instead of a "featureless future," instead of an aspiring vacuum, which ends in disappointment, we may see a more modest future, but one inhabited by living people. This is the great boon of the past, that it saturates thought with concrete images. And it leaves scope for imagination, for the control of nature and buoyant living. For by taking with a certain levity our schemes for improvement we shatter the sects and liberate thought.[49]

Here then was Lippmann's take on James and on the future; immoral godlessness could be mastered and filled with hope, be it godly or secular, but in doing so, the sorts of absolutist sects that prevented mastery had to be shattered in pursuit of truly liberating thought and action.

As we have seen, among those thinking about progressive improvement and the Social Gospel, there were those who saw the future of American religiosity as filled with positive associations of sects, social reform, and Christian values. Often split by denominational differences, they shared certain values nonetheless. Walter Rauschenbusch, who started his career preaching as a Baptist minister near Hell's Kitchen, wrote extensively about what he termed the "social role of Christianity." Others were more overtly political, like Congregationalist Washington Gladden, who was an outspoken labor leader. He advocated government activism and sought government oversight to regulate corporate malfeasance and reduce poverty. Powerful variants of these ideas were expressed by Christian socialists, the most radical of whom wanted to reclaim all of the land in the name of Old Testament values, for the use of all and not the favored few. An extreme perspective, to be sure, but characteristic of the small yet vocal group called the Christian Socialist League.[50]

Most of the Social Gospel–style religious reformers came from Protestant ranks. However, there were also many newly arrived and native-born Catholics and Jews who looked to the future. They often envisioned greater religiosity spreading throughout society as the way to reduce poverty and injustice and to increase moral behavior.[51]

Rauschenbusch echoed these basic precepts. His views were also representative of most of the broader perspectives that animated religious progressive reformers. They perceived American society as useful and generally good, but in need of far greater guidance and a more immediate sense of Christian morality. Most Social Gospel advocates argued that the nation was exceptional, yet in decline. America in particular, they often said, held the potential to be an instrument of great good in the world, and of hastening the second coming of the messiah, but to achieve such lofty ends the nation required repair via thoroughgoing social reforms. "There are two great entities in human life—the human soul and the human race—and religion is to save both," said Rauschenbusch. In this, his critique sounds similar to those heard before in different epochs, yet updated for an industrial America ravaged by the excesses of corporate capitalism.

> Our political economy has long been an oracle of the false god. It has taught us to approach economic questions from the point of goods and not of man . . . . Religious men have been cowed by the prevailing materialism and arrogant selfishness of our business world. They should have the courage of religious faith and assert that "man liveth not by bread alone," [but] by doing the will of God, and that the life of a nation "consisteth not in the abundance of things" which it produces, but in the way men live justly with one another and humbly with their God.[52]

Aiming to achieve these sorts of goals linked an array of new Christian organizations, including the Salvation Army, which fused religion and reform.[53]

What unified the Salvation Army and other similar groups of Social Gospel–minded reformers was a belief that the current trend was, achingly, toward greater immorality and suffering. In short, society seemed to be becoming more godless as it became more industrialized and urbanized. To alleviate this downward trajectory, men like Rauschenbusch argued for a Christian ethical approach to the industrial era's problems of poverty and progress. He said, though, that such an approach must be premised on a realistic sense of enacting meaningful change via individual Christian communal aid and by government intervention.[54] These reformers believed that shared Protestant values were essential for the creation of a better society.

The Lines Are Drawn

How these progressives viewed the direction of society depended on how they defined "mastery." Given elites' widespread fear of a crisis of faith, a rising interest in scientific mastery, and challenges to authority and received understandings of the need to submit to reality, the fate of religion lay in doubt. Ingersoll, James, and the Social Gospel progressives offered three possible futures, all aiming in part to fulfill what they believed was America's unique democratic, social, and ideological potential.

For Ingersoll, the ascent of secular belief and scientific methods indicated a beneficial decline of religious faith for the future. For James, religious belief was becoming experimental and open as a subject of study. In a modern, industrial America, an array of religious experiences should be embraced as possible ways to negotiate the uncertainties of existence. And for Social Gospelers, for example Rauschenbusch, the enactment of Christian progressive reforms was an instrument that expedited the inevitable historical march to build the kingdom of God on earth. After all, they said, it was to be a "Christian Century."

The sides were hardening on the way to the coming debates of the 1920s and 1930s. When religion was pitted against science, one or the other had to lose. James's complex combinations of emotion, science, and faith were untenable in the less nuanced realm of the general public. By the time of the high-profile battle of the Scopes trial, the resulting tensions revealed fissures in America's founding secular freedoms and undermined the coherency of the progressive program. It increasingly seemed that one effect of progress was the sort of poverty and inequality symbolized by the "tramp" or the existential uncertainty known as "modern doubt." Despite many successful progressive reforms, by the 1920s there appeared to be a diminished possibility of reconciling absolute forms of faith with more contingent understandings of civic values for science, society, and industrial progress.

In the coming decades, the challenges of Lippmann's call for mastery remained unsolved. By the 1960s, scientific arguments and progressive thinking were radically reoriented, often eliminating established religions as a source for building a better future. As the twentieth century approached its close, this battle no longer appeared to be a direct clash of reason and religion; the battle seemed to have come to an end. The new skeptics, voicing a postmodern twist on the old Progressive Era's modern doubt, said: "God is dead." Yet the resurgence of religion in the public square in recent years definitively shows that America continues to grapple with the future by thinking about the role of religion. From the late nineteenth century through the present, a central quandary has remained when Americans confront the idea of progress and the uncertain religious future: Will liberal democracy in the United States be able to hold these long-standing tensions in check?

NOTES

1. Henry George, *Progress and Poverty* (New York: Robert Schalkenback Foundation, 1949) (orig. pub. 1879), 7. Charles A. Barker, *Henry George* (New York: Oxford University Press, 1955), 270–71.

2. Charles Sheldon, *In His Steps* (Chicago: Advance, 1897).

3. See Jon Butler, Grant Wacker, and Randall Balmer, eds., *Religion in American Life: A Short History* (New York: Oxford University Press, 2003), 331; see also Paul Carter, *The Spiritual Crisis of the Gilded Age* (DeKalb: Northern Illinois University Press, 1971).

4. T. J. Jackson Lears, *No Place of Grace* (Chicago: University of Chicago Press, 1983), 44. Three good new studies of this era provide a place to start in understanding the period as a whole. See Rebecca Edwards, *New Spirits: Americans in the Gilded Age, 1865–1905* (Oxford: Oxford University Press, 2006); Alan Dawley, *Changing the World: American Progressives in War and Revolution* (Princeton: Princeton University Press, 2003); and Michael McGerr, *A Fierce Discontent: The Rise and Fall of the Progressive Movement in America, 1870–1920* (New York: Oxford University Press, 2003).

5. Walter Lippmann, *Drift and Mastery: An Attempt to Diagnose the Current Unrest* (Madison: University of Wisconsin Press, 1985) (orig. pub. 1914), 153.

6. Ibid., 163.

7. See Herbert Croly, *The Promise of American Life* (New York: Macmillan, 1909), 5–6.

8. Robert Crunden, *Ministers of Reform: The Progressives' Achievement in American Civilization, 1889–1920* (New York: Basic Books, 1982), 3.

9. On Adams's thought, see Henry Adams, *The Education of Henry Adams* (Washington D.C.: private printing, 1907), chap. 15, "Darwinism" (1867–68); see also Adams's later thought, published posthumously, *The Degradation of the Democratic Dogma* (New York: Macmillan, 1920).

10. Cited in Butler et al., *Religion in American Life*, 342.

11. For more on this see Lears, *No Place of Grace*.

12. Mark Twain, *The Adventures of Huckleberry Finn* (New York: Penguin Classics, 1991).

13. Walter Lippmann, *Drift and Mastery: An Attempt to Diagnose the Current Unrest* (Englewood Cliffs, N.J.: University of Wisconsin Press, 1985) (orig. pub. c. 1914), 92.

14. Lears, *No Place of Grace*, 41. In my analysis of secularization and the "crisis of authority" of this period I am indebted to T. J. Jackson Lears's work for its many insights into American culture during these tumultuous years.

15. Ingersoll's speeches and publications were extensive. Most have been compiled in *The Works of Robert Ingersoll* (Dresden, N.Y.: Dresden Publishing/C. P. Farrell, 1907–1915), known as the 12-volume Dresden memorial edition, named for its publication site in Dresden, New York (also where Ingersoll's father was born). The quote is from 9:93.

Also, for a concise overview of his most important works and on American themes, see Ingersoll, *On the Gods and Other Essays* (Buffalo, N.Y.: Prometheus Books, 1990), in particular "On Tom Paine." On Robert Green Ingersoll and the freethought movement, see Susan Jacoby, *Freethinkers: A History of American Secularism* (New York: Metropolitan Books, 2004), and MacDonald, *Fifty Years of Freethought* (New York, 1899). For a good account see Orvin Larson, *American Infidel* (New York, 1993). In recent years there has been a revival of interest in Ingersoll. See also *On the Gods and Other Essays* and *What's God Got to Do with It?* ed. Tim Page (Hanover, N.H.: Steerforth Press, 2005).

16. Ingersoll then went on to describe his own teleology of sorts. In many of his speeches, letters, and published works he cited the lessons of history as evidence that the nation was embarked on a progressive march away from organized, irrational religious belief. In a letter he summed the connection between history and religion, asking: "Thousands of religious have perished, innumerable gods have died, and why should the religion of our time be exempt from the common fate?" ("Col. Ingersoll to Mr. Gladstone," *Works of Robert Ingersoll*, 6:302).

17. See Jacoby on freedom of religion not being exempt from public criticism or ridicule, *Freethinkers*, 172.

18. To be fair, not all Enlightenment thinkers were radical skeptics. As David Ciepley notes in chapter 8 here, many of the luminaries of the Enlightenment—Kant, for example—had a powerful confidence in the existential reality of God and the need for "natural religion."

19. On the jeremiad form and Samuel Hopkins, see chapter 1 here.

20. Jacoby, *Freethinkers*, 84–85.

21. Ibid.

22. Robert Green Ingersoll, "Col. Ingersoll to Mr. Gladstone," *North American Review* 374 (June 1888): 639–40.

23. Vincent DeSantis, *The Shaping of Modern America: 1877–1920* (Arlington Heights, Ill.: Forum Press, 1973), quoting Beecher, 110.

24. From multiple sources. See section and quotation in Jacoby, *Freethinkers*, 173.

25. Ibid., 173. Also see the Dresden edition of Ingersoll's collected works.

26. Even Pope Leo XIII, when he issued the encyclical *Rerum Novarum* in 1891, evoked a progressive-secular cast in condemning the exploitation of the laboring classes and advocating state-led social justice. American Catholics (fully 16 percent of the population by 1910) responded to this encyclical, as did their Protestant Social Gospel brethren. See DeSantis, *Shaping of Modern America*, 108–12; for more detail, see John T. McGreevy, *Catholicism and American Freedom: A History* (New York: Norton, 2003).

27. William James, *Letters of William James*, ed. Henry James (Boston: Atlantic Monthly Press, 1920), 2:58. The two best biographies of William James are Ralph Barton Perry, *The Thought and Character of William James* (Nashville: Vanderbilt University Press, 1996), and Gerald E. Myers, *William James: His Life and Thought* (New Haven: Yale University Press, 1986). One good, brief collection of James's writings is *Pragmatism, A Reader*, ed. Louis Menand (New York: Vintage Books, 1997). For studies of William James's religious belief see Ellen Kappy Suckiel, *Heaven's Champion: William James's Philosophy of Religion* (Notre Dame, Ind.: University of Notre Dame Press, 1996); Henry Samuel Levinson, *The Religious Investigations of William James* (Chapel Hill: University of North Carolina Press, 1981); and Paul Jerome Croce, *Science and Religion in the Era of William James*, vol. 1, *Eclipse of Uncertainty, 1820–1880* (Chapel Hill: University of North Carolina Press, 1995).

28. James wrote privately of the importance of his father's blend of religious beliefs, in large part coming from the Swedish theologian Emanuel Swedenborg. "Father's cry was the single one that religion is real. The thing is so to 'voice' it that other ears shall hear,—no easy task, but a worthy one, which in some shape I shall attempt." January 9, 1883, cited in Perry, *Thought and Character of William James*, 41.

29. *Letters of William James* (1897), 2:58; also Perry, *Thought and Character of William James*, 40–41, and see chapter 28, on *Varieties of Religious Experience* and James's changing philosophy of religion.

30. Quotation from Theodore T. Munger, *The Appeal to Life* (Boston: Houghton, Mifflin, 1887), 33–34; Froude quoted in Lears, *No Place of Grace*, 42.

31. William James, "Pragmatism and Religion," lecture 8, in *Pragmatism: A New Name for Some Old Ways of Thinking* (New York: Penguin Books, 1907), 105–16.

32. For more detail see the excellent account provided by Louis Menand in *The Metaphysical Club* (New York: Farrar, Straus, and Giroux, 2001).

33. James, *Pragmatism*, 42.

34. *Letters of William James*, 2:58.

35. Perry, *Thought and Character of William James*, 41.

36. For more on this subject, see ibid., esp. chap. 28, and Levinson, *Religious Investigations of William James*, 209–39.

37. James, "Pragmatism and Religion," lecture 8, in *Pragmatism* (1907).Interestingly, Walter Lippmann observed that it was scientists who feared and tended to ridicule James most when his work provided legitimacy to the unscientific experiences of mysticism and in psychic research. See Lippmann, *Drift and Mastery*, 161–62.

38. James's friend and fellow Metaphysical Club member the philosopher Josiah Royce disagreed with James about the proper understanding of religious phenomena in human life. When James delivered the Gifford Lectures in 1901–2, many of his arguments attacked Royce's idealism (although he did not name his friend as an adversary). Royce believed that James, who never regularly affiliated with any established church or community of faith, was out of touch. Royce alleged that James placed too much emphasis on the extraordinary religious experiences of extraordinary individuals. Royce, in contrast, sought a philosophy of religion that would help understand and explain the phenomena of ordinary religious faith, as experienced broadly by whole communities. In contrast to James's expansive pluralistic and pragmatic concept of faith, Royce argued that both the "object and source" of religious experience were encompassed by an actual, infinite, and superhuman being. For more on this, see *The Letters of Josiah Royce*, ed. J. Clendenning (Chicago: University of Chicago Press, 1970), esp. 570.

39. *Will to Believe* (1896), in *Pragmatism, A Reader*, see 88–89.

40. See James, *Varieties of Religious Experience: A Study in Human Nature* (New York: Penguin Books, rept., 1982), Martin Marty, ed.; see especially lecture 11, on the types and character of saints, 259–61, 271–77; and lectures 14 and 15, "On the Value of Saintliness," 326–78.

41. James, *Will to Believe*, 92.

42. Ibid.

43. On W. K. Clifford's views, see "Ethics of Belief," *Contemporary Review* (1877), reprinted, in *The Ethics of Belief and Other Essays* (New York: Prometheus Books, 1999).On the development of American philosophy, distinctions between U.S. and continental philosophy at the time, and how the study of religious belief slotted into American philosophy, see Bruce Kucklick, *A History of Philosophy in America, 1720–2000* (New York: Oxford University Press, 2001); see also Kucklick, *The Rise of American Philosophy: Cambridge, Massachusetts, 1860–1930* (New Haven: Yale University Press, 1977).

44. See Suckiel, *Heaven's Champion,* on "faith ladder" in James's thought, 102–3.

45. James, *Varieties,* 17.

46. Ibid., 303; on his personal belief see Suckiel, introduction to *Heaven's Champion,.*

47. Lippmann, *Drift and Mastery,* 161.

48. Ibid., 164.

49. Ibid., 165.

50. For more on this, see W. D. Bliss's activities in organizing, writing, and preaching Christian socialism to bring about God's Kingdom on earth as part of the "left wing" of the Social Gospel movement (along with Walter Rauschenbusch and George Herron). Richard B. Dressner, "William Dwight Porter Bliss's Christian Socialism," *Church History* 47, 1 (March 1978): 66–82; see also Crunden, *Ministers of Reform,* and Eldon Eisenach, *The Lost Promise of Progressivism* (Lawrence: University of Kansas Press, 1994).

51. For a brief overview of some of the distinctions among Catholics, Jews, Protestants, and others in this period, see Edwards, *New Spirits,* chap. 8, "Faith," 171–95.

52. Walter Rauschenbusch, *The Social Role of Christianity* (New York: Macmillan, 1907), 367–72, and *Christianity and the Social Crisis* (New York: Macmillan, 1907).

53. The Salvation Army originated in England and came to thrive in the United States in the 1880s. By 1900, the organization was offering material aid to the poor, as well as spiritual upliftment and Bible study classes, while counting more than three thousand "officers" and twenty thousand "privates" in its ranks of Christian social workers.

54. For more on these views, see two of Rauschenbusch's other works: *Christianizing of the Social Order* (New York: Macmillan, 1912), and *A Theology for the Social Gospel* (New York: Macmillan, 1917).

7

World War I and After: Godlessness and the Scopes Trial

Kevin M. Schultz

Was the earth really created in six days? Did Jonah really survive inside the belly of a giant fish? Did Eve really emerge from Adam's rib? And where did Cain's wife come from, anyway? These typical village atheist questions are not mine but represent paraphrased quotations from the most important symbol of the religious-secular controversy of the interwar years and perhaps of the entirety of American history, the Scopes monkey trial of 1925. By publicly probing questions about the believability of miracles and the resurrection of Christ, and by doing so within the context of the larger cultural struggles then going on, the trial brought to the fore three claims of godlessness, two of which were polarized positions widely remembered today (albeit in a flawed way), the third a middling position that is unfortunately most often forgotten. These three traditions all have histories and futures, and they all meet in a courtroom in Dayton, Tennessee, in the summer of 1925.

The trial of John Thomas Scopes has become a symbol of the battle royal between an emergent fundamentalist Christianity and an expansive godless secularism, the immovable force versus the unstoppable object. The trial was supposed to test the constitutionality of a law the Tennessee legislature passed that outlawed teaching biological evolution in public schools. Seeing the law as an infringement on a teacher's capacity to choose his or her own materials, the American

Civil Liberties Union (ACLU), a new organization founded in 1920 to protect individuals from what its founders saw as provincial bouts of majoritarian rule, offered to defend any Tennessee teacher prosecuted for teaching evolution. To the ACLU, the antievolution crusade epitomized the closed-mindedness of those who resisted progress. The ACLU was certain that any teacher arrested for the offense would be found guilty, so it sought a procedural case that would be fought at the appellate level and maybe even the U.S. Supreme Court. The ACLU wanted a ruling on whether a legislature could dictate what could be taught when the legislative mandate contradicted the espousals of the knowledge community. A contemporary editorialist articulated the ACLU's position precisely when he said the case was supposed to be about "whether truth shall be limited by law."[1]

The ACLU's plan for a quiet procedural trial went awry from the start. Civic boosters in quiet Dayton recruited John Thomas Scopes, a young high school science teacher, to be prosecuted for breaking the law, even though Scopes did not teach biology and had substituted in the high school's biology class only when the usual teacher could not attend a review session. The civic boosters desired publicity for their sleepy New South town and, knowing that a protracted case fought in appellate courts would not serve their cause, sought to publicize the case as a battle between self-righteous secularists and self-righteous believers. Their prayers were answered when William Jennings Bryan volunteered to assist in prosecuting young John Scopes.

From the start, Bryan was the trial's star attraction. His presence assured national headlines, a "big" debate, and, he hoped, a powerful opposition he could debunk. With his entrance, the *Chicago Tribune* wrote: "The defendant, Scopes, is already a negligible factor. Nothing serious can happen to him. The contest is entirely over ideas."[2] This is exactly what Dayton's civic boosters had wanted. Bryan had run for president three times between 1896 and 1908, a loser each time. But he had served as Woodrow Wilson's secretary of state, resigning over the nation's entry into World War I, assuring his status as a serious voice in American life. More important, Bryan was defined not by party affiliation but by the causes he advocated: relief for farmers, rural self-sustenance, anti-imperialism, and a stern Victorian morality. Because his campaign platforms often demonstrated empathy for the poor, because of his unstinting belief in popular democracy, and because of his ability to frame complex issues simply, he was popularly called the Great Commoner.[3]

After leaving politics in June 1915, Bryan made the lecture circuit his vocation. To keep his bombastic voice in the headlines, he adopted one controversial cause after another, each touching sensitive cultural nerves. He successfully argued for four constitutional amendments, each controversial.

He advocated the direct election of senators, a progressive federal income tax, Prohibition, and female suffrage. In each case, he was a classic Progressive Era reformer, hoping to create a more vibrant democracy while removing the things he saw as potentially harmful to those with less moral clarity or personal conviction.

In 1921, he stepped up his long-standing support for the antievolution cause, an effort that aligned him with his conservative Presbyterian brethren. Bryan feared the implications of Darwin's theory for human morality, and he came to view the destructive violence of World War I as a result of the effect of Darwinist thinking on otherwise peace-loving men. He did not reject evolution in animals and plants, just human evolution. Indeed, more than human evolution, Bryan's enemy was evolution's perceived corollary, social Darwinism, or the idea that humans should unsympathetically eliminate or at the very least not provide support to those who seemed incapable of succeeding in America's market-driven economy. Bryan thought the concept of "survival of the fittest" inhumane and unjust. Thus, when it became a chief goal of a burgeoning Fundamentalist movement in the early 1920s to stop the teaching of human evolution in public schools, Bryan became an avid supporter. He did not want the dangerous ideas of social Darwinism to seep into the minds of American children. In his mind, protecting the sanctity of the Bible was the best way to prevent this from happening. So a man who had not practiced law in more than three decades signed on as one of the chief prosecutors of John Thomas Scopes.

The ACLU was not pleased with Bryan's entrance into the case. His presence meant publicity. It meant the case would focus on Genesis rather than individual rights. The quiet procedural case the ACLU wanted was not what Bryan had in mind when he decided to join the legal team.

The news rapidly worsened for the ACLU. Bryan's entrance piqued the interest of Clarence Darrow, the country's most famous defense attorney. Based in Chicago, Darrow was a famous agnostic who had defended the rights of labor and of communists. He was an advocate (and occasional practitioner) of free love, enjoyed urbanity and all its rebellious playfulness, and, more than anything else, loved the freedoms promised by modern living. Modesty was not his strong suit: when asked about his new marriage, Darrow responded that it was going well because "Marge and me, we both love Darrow." In 1925 he was at the peak of his power, having just successfully argued against the execution of Nathan Leopold and Richard Loeb, two wealthy Chicago teenage lovers who had murdered an unpopular kid in part just to see if they could get away with it. Riding high on this success, Darrow headed to Dayton to try to shake loose some of that old-time religion from the South.

And so, in short, an agnostic defender of communists and murderous homosexuals was coming from the North to challenge the way a small southern community wanted to educate its children. And the greatest defender of southern and western populism was coming to the rescue. The ACLU's goose was cooked. Hundreds of reporters descended on Dayton; people abandoned their homes in order to rent them to visitors. The "trial of the century" was on. And, save two episodes, the case proceeded as might be expected: after two hours of closely recorded testimony, Scopes was found guilty of violating the law. He was given a nominal fine and, never cuffed or imprisoned, walked away untouched.

What makes the case memorable, however, is that the two hours of official testimony took place over eight days of legal wrangling that brought to the surface bitter claims from all sides. And what protracted the case to eight days were the two interesting episodes of the trial. First, although the law in question prohibited the teaching of Darwinian evolution, the judge decided that the real issue was not the veracity of evolution but the right of a legislature to dictate what went on in its state. The judge therefore disallowed any testimony about the scientific community's opinion of evolution. Denied his chief weapon, Darrow sought tactical refuge in showing that it was impossible for rational thinkers to believe the Christian origin story; with no other course open to him, he tried to make a mockery of Christian mythology.

The second interesting episode resulted from the first. As Darrow cast about for biblical authorities who would have standing with Tennessee jurors, he looked across the aisle; and he proposed that Bryan himself take the stand. The two great personalities going toe-to-toe in the hot Tennessee summer was one of the most memorable episodes of the trial, and of the 1920s generally. During this inquisition, Darrow asked Bryan the village atheist questions posed at the beginning of this essay. Each man gave as well as he got, although Darrow did manage to get Bryan to hedge a good bit on several questions of biblical literalism—something Darrow took as a victory, but something not entirely out of the norm for conservative Christians of the 1920s. Biblical literalism of the 1920s was not what it came to be in the 1970s; it was more of a liberal literalism, suggesting the Bible was true because God was capable of anything, while humankind's ability to interpret those words was less secure. Bryan's rousing rhetoric masked these obfuscations, leading many who heard the debate firsthand to recall that Bryan had more than held his own.

In the end, of course, their jousting was irrelevant to the trial. The jury found Scopes guilty after just nine minutes of deliberation. A newspaper paid the modest fine of $100, Scopes was released, and he lived a quiet life thereafter, writing a jaunty memoir, *Center of the Storm*, of the event four decades later. Because of a legal technicality (the judge issued the $100 fine rather than the jury), the decision was thrown out on appeal, meaning the ACLU could not get a higher court to hear the case again. The trial of *Tennessee v. John Scopes* lived and died in Dayton, Tennessee.

Between Bryan and Darrow

But of course it did not. In history, context is everything; events are inexplicable without knowledge of the surrounding circumstances. And the context of the Scopes trial was the uncertain direction of Christianity in the modern world. The turn of the twentieth century was marked by tremendous changes— industrialization, urbanization, immigration, the expansive growth of the natural sciences, and of course secularization, which was partly attributable to each of these. Each of these watershed changes provoked questions about traditional sources of moral authority, such as rural community life, the taken-for-granted Anglo-Protestant hegemony, and the Bible as a source of inspiration and moral guidance. These traditional sources of authority had served as a moral foundation for Americans since the nation's origins. The very act of probing their veracity led to fundamental questions about what kind of America people wanted to live in. Would it protect the integrity of the past, resisting urbanity, cosmopolitanism, and humanism in favor of a known, if questionable, authority? Or would it take a progressive cast, rejecting the certainty of old dogmatisms in favor of the vague promises of the new? Or was there a third way, in which the rigor of old forms of authority could be adapted to align with new data?

Because of the breadth of these questions, smaller issues served as proxies for the larger debate. Because of the stakes involved—the fundamental sources of moral authority in America—small and local proxies became national events. And national events created polarized positions that evaded any middle ground. This is what happens in most battles over moral authority, and it was what happened in the Scopes case. And because the stakes seemed so high, godlessness—a concept at the heart of the larger cultural debate—moved to the center of each side's argument. With Darrow and Bryan representing either pole, neither man disputed that Bryan had God on his side. What was at issue was whether or not that was desirable. To Darrow and his followers, a victory for Bryan would be a win for parochial dogmatisms and a loss for enlightened tolerance. To Bryan and his followers, a victory for Darrow would affirm the increasing amorality and godlessness in America, and they relied on the tradition of the Puritan jeremiad to make their case. Quietly in the corner, a third tradition grew. It espoused the tolerance of Darrow's brand of godlessness and the faith of Bryan's. Between Bryan and Darrow was a burgeoning liberal Protestantism.

Between Darrow and Mencken

But first, the two poles. At one pole, Clarence Darrow reveled in his self-proclaimed godlessness. He believed religious dogma was inherently divisive; given the choice of living in a world with or without men who preached on behalf of God, Darrow's choice would be easy. "There is nothing else," he said in his opening statement of the Scopes case, "that has caused the difference of opinion, of bitterness, or hatred, of war, of cruelty, that religion has caused." Then he claimed that Bryan's type of biblical literalism and his dogged defense of nineteenth-century Protestant moral austerity was out "to kindle religious bigotry and hate" in America. He added emphatically: "To strangle puppies is good when they grow up into mad dogs. . . . Your life and my life and the life of every American citizen depends after all upon the tolerance and forbearance of his fellowman."[4] The stakes were so high that the wanton murder of puppies was a justifiable metaphor.

Darrow premised his legal argument on the assumption that Tennessee's antievolution statute was in fact establishing a particular religious viewpoint. Fearful of a new clerical order that would stamp out individual rights and any glimmer of freethinking, Darrow worried that if a legislative body began to restrict the way people were allowed to think, American society would be on a slippery slope toward intolerance. "We are marching backwards to the glorious age of the sixteenth century when bigots lighted fagots to burn men who dared to bring any intelligence and enlightenment and culture to the human mind," he said in one of the case's most arresting passages.[5] To be officially secular, then, was the only acceptable mode of tolerance in a diverse America. The alternative was frightening and, as he saw it, anything but filled with God's grace.[6]

Darrow was not alone in championing the godless future. He was joined, most articulately and enthusiastically, by H. L. Mencken, the famous Baltimore writer and skeptic. Mencken had a front row seat at the Scopes trial and expounded on it with daily dispatches. He called Dayton "a sort of Holy Land for imbeciles," referring to those he saw indiscriminately clutching to the certainty of a fading past. Of Bryan, Mencken said, "It is a tragedy, indeed, to begin life as a hero and to end it as a buffoon." Like Darrow, however, Mencken was not an avowed atheist, nor did he necessarily dislike people who professed a religion. The problem, he said, was that, on the whole, believers were hypocrites. They did not live by the creeds they avowed. They did not find humility and forgiveness in the Good Book but strict moral codes that led them to regard with wrath all those who did not share their views.[7]

Mencken most thoroughly examined the subject in his *Treatise on the Gods*, which appeared in 1930, after he had sifted through the varieties of religion that emerged in 1920s America. Sounding like the English Enlightenment philosopher David Hume, Mencken argued that religion originated in response to humankind's fear of the unknown. As humans increased their knowledge about the universe around them, religion was destined to occupy increasingly smaller space. There really was a turf war between science and religion, and science was winning. Enlightened people knew this, and had shed much of their belief in the supernatural. "Today," he wrote, "no really civilized man or woman believes in the cosmogony of Genesis, nor in the reality of Hell, nor in any of the other ancient imbecilities that still entertain the mob.... On the upper levels of the human race Christianity is plainly breaking down." Mencken acknowledged, however: "It may be that, by thus moving away from religion, man is losing something" and admitted that "illusions also have their uses" in providing comfort and assisting the weak by offering moral defenses for their actions. But for the most part, religion "tends to engender a smugness which is essentially anti-social." Worse, it is "always against that free play of human personality which is at the bottom of all progress." In this view, living without the need to believe in God was an invitation to human creativity, an end to bitter divisiveness, and a welcome substitute for the self-righteousness of the true believer.[8]

It was also, however, an invitation to lionize progress so much that harsh forms of social Darwinism became palatable. Like Darrow, Mencken also found use for Nietzsche, and promoted Nietzsche's thoughts in the first book on Nietzsche in English, *Philosophy of Friedrich Nietzsche* (1908), which called the German philosopher "a thorough Darwinian." Similarly, Mencken was well versed in the writings of Herbert Spencer and William Graham Sumner, two of the leading lights of turn-of-the-century social Darwinism. Mencken made comments throughout his life that were both racist and anti-Semitic, and it seems likely that these comments originated from his support of social Darwinist beliefs. Similarly, Mencken was also always an avid supporter of strict free market capitalism, leading him to even eventually denounce the New Deal because of its expansion of federal powers and its assistance for the poor. Thus, the cultural battles about evolution in the Scopes trial were layered with context that is easy to miss today, when social Darwinism is, thankfully, no longer intellectually respectable.

It is hard to know how representative Mencken's ideas were in 1920s America. Certainly large swaths of the literati, including John Dos Passos, F. Scott Fitzgerald, Ernest Hemingway, and Sinclair Lewis, resonated with his views. Echoing Jefferson and Emerson in earlier eras, these thinkers felt liberated from the dogmas of the past. Along similar lines, the most important institutional advocate of free thinking in the United States—the ACLU—was founded in 1920, although it was founded not out of a glorification of godlessness but out of respect for multiple perspectives. The small bands of American communists then in existence were more celebratory of what they saw as a coming godless era, although they had been pegged as anti-American during the Red Scare of the 1920s and remained on the run throughout the decade. Indeed, the Red Scare conflated atheism with communism, so anyone advocating a future godlessness, including Darrow and Mencken, was readily castigated as a Red (although in these men's cases, nothing could have been further from the truth). This kind of thinking was certainly reactionary, but it occasionally had (and has) political legs. This suggests that in the end, the thankful godlessness of Mencken and Darrow was relatively limited in the age of Babbitt. If these years really did represent "the end of American innocence" (as one historian has put it), then many Americans were all the more ready to grab onto the fixity of biblical doctrine.[9]

As wolves howling in the lonely wind, though, both Darrow and Mencken were also harking back to a prophetic tradition of godlessness. Both men saw themselves in line with Tom Paine and Robert Ingersoll as advocates of free thought. Despite their rhetorical flourishes, both men were not opposed to faith per se; they just felt it was too often misused. In this sense, their prophetic tradition emphasized more fully the capacity of humankind to live without voodoo and the wonderful knowledge that would when this happened. Theirs was an optimistic and progressive vision, although both men were deeply skeptical that America would choose this route, and both were deeply unaware of or indifferent to the dark side of the Nietzschean scheme of evolution.

Bryan and Machen

At the other pole sat Bryan. He claimed that Darrow, as the defendant of evolutionary theory, lacked any belief in God and that his lack of faith had left him without a moral center. As Bryan said, "the contest between evolution and Christianity is a duel to the death. The atheists, agnostics and all other opponents of Christianity understand the character of the struggle, hence their interest in this case."[10] A cartoon in the Memphis *Commercial Appeal*, a Fundamentalist magazine, showed Darrow sitting atop a dirt mound in the depths of hell, surrounded by the figures of "spiritual despair," "annihilation," and "agnosticism." The inscription on his dark throne read "Anti-Christ." To those within the Fundamentalist tradition, Darrow was nothing more than the devil in disguise, joyfully leading America down a perilous path of godless doom.

But of course, Darrow was just a symbol of the lurking evil. Science, and in particular human evolution, was the real evil. Why? Although it had no scheme of the origins of life, the scientific perspective was dislodging the Christian one, creating dire instability throughout Western civilization, as in a body with no skeleton. Speaking of the evolutionary scientists, Bryan said, "Not one of them can tell you how life began. The atheist says it came in some way without a god. The agnostic says, it came in some way, they know not whether with a god or not." Either way, "they shut God out of this world." This meant no miracles, no virgin birth, no resurrection, no eternal salvation—no authority derived from the Bible. In his one rousing speech at the trial, Bryan concluded:

> There is no place for the miracle in this train of evolution, and the Old Testament and the New are filled with miracles; and if [evolution] is true, this logic eliminates every mystery in the Old Testament and the New. And eliminates everything supernatural. And that means they eliminate the Virgin Birth. That means that they eliminate resurrection of the body, and that means that they eliminate the doctrine of atonement. And they believe that man has been rising all the time, that man never fell, that when the Savior came there was not any reason for His coming, there was no reason why He should not go as soon as He could, that He was born of Joseph of some other co-respondent and that He lies in His grave and, when the Christians of this State have tied their hands and said we will not take advantage of our power to teach religion to our children by teachers paid by us, these people come in from the outside of the State and force upon us, the people of this State and upon the children of the tax payers of this States, a doctrine that refutes not only their belief in God, but their belief in a Savior and a belief in heaven and takes from them every moral standard that the Bible gives us.

Talk about your slippery slope. Teaching evolution dissolves the resonance of the Bible, making one godless and therefore unable to locate any suitable morality. After this part of his speech, Bryan suggested that Nietzsche was the only major thinker who had sifted through the consequences of this line of thought, and that Nietzsche's theories had led to reckless affirmations of the validity of lawbreaking and murder—an intellectual journey that ultimately led the famous philosopher to lose any rational perspective on this world. Citing Nietzsche was a direct jab at Darrow, of course, because Darrow had used the violence inherent in Nietzsche's philosophy as an exculpatory reason to spare the lives of Leopold and Loeb, the wealthy teenage murderers. Throughout the Scopes case, Bryan continued to assert that if Christianity could not be taught to the next generation, Americans were setting themselves up to live in an amoral, godless community where violence, self-interest, and moral relativity would reign supreme. The stakes were high, the possibilities dire.

In these statements, however, it becomes clear that Bryan was not essentially an antimodernist buffoon rejecting the arrival of anything new. Rather, he was afraid that human evolution could not be connected to the teachings of the Bible and, worse, that would necessarily lead to social Darwinism and its dangerous practices. Nietzsche thus was relevant not only because Darrow had used Nietzsche in the case of Leopold and Loeb but also because Nietzsche's early protobrutalist, evolutionist views promised frightening results, especially as writers like Mencken amplified and supported those ideas in America. While many scholars tend to think of Darrow as an offshoot of the Enlightenment and Bryan as occupying a reactionary intellectual backwater, Bryan made it clear that he rejected the brutal form of social Darwinism that seemed to be the end product of human evolution, a fact that makes him appear all the more human, and humane.

Although he was one of the most explicit attackers of social Darwinism, Bryan was not alone in making these sorts of arguments during the interwar years. In fact, he tapped into a growing minority tradition. His most theologically astute ally was J. Gresham Machen, a disgruntled Presbyterian whose book *Christianity and Liberalism* (1923) attacked what he called "liberalism" as disingenuous and dangerous. To Machen, liberals were those who claimed to still believe the veracity of the Bible but resisted any literalist reading of it, seeing it instead as a book of morals or nice stories. Machen not only feared Darrow's brand of godlessness but also saw his fellow Christians softening their beliefs and allowing godless fools like Darrow to gain traction.

Machen began by labeling liberalism a "totally diverse type of religious belief, which is only the more destructive of the Christian faith because it makes use of traditional Christian terminology." The only thing that unified the liberals, Machen said, was their endorsement of a theory of "naturalism," which he defined as "the denial of any entrance of the creative power of God in connection with the origin of Christianity." To Machen, liberals denied that God had anything to do with the creation of Christianity, which made Christianity merely a religion that served the needs of humans. He saw these liberals as weaklings, searching for peace under the cowering pressure of growing scientific knowledge. But liberals would not find peace: "In abandoning the embattled walls of the city of God," Machen wrote, liberals had "fled in needless panic into the open plains of a vague natural religion only to fall an easy victim to the enemy who ever lies in ambush there." Taking God out of Christianity was fallacious; it was moral quicksand that denied sin and opened the door to the devil—which was, of course, the very definition of Christian godlessness.[11]

From there, Machen developed a systematic theology centered on the Westminster Confession, which, among other tenets, asserted the importance of biblical inerrancy and all that followed from that. The development of this hard-line theology led to a significant denominational schism in the middle 1930s, when Machen was thrown out of the Presbyterian Church and went on to form an alternate denomination, which has since folded but served as an ideological precursor to today's Presbyterian Church of America (as opposed to today's more liberal Presbyterian Church, U.S.A.).[12]

From a historical perspective, these fears of a coming godlessness tapped into a prophetic tradition in America that extends back to the first Puritans. These claims, or varieties of them, resurfaced numerous times throughout the eighteenth and nineteenth centuries. By the 1920s, however, the jeremiad tradition of American evangelicals had become avowedly antimodernist, rejecting the new world taking shape around them and harking back to an earlier time when Protestant morality supposedly had gone unchallenged. The jeremiad tradition also became antiprogressive. Throughout the nineteenth century, American evangelicals overwhelmingly believed in progress, viewing America as the location of the coming kingdom of God. By the 1920s, this hopefulness was gone. They fought hard against the consequences of secularization. They fought hard against secularization, which had the unintended consequence of allowing them to recoil from mainstream struggles and turn inward. This departure from the public realm allowed them to build institutions—universities, Bible schools, journals—that would allow evangelicalism to come back in force during the last third of the century. It is, however, important to recall the difference between that time, when people feared a Nietzschean interpretation of social Darwinism, and now, when people fear a supposed "moral relativism" that arises when the Bible is left behind.

New Prophesies of Liberal Protestantism

In popular imagination, Bryan and Machen's turn to the gospel and Darrow and Mencken's celebration of secularity are the two most visible traditions of the 1920s. These were the two main camps in the post–World War I culture war, which was being fought over the rightful foundation of moral authority, once it seemed that the forces of modernity had seemingly dislodged all previous contenders. And although both sides had long-standing antecedents, both claims of godlessness were new in force and resonance, perhaps because the stakes suddenly seemed so high. There had been little biblical literalism in the eighteenth and nineteenth centuries, and Machen's brand of Fundamentalism emerged in direct response to the forces of modernization. Similarly, there had been only a short tradition of gleeful godlessness in the American past, and Darrow and Mencken's raucous affirmation of godlessness struck a chord with many prominent voices during the interwar years.

These poles, however, excluded the large middle of American society, and much of our understanding of the past has subsequently missed this large middle. This is problematic because this third position, often labeled liberal Protestantism, was destined to become one of the most important intellectual traditions of the twentieth century, due to its espousal of tolerance, forgiveness, and weak ontology. For instance, having been founded in part by a scattering of liberal Protestants, the ACLU was well aware of the appeal of this middling position. Trying to avoid the polarization of a culture war, the ACLU's leaders actually *opposed* Darrow's participation in the Scopes trial, not only because of the publicity he would attract but primarily because his presence meant the trial would become a litmus test of one's thoughts on God. As one of Darrow's cocounselors said, "If the fight of liberalism and honest thinking is to be won it must have the support of millions of intelligent Christians who accept the Bible as a book of morals and inspiration."[13] Darrow's brand of godlessness would not lead to victory in twentieth-century America. Laugh as they might at the words of Darrow and Mencken, most Americans did not quite feel that the haughty, perhaps morally ugly position of these two iconoclasts represented Americans' true beliefs. The ACLU wanted someone who could reclaim the vital center between Fundamentalism and secularism. But John Scopes, because of his fears of the emotional fury Bryan might provoke, chose Darrow as his primary defender. Thus liberal Protestantism was shut out of the Scopes case.

Twentieth-century liberal Protestantism has not yet had its historian, but a tentative conclusion about its basic ideals suggests that its prominent thinkers were willing to accept the fallibility of the Bible, reading it instead as an inspired book of morals. Liberal Protestants also hedged on the reality of miracles, sensing that science was a more robust source of knowledge about the material world. Some of the more liberal thinkers even resisted (or avoided discussing) the idea of the resurrection—the central miracle of them all. What did they believe in? Most liberal Protestants of the 1920s were evangelicals—

that is, insistent on a Christlike rebirth experience and Spirit-filled worship and devoted to spreading the gospel and professing an austere moral stance. Otherwise, their beliefs are less clear, principally because they never made up a single movement and were strictly antidogmatic. At root, though, most liberal Protestants believed in the moral lessons taught in the Sermon on the Mount. They professed and even demanded tolerance of other faiths. And they advocated an appreciation of the dignity of man, which sometimes led them to side with the proletariat in labor disputes and other liberal political causes. More than anything, however, liberal Protestants embraced Christlike love rather than a strict doctrinaire code. It was the spirit of the law, not its letter, that mattered.[14]

A large number of liberal Protestant pastors rose to prominence during the interwar years, including Shailer Mathews, Earnest Freemont Tittle, and John Haynes Holmes, but the most famous was Harry Emerson Fosdick. Like other liberal Protestants, Fosdick fashioned his beliefs in opposition to the Fundamentalist movement. He thought he had a better understanding of what Jesus would want, should he return to earth anytime soon. The host of intolerant dictums preached by the Fundamentalists was certainly not it.

Harry Emerson Fosdick was a near-celebrity in interwar America, reaching fame through a series of sermons published between 1908 and 1920. His central theme was keeping the Christian message pertinent to the modern world, and this desire led him to be associated with a burgeoning group of social activists and Protestant pastors who claimed to be following the Social Gospel, improving living conditions in industrializing America. In his mind, the Fundamentalists were more interested in being right than in asserting rights, and so in 1922, three years before the Scopes trial, Fosdick gave a sermon entitled "Shall the Fundamentalists Win?" This sermon made him the figurehead of liberal Protestantism, and the principal target of Fundamentalists.

In the sermon, Fosdick described a key difference between faithful conservatives and the Fundamentalists: the faithful conservatives possessed "true liberality of spirit," while Fundamentalists were "illiberal and intolerant." Indeed, tolerance and humility were the central themes of the sermon. To Fosdick, Fundamentalism *meant* intolerance. There were, he said, inevitable differences of opinion about matters such as virgin birth, the divine inspiration of the Bible, and whether or not Christ was literally going to return to earth in a messianic moment of awe-inspiring deliverance (referred to as millennialism). What separated liberals from Fundamentalists, however, was the question of what to do with those whose opinion differed from one's own. Fundamentalists wanted to drive out their opposition. They wanted more separation, not less. This attitude was dangerous, Fosdick warned, for two reasons. First, it lacked the "spirit of tolerance and Christian liberty" that was central to the meaning of Christ. "If He should walk through the ranks of this congregation this morning," Fosdick asked, "can we imagine Him claiming as His own those who hold one idea of inspiration and sending from Him into outer darkness those who hold another?" The question was rhetorical. "You cannot fit the Lord Christ into that Fundamentalist mold." The worst part of this intolerance was that it prevented young people from coming to the Church. "Science," Fosdick said, "treats a young man's mind as though it were really important." On the other hand, "Can you imagine any man who is worthwhile turning from that call to the church if the church seems to him to say, 'Come, and we will feed you opinions from a spoon. No thinking is allowed here.'" Strict dogma and intolerance of intellectual exploration were anathema in the modern world.

The second problem with Fundamentalist intolerance was that it high-lighted esoteric yet unexciting issues—rather than more lofty ones. Christians, he said, were forced to ponder the feasibility of virgin birth rather than figuring out how to save souls in the aftermath of a brutal world war. Christians were arguing about the verbatim truth of Genesis rather than working through "the weightier matters of the law, justice, and mercy." To Fosdick, the Funda-mentalists' concern with unimportant issues led them to miss the real meaning of the Bible. Love, not legalisms, was what was devout.

Fosdick expanded these ideas in many of his books, the most famous of which was *Christianity and Progress* (1922). He was a serious scholar of the Bible, and it was incredible to him that people were beginning to read the Bible literally, with all its contradictions and historical inaccuracies. In fact, the tendency to read the Bible literally was only increasing with the rise of Fun-damentalism.[15] Like Mencken, Fosdick believed that intelligent people were rejecting biblical dogmatism; unlike Mencken, he argued that this challenge left the true Christian no choice but to create a new theology that would make the life of Jesus resonate in a scientific age. The alternative was insignificance. As he put it: "The decision no longer lies between an old and a new theology, but between a new theology and no theology." To keep spouting the intolerant Fundamentalist rhetoric was to languish in irrelevance, leaving the world an entirely godless place.[16]

These thoughts made Fosdick an easy target in the larger cultural battles over questions of morality during the interwar period. Espousing a middle way made him vulnerable to the big guns located at either pole with their ruthless certainties. Fosdick's problem was compounded by the fact that he was a Baptist minister preaching in a Presbyterian church—the same denomination Machen was doing so much to define dogmatically. And (bringing this essay full circle), after "Shall the Fundamentalists Win?" Fosdick was attacked in a show trial by none other than William Jennings Bryan, who led the Presbyterians in an inquisition similar to the one at Dayton. After Fosdick refused to assent to any creed, he was forcibly removed from his Presbyterian pulpit. Bryan won this round. In a testament to the popularity of Fosdick's middling position, though, he was quickly embraced by John D. Rockefeller Jr., who built New York City's famous Riverside Church so that Fosdick would continue to have a pulpit; Riverside quickly developed a congregation that numbered in the thousands.

Fosdick's removal from the Presbyterian ranks is a fitting symbol of the 1920s, when the polarized positions of freethinkers and Fundamentalists tended to grab the headlines. But Fosdick's fear that godlessness would emerge if either side won, and his notion that Christian love was more important than any creed, continued as a key component of American intellectual life for the remainder of the twentieth century.[17] Whether or not this position has any intellectual coherence—how are we to know what Jesus would want if he were to return? How does one clarify an antidogmatic position other than by scapegoating an opposition? How does an unorganized, deinstitutionalized belief find and retain advocates?—its importance lies in the fact that its chief ideals have become central to American politics and culture. One might say its defeat in the 1920s was temporary; its victory, if one might call it that, was more subtle.

But beyond recalling the birth pangs of liberal Protestantism, it is also useful to remember that the culture wars of the 1920s do not exactly mirror those of today. Despite the fact that the terms seem to align so nicely, Bryan was clearly not an unfeeling antimodernist throwing stones at all reformers; his worries about social evolutionism are common currency today, after eugenics culminated in the Nazi Holocaust. Nor was Mencken an avatar of Richard Rorty and other advocates of secular humanism; his frank racism and anti-Semitism mark him as an ambiguous ancestor for them. The terms of the debate were different then. That social Darwinism has fallen from grace as a respectable intellectual position is a piece of progress that Americans should be thankful to have achieved. That Americans are still debating the place of human evolution in the classroom is a reminder that battles over moral authority do not take place quickly or end quietly.

NOTES

1. This quotation and many others cited here are found in the indispensable guide to the Scopes trial, Edward J. Larson, *Summer of the Gods: The Scopes Trial and America's Continuing Debate over Science and Religion* (Cambridge: Basic Books, 1997),

125. For a look at many of the primary source documents surrounding the case, see Jeffrey Moran, *The Scopes Trial: A Brief History with Documents* (Boston: St. Martin's, 2002). See also Paul Conkin, *When All the Gods Trembled* (Oxford: Rowman and Littlefield, 1998).

2. Larsen, *Summer for the Gods*, 142.

3. For Bryan in these years see Lawrence W. Levine, *Defender of the Faith: William Jennings Bryan; The Last Decade* (New York: Oxford University Press, 1965), and Michael Kazin, *A Godly Hero: The Life of William Jennings Bryan* (New York: Knopf, 2006).

4. Larson, *Summer for the Gods*, 163–64.

5. Ibid., 164.

6. For Darrow's life, see Arthur and Lila Weinberg, *Clarence Darrow: A Sentimental Rebel* (New York: Putnam, 1980).

7. For a good new biography, see Marion Elizabeth Rodgers, *Mencken: An American Iconoclast* (New York: Oxford University Press, 2005), quotations 282 and 295.

8. H. L. Mencken, *Treatise on the Gods* (New York: Knopf, 1930), 297, 327, 350, 332, 320, 321.

9. On the idea that the 1910s and 1920s were a liberating and secular time, see Henry F. May, *The End of American Innocence: A Study in the First Years of Our Time* (New York: Knopf, 1959), and Christine Stansell, *American Moderns: Bohemian New York and the Creation of a New Century* (New York: Metropolitan Books, 2000). See also Susan Jacoby, *Freethinkers: A History of American Secularism* (New York: Owl Books, 2004), 186–267.

10. Larson, *Summer for the Gods*, 143–44.

11. J. Gresham Machen, *Christianity and Liberalism* (New York: Macmillan, 1923).

12. For the rise of the Fundamentalist movement, see George M. Marsden, *Fundamentalism and American Culture: The Shaping of Twentieth-Century Evangelicalism, 1870–1925* (New York: Oxford University Press, 1980), and Joel A. Carpenter, *Revive Us Again: The Reawakening of American Fundamentalism* (New York: Oxford University Press, 1997).

13. Larson, *Summer of the Gods*, 134.

14. For the origins of these ideas, see William R. Hutchison, *The Modernist Impulse in American Protestantism* (Cambridge, Mass.: Harvard University Press, 1976), and Susan Curtin, *A Consuming Faith: the Social Gospel and Modern American Culture* (Baltimore: Johns Hopkins University Press, 1991). For good sources for thinking about liberal Protestantism, see Gary Dorrien, *The Making of Modern Liberal Theology*, vols. 1–3 (Louisville, Ky.: Westminster, 2001–5), and Martin E. Marty, *Modern American Religion*, vol. 2, *The Noise of Conflict, 1919–1941* (Chicago: University of Chicago Press, 1997).

15. For the argument that literal reading of the Bible was a late nineteenth-century development, see Hans W. Frei, *The Eclipse of Biblical Narrative: A Study in Eighteenth and Nineteenth Century Hermeneutics* (New Haven: Yale University Press, 1974).

16. Harry Emerson Fosdick, *Christianity and Progress* (New York: Fleming H. Revell, 1922), 246.

17. Indeed, one might speculate that the importance of the idea of tolerance in liberal Protestantism helped open the door to an acceptance of minority faiths and minority people, thus helping to bring about the decline of the Anglo-American hegemony in American history. For a good biography, see Robert Moats Miller, *Harry Emerson Fosdick: Preacher, Pastor, Prophet* (New York: Oxford University Press, 1985).

8

The Thirties to the Fifties: Totalitarianism and the Second American Enlightenment

David Ciepley

In 1961, Gabriel Almond, chairman of the highly influential Committee on Comparative Politics of the Social Science Research Council (SSRC), distributed a memo to his committee colleagues. In it, Almond acknowledged the growing doubts among them that the nations of the world were converging on a common end-state. But he followed this with an observation that would keep his colleagues committed to the committee's program of formulating a universal theory of political development: however divergent were the trajectories of modernization their studies were uncovering, they were nevertheless converging on a common definition of the modernizing *process*: "Modernizing change...refers either to structural differentiation or cultural secularization, or both."[1]

At first blush, one can hardly imagine a more straightforward translation, into twentieth-century language, of the Enlightenment story of progress through the division of labor and the retreat of superstition. Of course, closer inspection inevitably qualifies this initial reaction. The vision of the future projected by Almond and other modernization theorists of the postwar period did not exactly replicate of any of the visions of the future coming out of the Enlightenment. From the perspective of this book, a particularly significant point of difference concerns the place of the transcendent in their respective vision. While the Enlightenment produced a few noteworthy "infidels"—Hume, d'Alembert, Voltaire—its signal religious stance was not atheism but what was then referred to as natural religion. Even at its Deist, post-Christian extreme, natural religion continued to affirm God's law as a transcendent guide for human conduct. When Thomas Jefferson, in the Declaration of Independence, invoked "the Laws of Nature and Nature's God" and asserted that all men are "endowed by their Creator with certain unalienable Rights," he spoke in typical Deist fashion.

The same quotes from Jefferson also point up a fact already shown in this book: with regard to morality, Enlightenment thinkers were rarely skeptics. Rather, these thinkers expressed *confidence* in the existence of universal moral laws (such as the "laws of nature") and in the ability of individuals to know and act on these laws. Indeed, it was precisely this confidence that spurred Enlightenment thinkers' critique of paternalistic political and religious authority. A common morality was a sufficient bond of society: one didn't need religious and political conformity on top of it.

By the mid-twentieth century, American social scientists inhabited a very different cosmological space. They were posttranscendent, even antitranscendent, thinkers.[2] They agreed with the Enlightenment critique of moral tutelage, but not out of confidence in the accessibility of universal moral laws. They agreed with it because they doubted the *existence* of such moral laws, and *this* made tutelage unjustifiable. As we will see, this moral skepticism, which we will call "relativism," was integral to their reworking of the theory of democracy and their antipathy to the presence of religion in politics—the central focus of this chapter. Belief in moral absolutes, an attitude of moral certitude—these, they held, were the traits of totalitarians, people anxious to impose their values and worldview on others. The attitude of democrats, in contrast, was one of moral "openness" and skepticism—an attitude that produced the toleration and compromise essential to a democratic order. To be modern was to be antiabsolutist—that is, to be democratic and secular. The safety and progress of liberal democracy depended on removing religion and its absolute moral claims from the public sphere. Accordingly, while postwar social scientists would strike many Enlightenment chords, they transposed them into a more morally skeptical key.

Still, even after registering all these caveats, and recognizing how complex and contested is the category of "Enlightenment," it remains hard to deny the resonance between modernization theory and the Enlightenment story of the march of reason.[3] What is harder to appreciate is how *surprising* it is that a secular Enlightenment narrative gained ascendance among midcentury American intellectuals. It is surprising when one considers that (1) only a decade earlier, what there was of Enlightenment in western Europe was nearly snuffed out by Nazism and fascism; (2) construing value skepticism as the guarantor of democracy and progress flew in the face of the enormous moral commitment to democracy involved in the waging of the Cold War; and (3) a secular narrative was such a dramatic departure from mainstream American intellectual traditions, which, as already shown here, thought Christianity lent positive support to democracy and progress.

Prewar progressives, for example, advanced a theory of modernization, but one in which Christianity was given a central constructive role. They saw modernization as a two-step process. First, religion—and more particularly, Christianity—would be modernized, meaning it would drop its emphasis on dogma and creed and intensify its emphasis on ethics. Second, this modernized religion would infuse the broader culture and "redeem" it from the ills of corrupt politics, cutthroat capitalism, and urban overcrowding. The "apparent paradox," political theorist Eldon Eisenach notes, is that "among all those active in national political affairs . . . the most cosmopolitan, scientifically trained, philosophically sophisticated, informed, and deeply critical of prevailing institutions and practices [were] *also* the most moral, religious, spiritual, and even romantically mystical in their public doctrines."[4] Far from advocating secularism, progressive intellectuals were enlightened Christianizers.

Even those who had lost their Christian faith, as had many of the country's leading sociologists, still saw a positive role for religion in society. They criticized religion as "dogmatic," "hierarchical," "theological," "legalistic," and "prohibitive." But religion had one undeniable virtue: "To the sociologist, what keeps the church most alive is its power to fit human beings for harmonious social life."[5] In an era preoccupied with the violent conflict between labor and capital—and the sharp struggle between urban and rural, immigrant and native, small producer and large producer—this counterbalanced all of religion's other drawbacks. Some secular sociologists even spoke in rather mystical terms of a future unity of science and religion on a reform basis:

> While sociology is not a religion . . . it finds much in common with the ethical aspirations of the church, so that the two will inevitably unite in ethical policy in coming years. The ethical generalizations of the great religions are broadened out into a common teaching, and their ethical applications in details are more and more compatible with scientific conclusions. The ethical aims of all religions and sociological teachings will increasingly harmonize.[6]

Postwar American academics' ready embrace of the modernization-secularization thesis was part of a broader midcentury reevaluation of the place of religious values in public life, which in turn was part of a yet broader reevaluation of the place of idealism and ideology in public life. Motivating these reevaluations was a reaction against "totalitarianism"—against its practice of ideological imposition, and against the putative "value absolutism" that lay behind it. Antitotalitarianism was not the only factor involved. World War I, the Treaty of Versailles, the lost battle for the League of Nations, the Red Scare, Prohibition: all these led American intellectuals to reconsider the political use of Christian millenarianism and the tactics of the moral crusade. The ascent of Jewish intellectuals within American academia also played its part in the adoption of the modernization-secularization thesis. But when we look at the specific terms in which postwar modernization theory was cast and trace their genealogy, what we come back to is the rhetoric of antitotalitarianism. Modernization-secularization theory projected onto the future of world history a new image of American democracy—a pluralist, skeptical democracy. And as the following sections show, this new image of democracy was forged in the late 1930s in an academic debate over the origins and etiology of totalitarianism. In the modernization theory that resulted, Americans' prophesies of godlessness were, for the first time, projected globally, even as they retained their distinctive American characteristics.

The Crisis of Democracy

In a time when scholars have discussed liberal capitalist democracy as the "end of history," it is easy to forget that in the 1930s, it hung by a thread. The European powers had never deemed these principles suited to the dark-skinned, non-Christian peoples they ruled; nor did Japan as it began its own territorial conquests. The world's dominant form of political and economic organization, from the nineteenth century well into the twentieth, was empire. The Russian Revolution was certainly not hospitable to liberal capitalist democracy. Then came the Great Depression, which shook the foundations of capitalism and raised anew questions about liberal democracies' capacity to manage the industrial economy. In western Europe, a new breed of dictators took advantage of the crisis to seize power and discard the liberal capitalist democratic order in their own countries, and they soon revealed their ambition to wipe it from the earth.

Even in the United States, liberal democracy was placed in question. In 1932, there were widespread calls, across the political and journalistic establishment, for President Franklin D. Roosevelt to assume dictatorial powers, at least temporarily, to resolve the economic crisis.[7] This came on top of the disenchantment many progressive intellectuals already felt toward popular democracy, in light of the willingness of the American middle classes to abandon progressive and economic reforms for the sake of "normalcy." "To attempt a defense of democracy these days," one observer wrote, "is a little like defending paganism in 313 or the divine right of kings in 1793."[8] By 1934, after a decade of depression in the agricultural sector and almost five years in the industrial sector, without any sign of recovery, even Frank Knight, the hardboiled godfather of the Chicago school of economics, was raising the white flag: "We are actually in the course of one of the world's great economic and political revolutions.... The nineteenth-century liberal system is played out, and the world of West-European civilization, based on political 'democracy' and economic 'freedom,' will go through a drastic revaluation of its 'modern' ideas and values."[9]

Yet in the late 1930s, American intellectuals underwent a reaction against the reaction. News of Stalin's purges shocked the political Left, and Hitler's murderous racism shocked everyone. Confronted with the barbarity of these regimes, intellectuals of all stripes rallied to the defense of the "American way of life" and trimmed much of their progressive agenda for transforming it. With regard to economics, they again embraced free enterprise and distanced themselves from the progressive ideal of a "cooperative commonwealth." With regard to the law, they again embraced the rule of law and distanced themselves from the progressive ideal of judicial deference to legislatures and executives, especially in the areas of civil liberty, civil rights, and due process. Civic republican values came under scrutiny as well. With regard to politics, American intellectuals again embraced popular democracy (although not populist democracy) and distanced themselves from the progressive ideals of social control and citizen transformation.[10]

However, to agree on the virtue of democracy was not necessarily to agree on the virtues that sustain it. No sooner had American intellectuals rallied to the defense of democracy than they found themselves locked in a bitter fight over the terms in which this defense should be made. Many of the participants depicted it as a contest between medievalism and the Enlightenment. Which offered the true philosophy of democracy, and which was the slippery slope to totalitarianism? This debate generated new assumptions about the basis of democracy, and these assumptions provided fertile soil for a modernization-secularization narrative to take hold.

Debating the Foundations of Democracy and Totalitarianism

Conflict had been brewing within academia for some years, centering on issues of social scientific methodology. In the interwar years, social scientists, grown wary of moral crusading, had adopted a more thorough naturalism, with the younger of them inclining toward positivism. They rejected the idea that ethical ideals could be rationally demonstrated and advocated replacing such exercises with "value-free" studies of the way politics, the law, and other social phenomena "really work." In practice, an ethical impulse generally remained behind their work—they would use scientific naturalism either to clear the way for reform by debunking existing "folkways" or to create an instrumental social science that would be of use to reforming legislators.[11] But the change in language suggested a major departure from ethical moorings.

Opposed to this departure were the "value absolutists." A pair of encyclicals from Pope Leo XIII—*Aeterni patris* (1879) and *Rerum novarum* (1891)—had established Thomist scholasticism and natural law theory as the proper Catholic framework for addressing modern social problems. Catholic intellectuals thus took a leading role in criticizing scientific naturalism. They were joined in this by an influential group of rationalists, among them Robert Hutchins and Mortimer Adler of the University of Chicago, who—analogously to the Catholics—held that human reason could discover universal principles of justice through philosophical analysis of the nature of reality.

The rise of fascism brought this quarrel to a fevered pitch by injecting each side with the conviction that the fate of Western democracy depended on the other side's defeat. While the scientific naturalists had numbers on their side within academe, in the court of public opinion they found themselves pushed back on their heels.[12] The most basic charge leveled at the naturalists was that their work propagated moral relativism—with its logical implication of "that which is, is right"—and that it was on this relativism that totalitarianism fed.[13] The legal realists, who brought naturalist sensibilities to the study of law, came in for especially harsh condemnation. Father Francis E. Lucey, regent of Georgetown University School of Law: "Democracy *versus* the Absolute State means Natural Law *versus* Realism."[14]

The real polemical gold was struck when Catholic critics recruited the Founding Fathers to their side against the naturalists. Jefferson, after all, had invoked the "law of nature" to justify the people's "inalienable rights." If the country was founded on natural law, what perils would follow from abandoning it? Despite significant differences with the founders regarding the *content* of natural law, continuity in the *form* of argument allowed Catholic intellectuals to cast themselves as the defenders of the American faith against the onslaught of naturalist, "secular humanist," godless apostates.[15]

This was rhetorically powerful stuff, and it helped secure Catholic intellectuals a surprising degree of influence, especially in the growing conservative movement. But within the academic mainstream, the scientific naturalists were able to turn the tables. Ever since the early decades of the twentieth century, John Dewey had been arguing that democracy was the "experimental attitude" in science writ large.[16] By the late 1930s, he was also emphasizing the converse: that science's opposite—philosophical and theological absolutism— leads to political absolutism, since the pretense of eternal verities licenses an authoritarian caretaker.[17]

This was the flag the besieged naturalists rallied around. Totalitarianism, as the naturalists construed it, stood for the imposition of values, and was brought on by an attitude of moral absolutism. Democracy, in contrast, stood for discussion, change, and diversity, and it flowed from a scientific, experimental, skeptical attitude. As the Chicago philosopher Charles Morris put it, "The democratic attitude involves flexibility, experimentation, correction of beliefs in action, respect for individuality, ability to live with diversity; and dogmatism in any form is an enemy to this attitude and a friend to its rival, the authoritarian attitude."[18] This position had two signal benefits for the naturalists. First, it allowed them to associate their methodological opponents with totalitarianism. Second, it meant that they could denounce totalitarianism without violating their own value agnosticism. The *mere fact* that values were being imposed was objectionable, whatever the values might be. Since moral-political demonstration is impossible, such imposition can never be justified.

The implications for democracy were dramatic. As late as 1937, Carl Friedrich of Harvard's Department of Government was still quoting Lord Balfour's dictum that democracy is only possible where citizens agree on fundamental values. Two years later, he was asking rhetorically: "May it not be that modern constitutional democracy is the endeavor precisely to organize government in such a way that agreement on fundamentals need not be secured?"[19] Thomas V. Smith, a leading ethicist, was more blunt: "Democracy does not require, or permit, agreement on fundamentals."[20]

In this new understanding, democracy was the system of government that accepted the relativity of all value positions and did its best not to impose values on anyone. "Organized skepticism," the Columbia University sociologist Robert Merton called it.[21] Edward Purcell Jr. has dubbed this view the "relativist theory of democracy." Throughout the war years and well into the postwar period, it spread far and wide within the university system, and spilled out into educated liberal opinion. Leading historians, for example, read the relativist theory of democracy into American history. Since Americans have more or less always been good democrats, they must always have been secular, skeptical, and driven by material interests rather than moral ones. As Arthur Schlesinger Jr., a dean of the American historical profession, boldly argued,

"The American mind is by nature and tradition skeptical, irreverent, pluralistic and relativistic." "Relativism," he added, "is the American way."[22]

In short, over the course of World War II, American social scientists and legal scholars translated the Weberian ideal of value-neutral *science* into an ideal of a value-neutral *political-constitutional order*—or at least, a political-constitutional order in which values are not imposed on anyone. Even more stunning, they presented America as the embodiment of this ideal. Academics dropped the covenantal conception of America as a moral project, and re-interpreted it as a regime of neutral process.

Totalitarianism and Religion

Religion occupied a central role in this contest over the meaning of American democracy. In the popular mind, the association between religion and democracy was arguably strengthened, consistent with the position of Catholic intellectuals. The antidote to godless communism was God. "If you will not have God (and He is a jealous God)," T. S. Eliot wrote, "you should pay your respects to Hitler or Stalin."[23]

But within academe—especially among naturalist social scientists and legal scholars—religion and democracy were increasingly disassociated, and even placed in opposition. The Catholic theologians' neo-Thomism was the particular object of naturalist ire. Despite the cultural clashes between Fundamentalists and secular liberals symbolized by the Scopes trial, the 1920s and early 1930s had been a period of warming relations between the liberal intellectuals and the Catholic intelligentsia, as they put aside their philosophical differences to cooperate on reforming the competitive market order.[24] But the quarrel over methodology and totalitarianism ended this rapprochement. The fact that American Catholic bishops had come out so strongly in support of Mussolini didn't help either.[25] In a 1943 essay, "Freedom and Authoritarianism in Religion," Horace Kallen, the erstwhile exponent of cultural pluralism, turned against his former ally on issues of economic reform, John A. Ryan, the leading American Catholic social theorist of the first half of the twentieth century. Speaking of Ryan's works *The State and the Church* (1936) and *Catholic Principles of Politics* (1940), Kallen argued:

> In principle and in practice their intent is a spiritual fascism, a moral and intellectual totalitarianism, which has its peers in those of the Nazis and their ilk.... Behind the authoritarian assault on democracy wherever it occurs, you will find the pretension to an exclusive

monopoly of religious truth and moral wisdom put in the possession of its keeper by God above, and making of the keeper the infallible master of the children of men, who are bound to believe, to obey and to fight for this master.[26]

Nor was Kallen about to surrender Jefferson to the opposition: citing Jefferson's authorship of the Virginia Statute of Religious Liberty and quoting his pronouncement "History furnishes no example of a priest-ridden people maintaining a free civil government," he argued for Jefferson as a founding father of the relativist tradition.[27]

This suspicion of the Catholic Church remained typical of liberal intellectuals until the mid-1950s, as reflected in the popularity among the liberal university establishment of Paul Blanchard's book *American Freedom and Catholic Power* (1949).[28] It was part of the dichotomy, or set of dichotomies, that structured thought in almost every field in the postwar period: Totalitarianism-dogmatism-Catholicism was set in opposition to democracy-science-skepticism-Enlightenment. And if the brunt of naturalist ire was directed against neo-Thomism, it nevertheless could easily extend to Niebuhr's "neo-orthodox" theology, and indeed, to any creed that still made a place for the supernatural.[29]

Throughout the nineteenth century, most Americans had supposed that Christianity was the foundation of morality, and morality the foundation of the republic, guaranteeing that liberty did not run into license. But by the early 1940s, American academics had turned this supposition on its head. Moral absolutism was the source of *totalitarian* government, and supernaturalism was the leading source of moral absolutes. Indeed, the medieval Catholic Church was, they argued, the *prototype* of totalitarian government.[30] Moral skeptics and secularists were the true democrats.

Offspring of the Relativist Theory of Democracy

The academics who embraced this new relativist understanding began at this point to pursue three important intellectual projects: *religious disestablishment*, the *pluralist theory of democracy*, and *secularization theory*. We will discuss each of these in turn.

Religious Disestablishment

Liberal academics' new misgivings about religion in public life, and about Catholicism in particular, were quickly reflected in the work of the Supreme

Court, which, of all the branches of the federal government, maintains the closest ties to academe. In *Everson v. Board of Education* (1947), the Court "incorporated" the religious clauses of the First Amendment through the Fourteenth Amendment, prohibiting the states, no less than Congress, from making laws establishing religion. Justice Hugo Black, writing for the Court, invoked "the words of Jefferson" to argue that "the clause against establishment of religion by law was intended to erect 'a wall of separation between Church and State.'" *Everson* was followed by a line of cases disestablishing religion, especially in America's schools, by cutting off the public subsidizing of parochial schools and removing prayer and other expressions of religion from the public classroom. The first reflected the Court's concern with the "Catholic problem."[31] The second reflected their more general concern about public religious indoctrination.[32]

The liberal elite's anti-Catholic animus faded by the mid-1950s, as registered by Will Herberg's *Protestant-Catholic-Jew* (1955). And with time, the Court would loosen its strictures on the public subsidy of parochial schools. But the stricture on religion in the classroom would remain firmly in place, as part of the more general antitotalitarian aversion to government imposition of values. This view would achieve its most formal expression in the writings of liberal theorists such as Rawls, Dworkin, Ackerman, and Nozick. Despite their disagreements on certain details, all held that the touchstone of liberalism was the neutrality of the state toward "theories of the good" or "comprehensive doctrines," of which religion was the paradigmatic example.

The Pluralist Theory of Democracy

In addition to this literature on "state neutrality," another line of postwar political theorizing even more directly incorporated the new assumptions about democracy generated in the 1930s debate over totalitarianism. This was the "pluralist theory" of democracy, as developed by the likes of David Truman and Robert Dahl. The dichotomy between morally absolutist totalitarianism and scientific-skeptical democracy was one of its key organizing tropes.[33]

For starters, the postwar pluralists redoubled their commitment to scientific naturalism. Dubbing themselves "behavioralists," they dismissed the traditional focus of political scientists on issues of right, legitimacy, and the public good in favor of nonnormative descriptions of the "political process." What is more, they did this without compunction. On the new understanding of democracy, moral skepticism was not a vice but a virtue; thus, in their formal agnosticism, scientific naturalists were being good democrats as well as good scholars.

Second, having accepted the association between moral absolutism and totalitarianism, they inferred that a politics based on absolutist claims—moral, theological, or ideological—was undemocratic and un-American. Even in the face of overwhelming evidence on the centrality of evangelical Protestantism in nineteenth- and early twentieth-century American politics, pluralists insisted that Americans were basically of a skeptical cast of mind and American politics is pragmatic and practical, devoted to brokering mundane "interests."[34] David Truman said his opus *The Governmental Process* was "an effort to take the concept of group, especially the interest or 'pressure' group, as a primary unit of analysis, and to examine patterns of action on the governmental scene in such terms." Of course, progressives had been keenly aware of the influence of pressure groups, or "special interests," on the legislative process. But they roundly condemned it and looked to a combination of moral uplift and expert-guided executive governance to minimize its influence. Postwar pluralists, in contrast, saw the influence of organized interests as largely beneficent. It was moral crusades and executive government that they saw as the source of danger. Interest groups were a device for making government responsive to societal needs. They also guaranteed that power would be dispersed in the political system. Government by interest groups avoided the tyranny of a stable "minority rule" or "majority rule" in favor of a minimally coercive and shifting "minorities rule."

Finally, there was the question of what held this congeries of competing interests together. What prevented society from disintegrating into a war of each against all? Totalitarian regimes might be held together by a common ideology, but ideology is what democratic countries abjure. Pluralists proposed instead that Americans are held together by a common "political culture." This was different from an ideology, they argued, because, at least in the American case, it consisted of shared attitudes and habits rather than shared beliefs, resulting in a consensus, not on ends and values but on procedures, on the rules of the game. In keeping with the assumptions of democratic relativism, it was described as a "scientific," "experimental," "skeptical," "pragmatic" culture, characterized by voting, bargaining, compromise, accommodation, and coexistence. Perhaps the most important implication of this view was that it turned the one thing prewar secular social scientists had seen as religion's saving grace—its ability to formulate unifying ethical ideals—from a positive into a negative.

As with so many postwar theoretical frameworks, pluralist theory was understood to be an Enlightenment revival—in this case, a revival of Madison's theory of factionalism. But it was Madison's theory recast in relativist, neutralist terms. Madison supported the multiplication of factions on the ground that they would check one another, allowing virtuous statesmen to rise above them and pursue the public good. Now political theorists dismissed the notion of the public good and argued that the pushing and pulling of interest groups was itself the means to determine policy. By pluralist lights, a properly democratic state has no values of its own to pursue—that would be authoritarian, even totalitarian. Whatever values find their way into legislation or executive action should be the values of "society." The state itself should be neutral, providing a neutral framework for the social bargaining of others, and merely placing its imprimatur on the upshot of the interest group struggle.

Secularization Theory

At the same time the relativist theory of democracy was being worked up into pluralist theory, it was providing a docking station for the secularization narratives of European social theory. Late nineteenth-century American intellectuals largely had fought off Comte's positivism, and with it, his vision of a coming secular, "positive" age. But his legatees, Durkheim and Weber, now found a ready American audience for their own theories of secularization, which emphasized the secularizing acids of "social differentiation" and "rationalization." However, these secularization narratives were not received cleanly. In entering via pluralist theory, they were inflected with the scripts of coming American godlessness noted earlier in this book.

One vehicle for this intellectual transfer was the cohort of Jewish émigré intellectuals who fled Germany and Austria in the 1930s. But an even more important vehicle, and a more revealing one, was Talcott Parsons, the son of a Methodist minister.[35] Before the war, Parsons was an obscure young commentator on European social theorists no American read. After the war, thanks to new assumptions about how the United States worked, he was catapulted to the status of the country's leading social theorist. His structural-functionalist account of society as a self-regulating system of social roles provided an exciting new conceptual tool kit for the postwar social scientists who were dedicated to the study of procedure and agnostic on substantive ends. The broader theoretical frameworks of Durkheim and Weber that Parsons propagated fit with this agnosticism as well, at least as he presented them.[36]

Forging Modernization Theory

Modernization theory, in the form in which it came to dominate American sociology and political science at midcentury, was a hybrid of pluralist democratic theory and secularization theory.[37] Secularization theory brought with it the assumption of a universal movement from the sacred to the civil and secular, from *Gemeinshaft* to *Gesellshaft*, from traditional to modern. Pluralist theory fleshed this out by providing an image of what "the modern" was supposed to look like. It was supposed to look like American pluralist capitalist secular democracy.

Edward Shils, University of Chicago sociologist and polymath, was a seminal figure in forging this synthesis.[38] But the synthesis can be seen most clearly in the work of Gabriel Almond, Shils's old University of Chicago office-mate, who became the postwar era's foremost theorist of political development. His theory was in fact a sophisticated projection of the relativist, pluralist image of American democracy onto the world historical stage, which he accomplished by lodging it within the Parsonian secularization-modernization framework.

To begin with, Almond accepted the democracy/totalitarianism dichotomy as the organizing principle for comparative work. Democracy and totalitarianism formed the poles of a spectrum of "political systems," including as principal types "the Anglo-American [i.e., the democratic]...the Continental European...the pre-industrial, or partly industrial...and the totalitarian political systems."[39] Second, Almond adopted the pluralists' account of the democratic, Anglo-American political system, which he used not only to distinguish democracy from totalitarianism but also to distinguish a "modern" from a "traditional" political system. In other words, Almond presented a supposedly objective description of the American political process as the ideal terminus of a process of political modernization taking place the world over. Furthermore, a crucial part of this modernizing process involved eliminating the "absolute-value" demands of ideology and religion from the political system. Postwar America—skeptical and secular—was the world's destiny.

The keystone of Almond's ambitious analytical framework was the pluralist ideal of a political system that is maximally open and responsive to the (nonideological) interests of the populace—a system that smoothly "converts" the multifarious narrow demands of citizen groups into uniform, moderate public policy. Whether speaking of the difference between "traditional" and "modern" political systems, or between totalitarian and democratic ones, the central contrast Almond draws is in the ease, even fluidity, of this conversion.

What is more, all the variables Almond identifies as conditioning this fluidity come straight out of pluralist theory—the theory of interest group politics—though now translated into the idiom of structural functionalism.[40] Most important for Almond is the "political culture" that pervades the political system, and nowhere is his participation in the relativist democratic persuasion clearer than here. "The Anglo-American political systems," he wrote, "are characterized by . . . a secular political culture . . . I mean a multi-valued political culture, a rational-calculating, bargaining, and experimental political culture." In describing the spirit such a culture imparts to politics, Almond invoked classic relativist and pragmatist metaphors of market and laboratory:

> The political system is saturated with the atmosphere of the market. Groups of electors come to the political market with votes to sell in exchange for policies. Holders of offices in the formal-legal role structure tend to be viewed as agents and instrumentalities, or as brokers occupying points in the bargaining process. The secularized political process has some of the characteristics of a laboratory; that is, policies offered by candidates are viewed as hypotheses, and the consequences of legislation are rapidly communicated within the system and constitute a crude from of testing hypotheses.[41]

Totalitarian political systems, in contrast, exemplify just the kind of logical simplism the Anglo-American system avoids. They are characterized by a "synthetically homogeneous" political culture—a monovalent political culture imposed upon the main body of a people by a charismatic dictator and his following, by means of the monopolization of the technology of communication, and violence.

Noteworthy is the fact that the contrast between democracy and totalitarianism that organizes Almond's discussion of political culture is couched in the exact terms of the 1930s debate between "scientific naturalists" and "ethical absolutists." Were ethical relativists the midwives of totalitarianism and ethical absolutists the guardians of democracy, or the other way around? By now, among social scientists the latter view was the consensus.

Almond's theory of political development was frankly more typological than developmental. This was the case despite Almond's intent that, as declared in the minutes of the SSRC's Committee on Comparative Politics, "the main concern of the Committee [is] to move toward a theory of political development."[42] The absence of a clear developmental story was an artifact of the theory's origins in a static polemical dichotomy contrasting totalitarianism and democracy. Since this dichotomy was built on a putative contrast between value-absolutist polities and value-skeptical ones, modernization theorists, in their subsequent effort to give this dichotomy a developmental underpinning— to explain how polities move from absolute-valued to scientific and skeptical, from traditional to modern—naturally looked to European secularization theory for help. The relativist, pluralist interpretation of America provided the image of what was modern, while European social theorists such as Durkheim and Weber—rather than the actual history of the United States—were looked to for the mechanisms by which one arrived there. This is just the move we see prefigured in Almond's 1961 memorandum, quoted at the outset of this chapter: "Modernizing change . . . refers either to structural differentiation or cultural secularization, or both." The result, from the 1960s and beyond, was a vast literature on modernization and secularization, replete with Enlightenment overtones, as discussed in the next chapter. Typical is the claim by Daniel Pipes, writing on the Middle East, that "Islam does not offer an alternative way to modernize. . . . Secularism cannot be avoided. Modern science and technology require an absorption of the thought processes which accompany them; so too with political institutions."[43]

But is it so? Understandably, Western intellectuals have long seen a contradiction between the scientific postulate of a world that operates according to uniform, constant laws and the religious postulate of a world guided by a divine will. In the eighteenth century, an uncertain peace was made through the mediation of "natural religion," with its image of God as a clock-maker. In the late nineteenth century, an even less stable peace was made through liberal-modernist theology, with its image of God unfolding in history. The inconvenient fact that confronts Pipes and other advocates of the modernization-secularization thesis is that today's global revival of religion, including the revival of Islam, is at its very strongest among the technically educated youth— "the students in technical institutes, engineering faculties, and scientific departments" who are in closest contact with the scientific ethos that is supposed to be the antithesis of supernatural religion.[44] Their religion is, and aims to be, unflinchingly supernatural. Yet they seem to find in this no contradiction at all.

In its heyday, the modernization-secularization thesis was not obviously wrong. Secularization was certainly the trend in the postwar decades among postcolonial elites—the kind of natives American social scientists were most likely to encounter and to assume were trendsetters for their societies. Even today, one might reasonably argue that the global revival of religion is a temporary phenomenon; after all, the revival's greatest strength is among the recently urbanized, and thus it could be interpreted as a stopgap search for identity and belonging in the face of social dislocation.[45] Yet the polemical nature of the debate over totalitarianism that gave rise to the modernization-secularization thesis raises doubts about the theoretical soundness of the thesis itself. In retrospect, one wonders how much of postcolonial secularization reflected "natural" developments accompanying modernization, and how much of it reflected the influence of the Western and communist *recipes* for modernization on a developing world anxious to catch up to the leading nations. When accompanied by evidence on the global revival of religion, with the sharpest revival among the scientifically minded, these considerations strongly suggest the need for an overhaul of our assumptions about secularization, and of the social scientific framework that generated them, in favor of a more discriminating account of the vicissitudes of religiosity and its place in the polity.

Conclusion

In many respects, the encounter with totalitarianism can be seen as sparking a second American enlightenment. Social scientists strongly concurred with the Enlightenment's critique of moral tutelage. They even shared its special animus against Catholic tutelage, which they viewed as the archetype of totalitarian indoctrination. But they went further, rejecting both Catholic and Enlightenment notions of higher law, on the ground that belief in such "moral absolutes" is precisely what licenses totalitarian control. These social scientists saw moral certitude, whether stemming from godly religion or from atheistic philosophy, as the attitude of totalitarians and moral "openness" and skepticism, in contrast, as the attitudes of democrats. Accordingly, while postwar social scientists often identified with the Enlightenment against Nazi irrationalism and communist suppression of human rights, theirs was an Enlightenment recast in relativist terms.

The modernization-secularization thesis was one of the signal products of this "Enlightenment" revival. American social scientists embraced an exaggerated view of the atrophy and privatization of religion in the United States; then they projected this image of a secularized America into the world's future. Nonetheless, notwithstanding the momentum previous generations' prophesies provided, the modernization theorists' confident prediction of religious privatization and public godlessness was clearly flawed, as was the social scientific framework that generated it. Not only has the global revival of religion given it the lie but also, since the 1960s, it has become clear that the pluralist image of America as skeptical and secular was itself a distortion. In what midcentury social scientists took to be the world's most modern country, religion continued, and continues, to hold sway over large swaths of the politically engaged public. Theory propelled them, as it had Jefferson more than a century earlier, to make claims beyond what the evidence allowed. As the following chapters will show, those who came after the modernization theorists were forced to grapple with their legacy of confident, overreaching predictions.

NOTES

1. Almond memo, November 22, 1961, 1, accession 2, ser. 1, box 739, folder 8937, Committee on Comparative Politics, SSRC Archive, Rockefeller Archive Center, Sleepy Hollow, New York. By "cultural secularization," it should be noted, Almond and the modernization theorists meant the privatization of religion, not its disappearance. Not private godlessness but public godlessness was their prophecy and prescription.

2. This is true notwithstanding the admiration of some for the writings of Reinhold Niebuhr.

3. For excellent discussion of the interpretive ambiguity yet historiographical indispensability, of "the Enlightenment," see David Hollinger, "Enlightenment and the Genealogy of Cultural Conflict in the United States," in Keith Baker and Peter Reill, eds., *What's Left of Enlightenment?* (Stanford: Stanford University Press, 2001).

4. Eldon Eisenach, *Lost Promise of Progressivism* (Lawrence: University Press of Kansas, 1994), 46.

5. Charles Henderson, *Social Elements* (1898), quoted in Christian Smith, ed., *The Secular Revolution: Power, Interests, and Conflict in the Secularization of American Public Life* (Berkeley: University of California Press, 2003), 133.

6. Dealey, *Sociology* (1909), quoted in ibid., 149.

7. For examples, see Arthur M. Schlesinger Jr., *The Crisis of the Old Order: 1919–1933* (Boston: Houghton Mifflin, 1957), 268, 461, and *The Coming of the New Deal* (Boston: Houghton Mifflin, 1959), 3, 19; William E. Leuchtenburg, *Franklin D. Roosevelt and the New Deal, 1932–1940* (New York: Harper and Row, 1963), 30; Ronald Steel, *Walter Lippmann and the American Century* (Boston: Little Brown, 1980), 299–300.

8. Quoted in E. Digby Baltzell, *The Protestant Establishment: Aristocracy and Caste in America* (New York: Random House, 1964), 233.

9. "Social Science and the Political Trend" (1934), reprinted in Frank H. Knight, *Freedom and Reform: Essays in Economics and Social Philosophy* (Indianapolis: Harper, 1982), 27–28.

10. For documentation of these shifts, see David Ciepley, *Liberalism in the Shadow of Totalitarianism* (Cambridge, Mass.: Harvard University Press, 2006).

11. For examples of each use of naturalism, see, respectively, *Thurman W. Arnold, The Symbols of Government* (New Haven: Yale University Press, 1948), and George E. G. Catlin, *A Preface to Action* (London: Allen and Unwin, 1934).

12. See, for example, the complaints of Sidney Hook, "Democracy and Education," in Jerome Nathanson, ed., *The Authoritarian Attempt to Capture Education* (New York: King's Crown Press, 1945), 12.

13. For what is probably the first sustained accusation of this sort, see William Y. Elliott, *The Pragmatic Revolt in Politics: Syndicalism, Fascism, and the Constitutional State* (New York: Allen and Unwin, 1928). Elliott associates Deweyan pragmatism with scientific objectivism, scientific objectivism with the denial of a public good, and this denial with the rise of Mussolini's fascism.

14. Quoted in Edward A. Purcell Jr., *The Crisis of Democratic Theory: Scientific Naturalism and the Problem of Value* (Lexington: University Press of Kentucky, 1973), 168 (see chap. 9 for further examples).

15. See John T. McGreevy, *Catholicism and American Freedom* (New York: Norton, 2003), 192–93.

16. John Dewey, *Reconstruction in Philosophy* (Boston: Beacon, 1957) (orig. pub. 1920), and *The Public and Its Problems* (Chicago: Swallow Press, 1954) (orig. pub. 1927).

17. John Dewey, *Freedom and Culture* (New York: Putnam, 1939). Dewey was more the popularizer than the progenitor of this view. Similar claims can be found in the writings of the early sociologists and in William James.

18. Charles Morris, "The Teaching of Dogmatic Religion in a Democratic Society," in Jerome Nathanson, ed., *The Authoritarian Attempt to Capture Education: Papers from the Second Conference on the Scientific Spirit and Democratic Faith* (New York: King's Crown Press, 1944), 141.

19. Carl J. Friedrich, "Democracy and Dissent," *Political Quarterly* (October–December 1939): 571–73, quoted in Purcell, *Crisis of Democratic Theory*, 213–14.

20. From T. V. Smith, *Discipline for Democracy* (Chapel Hill: University of North Carolina Press, 1942), 124, quoted in ibid., 209.

21. Quoted in McGreevy, *Catholicism and American Freedom*, 179.

22. Quoted in James Davison *Hunter, Culture Wars: The Struggle to Define America* (New York: Basic Books, 1991), 113.

23. Quoted in Samuel Huntington, *The Clash of Civilizations and the Remaking of World Order* (New York: Simon and Schuster, 1996), 95.

24. McGreevy, *Catholicism and American Freedom*, 148–53.

25. Ibid.

26. Horace Kallen, "Freedom and Authoritarianism in Religion," in Eduard C. Lindeman, ed., *The Scientific Spirit and Democratic Faith* (New York: King's Crown Press, 1944), 10–11.

27. Ibid., 11, 6.

28. See McGreevy, *Catholicism and American Freedom*.

29. Max C. Otto, "Authoritarianism and Supernaturalism," in Lindeman, *Scientific Spirit and Democratic Faith*, 19; see also Horace L. Friess, "The Teaching of Dogmatic Religion in a Democratic Society," in Nathanson, *Authoritarian Attempt*, 135.

30. See, for example, Sidney Hook, "Integral Humanism," in *Reason, Social Myths, and Democracy* (New York: John Day, 1940), 76.

31. McGreevy, *Catholicism and American Freedom*, 182–88.

32. Ciepley, *Liberalism in the Shadow of Totalitarianism*, chaps. 12, 16.

33. For more extensive documentation, see ibid., chap. 10; Purcell, *Crisis of Democratic Theory*, chap. 13.

34. See, for example, David B. Truman, *The Governmental Process: Political Interests and Public Opinion*, 2nd ed. (New York: Knopf, 1971), xix.

35. Charles D. Cashdollar, *The Transformation of Theology, 1830–1890: Positivism and Protestant Thought in Britain and America* (Princeton: Princeton University Press, 1989). See also chapter 5 here.

36. On early Parsons, see Charles Camic, ed., *Talcott Parsons: The Early Essays* (Chicago: University of Chicago Press, 1991). On the appeal of Parsons's structural functionalism to devotees of the relativist theory of democracy and on the use of Parsons in the development of modernization theory, see David Ciepley, "Why the State Was Dropped in the First Place: A Prequel to Skocpol's 'Bringing the State Back In,'" *Critical Review* 14 (2000): 193–95. See also Nils Gilman, *Mandarins of the Future: Modernization Theory in Cold War America* (Baltimore: Johns Hopkins University Press, 2003). On Parsons's distortion of Durkheim and Weber, see Donald N. Levine, *Visions of the Sociological Tradition* (Chicago: University of Chicago Press, 1995).

37. Contrast Gilman, *Mandarins of the Future*, who finds the origins of modernization theory in an effort to overcome the failures of development economics. I believe this is true only of the economic modernizers, not the political modernizers.

38. Ibid., 1–3, 86–87, 139–41.

39. Gabriel A. Almond, "Comparative Political Systems," *Journal of Politics* 18 (1956): 392–93, 408.

40. See especially Gabriel Almond and James S. Coleman, eds., *The Politics of Developing Areas* (Princeton: Princeton University Press, 1960). For more extensive documentation of this connection, see Ciepley, "Why the State Was Dropped in the First Place."

41. Ibid., 398.

42. From 1957 minutes of *Committee on Comparative Politics* meeting, cited in Gilman, *Mandarins of the Future*, 137.

43. Cited in Huntington, *Clash of Civilizations*, 73.

44. Ibid., 112; see also 113.

45. This is Huntington's explanation of "la revanche de Dieu," although he makes no suggestion that it might be temporary. See ibid., chap. 4.

9

The Sixties: Secularization and the Prophesies of Freedom

Slavica Jakelić

As previous chapters have shown, the idea that the importance of religion decreases as societies become more modern was neither uniquely American nor an idea that emerged only in the twentieth century. But earlier American thinkers did develop a distinctive vision of the process of religious "decline" that was premised on a belief that the "deinstitutionalization" of religion, which had been traditionally understood as an indicator of religious decline, is, in fact, good for religion. This process, many thinkers believed, would lead not toward the disappearance of religion but toward *true* religion. Jefferson, for one, wrote that the removal of the exclusive position of one religious institution—expressed in the wall of separation between church and state—was not just a precondition of religious tolerance. It was also a key to progress in which the freedom of reason and free enquiry would purify Christianity and return it to its origins. Religion that is not shaped by religious institutions and protected by the state, Jefferson insisted, will lead to true religion. Like Jefferson, Emerson concluded that God would not disappear when the churches and religions (as systems) were gone but that God would build on their ruin "his temple in the heart." Many American prophets of godlessness understood themselves, that is, to be prophesying god*li*ness.

The 1960s brought to the surface this same idea about the deinstitutionalization of religion, but as a particular interpretation of (what became known as) the "secularization thesis." Moreover, the

1960s brought about what Jefferson, Emerson, and others hoped for—an affinity between the idea that deinstitutionalized religion is something good and the intellectual and social sensibilities of the period.

Two views on secularization and deinstitutionalization of religion, those of Christian theologian Harvey Cox and sociologist Peter L. Berger, crystallized the intellectual and social climate of the time and were broadly discussed and debated. Some academic critics indicted Cox's *The Secular City* (1965) as a young book that lacked intellectual nuance—a sin Cox himself confessed two decades later.[1] But *Secular City* did stir everybody's minds: academics responded to it with *The Secular City Debate* in 1968, and broader audiences liked the book so much that it sold almost a million copies in different languages.[2] Peter Berger's colleagues, on the other hand, agreed that Berger's ideas on religions in modern societies demonstrated his remarkable breadth of knowledge and original synthesis of a large body of social thought.[3] And although his *The Sacred Canopy* (1967) did not sell millions, Berger, like Cox, was an academic celebrity in the 1960s, and his thoughts on secularization enjoyed significant popular attention and appeared in many leading American newspapers.

For all of these reasons, the ideas of Berger and Cox provide a useful framework for understanding both the 1960s' scripts about secularization and the structural and cultural conditions of their broad appeal. Berger and Cox were representative of the paradigms and the rhetoric of their disciplines on the topic of secularization, in that they endorsed the very 1960s idea that secularization was inseparable from modernization. Berger and Cox advocated the secularization thesis at a time when secularism as a worldview was progressively taking the central social stage and captivating the minds of intellectual and academic elites in particular. Our concern here is not with the political and power struggles of the 1960s or the ideological background of Berger and Cox but the differences and commonalities in Berger and Cox's secularization theses and the intellectual and social sensibilities they expressed. This essay asks two questions: *what* were Berger and Cox's secularization theses about, and *why* were their scripts of secularization so widely accepted in the 1960s?

"Everything Seemed Possible"

The 1960s in America, historian Howard Brick argues, were years not so much of revolution as of contradictions.[4] They were the years of the hippies but also of the conservative mood inherited from the 1950s; the age of the movements for racial and gender equality as well as the age when numerous public officials defended racial and gender inequality and separation. The 1960s gave us the miniskirt, the Rolling Stones, and the Pill but also defined the sexual counterrevolution and its images of the ideal American woman. The period saw escalation of a war in Vietnam and resulting conflict at home. It witnessed urban uprisings in many American cities, as well as the birth of a suburban ideal.

Contradictions characterized religion in 1960s America as well. Religion was an important topic, if not *the* topic, of the election in which John Kennedy was the second non-Protestant ever in American history to be nominated for the presidency. It was one of the central components of the civil rights movement, which adopted the principles and symbols of nonviolence that could be traced to Gandhi and Christianity. But religion as people had come to know and live it over the centuries—religion as an institutional phenomenon—*was* in decline. Participation and membership in churches was decreasing from a peak in the 1950s, and the authority of religious leaders, religious doctrines, and religious teachings was diminishing. Increasingly behaving as if they were on the market of beliefs, the churches in the 1960s were taking their believers as consumers with preferences, thus "secularizing themselves from within" in order to gain and maintain members.[5] The churches were less and less defined by individuals' loyalties to religious traditions. This process was shown in the ideas of such radical religious leaders as James A. Pike, the Episcopal bishop of California, who advocated "more belief, fewer beliefs" and affirmed "essential" Christianity by rejecting the importance of its doctrinal and institutional "packaging."[6] American Catholicism was also renegotiating its own traditions—defining its own social and political vocabulary in a dialogue with Protestantism but also reshaping its liturgical and doctrinal expressions in accordance with the *aggiornamento* of the Second Vatican Council.[7] And, while traditional, ritualized, and institutional religion was weakening—so much so that even theologians spoke of the godlessness of the age—New Age spirituality was being born. Religious life on American campuses is a case in point. College students in the 1960s practiced Asian philosophy, meditation, yoga, Zen, astrology, and witchcraft, to name only a few spiritual quests that captured the attention of the baby boomers.[8] The "new religions" might not have captivated a wide range of Americans, but they did reflect the general spirit of the cultural upheaval in the 1960s and, as sociologist of religion Robert Wuthnow writes, served "to redefine the outer limits of religious respectability."[9]

Behind the contradictions of religious life—behind the dying churches and "dead God" on the one hand and "the new pursuit of the sacred" on the other—was a common pattern. Both those leaving traditional churches and those practicing Zen—often the same persons—went against the religious traditions with their respective historically embedded heritages. They challenged the authority of religious leaders and doctrines with "words like 'honesty,' 'integrity,' 'fidelity,' 'love,' 'openness' and 'community.'" In 1969, Andrew Greeley quoted one of his students as saying: "Who in the world would expect to find anything sacred in the church?"[10]

The rhetoric of "the return to the sacred" in the religious realm closely resembled the rhetoric of the radical political movements. These challenged various social institutions' status quo in order to shake up the existing division of labor and clearly delineated social roles, which for many stood as the embodiment of gender, racial, or economic inequality. Saying "good-bye to all that,"[11] the social movements of the 1960s resulted in the decline of individuals' loyalties to group identities that had institutional frameworks, traditions, and histories.

Sociologists had long seen the deinstitutionalization of social life as one of the major characteristics of modernity. German social theorist Arnold Gehlen offered a particularly clear statement of this thesis when he described modernity as a deinstitutionalizing force that removes the taken-for-grantedness, or "background," of the individual's life and emphasizes its "foreground." In a process in which the authority of social institutions is decreasing and these institutions themselves are becoming negotiable, the relation of individuals to the world becomes more and more reflexive.[12]

But the 1960s offered more than just proof of the patterned social process of Western modernity that were leading toward the deinstitutionalization of social life. The 1960s also brought about the democratization of a very distinctive—and, perhaps, distinctly American—sensibility, according to which the deinstitutionalization of social life was something good. It is impossible to even begin to understand the arguments about the decline of religion and the claims about its deinstitutionalization in the 1960s outside this sensibility of the age.[13] It was the understanding of why the deinstitutionalization of social life *should* happen that was in the background of the ideas and actions of the reformers who advocated or fought for social changes in the 1960s. Both their ambitious goals and the way they pursued these goals reveal the views about the deinstitutionalization of life that were widespread at the time. The reformers wanted "to *redefine* and *enrich democracy*, *eliminate poverty*, enhance popular participation in government, *expand* opportunities for *self-fulfillment* . . . and make *flexibility and variation* keys to a new order of social roles."[14] Captivated by the hopefulness and confidence of the period, historian Howard Brick suggests, the reformers were mostly unable to identify the relationship between the political means they needed to transform the social order and the already existing power relations.

The optimism traceable in these plans and actions was not unfounded. The 1960s saw an increase in material prosperity; for the average American, life in the post–World War II era was only getting better. The total unemployment rate in 1966 was 3.8 percent.[15] And, while the younger generation of Americans was certainly the carrier of idealism, the optimism was actually much more widespread. Even the thinkers who challenged the notion of affluence had an optimistic outlook.[16] Robert Theobald thus predicted that the average working week by the end of the twentieth century would be fifteen hours. Together with David Riesman, Theobald suggested that society was showing less desire for additional goods.[17] Similarly, some American students professed a belief that the world and humanity were "on the verge of a great leap into a much better form of human life."[18]

Put simply, people believed that progress was guaranteed, and that this progress would be achieved through the deinstitutionalization and individualization of social roles and social life. The agents of reform and advocates of change in the 1960s both shaped and were shaped by this optimism; they identified institutional authority with oppression and saw the process of deinstitutionalization as a path to a better, more just society—in short, to freedom.

Without recognizing this conviction that progress was to be achieved through deinstitutionalization, one cannot grasp why thinkers in the 1960s— both the few who opposed and the majority who advocated the secularization thesis—understood their age as characterized by the rise of "religionless religion." To be sure, to different people, this freedom had different meanings. For secularists, for example, freedom from religion was freedom as such. But for some theologians, especially the sensationally dubbed "death-of-God theologians," freedom *from* religion often meant the freedom *for* religion and a chance to embrace the world as it was. "No one else," Robert S. Ellwood writes, "quite got the hopeful, secular-as-sacred spirit" of this stream of 1960s theology as Harvey Cox.[19] The diminishing of traditional religiosity, which for many in the Christian churches was a sign of godlessness, for Cox was a possibility for true religion. One can clearly hear an echo of Jefferson's and Emerson's ideas in Cox's prophesies.

Harvey Cox and "Religionless Religion"

Cox did not think of himself as one of the "death-of-God theologians."[20] But it is not surprising that he is always included in this group, together with Thomas J.

J. Altizer, Paul van Buren, William Hamilton, Ronald Gregor Smith, and Gabriel Vahanian. The Marxist influences that can be traced in the works of most of these thinkers also shaped Cox's concern for the problems of the world. A participant in the civil rights movement and a vocal opponent to the Vietnam War, Cox was troubled by the voicelessness and powerlessness of the oppressed, and the economic injustices, racial discrimination, and grave problems in urban communities. He was concerned about the church's inability to see those concerns as structural social problems.

Arguably, the clearest theological link between Cox and other death-of-God theologians is the influence of the Protestant German theologian Dietrich Bonhoeffer on their ideas. Several of Bonhoeffer's concepts—"man's coming of age," the church needing to accept the world as it is, the "nonreligious Christian language," and "religionless Christianity"—served as the departure point for the message the death-of-God theologians brought about the role of theology in the modern world. These ideas also served as a framework for Cox's questions and answers about secularization. He thought that the main problem for the church was not the times but its inability to engage with the times. According to him, two processes characterized the 1960s: "the rise of urban civilization and the collapse of traditional religion."[21] Instead of condemning these developments, Cox maintained, the church needed to face and understand they made up the reality of every day life. Even more important, Cox said these developments had profoundly religious roots and consequences.

In Cox's theological perspective, the historical and the providential were not separated. He recognized that urbanization transformed traditional human communities by establishing "an impersonality," "functional relationships," and "anonymity and mobility."[22] But these developments were ultimately *good*, Cox argued, because they were congruent with biblical faith. When the apartment dwellers refused to socialize within church groups or neighbor communities, they did not show a lack of religion but, rather, freedom to select and cultivate their own friendship networks. By becoming free *from* collective commitments, they used their freedom *of* choice to live in more diverse human communities. In consequence, the city actually transformed the strangers and outsiders into fellow citizens—into the Samaritans of their age. City life brought people closer to the early church, Cox asserted, the church that was detribalizing from its beginnings and moving toward the world in which there was no longer Jew or Greek. This was for Cox precisely what the New Testament was about—the possibility of universal citizenship.

The city was the necessary structural precondition for the historical unwrapping of secularization. While urbanization changed ways of life—it caused the deterioration of close-knit communities, introduced heterogeneous societies, and compartmentalized all spheres of life—secularization changed the way people understood their life together; it dissociated human soul and resulted in the disenchantment of the world.

Once we moderns entered this rationalized and disenchanted world, Cox argued, we could not go back. Secularization, like urbanization, rolled on, and as the latest phase in the course of human progress, it could not be reversed. Moreover, Cox saw this modern development as the fruition of the kernel of secularization already planted in the biblical tradition. Cox wrote that the three aspects of secularization—the *disenchantment of nature*, the *desacralization of politics*, and the *deconsecration of values*—were pivotal aspects of biblical faith. The disenchantment of nature began with the Creation, the desacralization of politics with the Exodus, and the deconsecration of values with the Sinai Covenant.

Cox's argument that secularization was built into the biblical traditions was central to his understanding of the "secular city." When approached as part of the biblical tradition, modern secularization, in Cox's mind, ceased to be the demise of religion and became the latest stage in the "defatalization of history," the latest phase in the transformation of human beings from dependent creatures into agents. From the Creation account to the modern secular city, Cox traced the same process—the gradual realization that the world has been left to human beings and they are responsible for it.

For Cox, secularization implied progress par excellence—the betterment of human beings and the creation of a more just society. Secularization was not antireligious but offered the possibility of religious emancipation, because it delivered the world "from religious and quasi-religious understandings of itself," disposed of "all closed world views," shattered "all supernatural myths and sacred symbols," and liberated "man from religious and metaphysical tutelage" by turning "his attention away from other worlds and toward this one."[23] The removal of traditional gods from the central stage of secular cities was good, Cox concluded, because it brought about "man's coming of age" (Bonhoeffer's term).

Cox recognized that the secular man who lived in a world in which there are no sacred values—Paul Tillich's "land of broken symbols"—encountered the problems of relativism of values and of nihilism. Cox also understood that the decline of institutionalized values and sacredness could undermine the maintenance of social order, because it brings about the relativization of values and creates the need for a different kind of social integration. Nonetheless, Cox remained optimistic, suggesting that

despite claims to the contrary, the relativization of values does not make impossible human society with its prerequisite of some degree of social consensus. . . . First of all it requires real maturity. It demands that all men be drawn into the secularization process so that no one clings to the dangerous precritical illusion that his values are ultimate.[24]

Cox's optimism about the potential of human beings to use their freedom from authority and institutions responsibly reflected the sensibility that was behind the social movements of the 1960s.[25] Just like the other reformers in this period—in fact, *as* one of them—Cox believed that the changing of social conditions opened the way to a better society. While recognizing that relativism of values could be a problem, he also emphasized that relativism could provide "the philosophical basis for a pluralist society" in which "no one has the right to inflict his values on anyone else."[26]

Unlike many 1960s reformers, however, Cox located the origins of the relativism of values in biblical tradition. The relativization of all human values, he argued, comes together with secularization and has some of its origins in the biblical rejection of idolatry. This is an important point, as it highlights the theology behind Cox's secularization thesis, wherein secularization as a history of progress and rise of human agency cannot be separated from its providential origins. The call for the church to "support and nourish" secularization rather than oppose it was in Cox's case more than just a liberal theologian's attempt to affirm the ways of the world instead of rejecting them. Echoing Bonhoeffer, Cox believed that the church needed to learn "to speak of God in a secular fashion" and find "a nonreligious interpretation of biblical concepts"[27] because that would imply trusting people's ability to fashion better lives, better societies, and better selves, precisely *by* fulfilling the gospel. In other words, by bringing about freedom from primordial communities and institutional organization, secularization established the freedom of responsible choice in order to reach true religion. As Cox put it,

> secularization is not without danger. It is not the Messiah. But neither is the anti-Christ. It is rather a dangerous liberation; it raises the stakes, making it possible for man to increase the range of his freedom and responsibility and thus to deepen his maturation. At the same time it poses risks of a larger order than those it displaces. But the promise exceeds the peril, or at least makes it worth taking the risk.[28]

Peter Berger's theory of secularization in the 1960s built on these ideas and shared a number of elements with Cox's thesis. Berger thought that religious ideas of the Hebrew Bible and the New Testament prepared for secu-

larization; he understood it as a part of modernization, as shaped by pluralization of worldview and sources of legitimation, and as manifested, among
others, in the deinstitutionalization of religion. Berger anticipated that this
deinstitutionalization would cause problems for modern societies and was less
optimistic about human beings' ability to maintain their social life while undermining its symbolic and institutional certainty. But during the 1960s,
Berger remained confident about the progressive and joint march of modernization and secularization.

Peter Berger: Pluralism as Freedom, Freedom as Choice

Berger's ideas on secularization in the 1960s stem from Max Weber's sociological tradition, according to which the rationalization of modern societies
leads to the disenchantment of the world. For Berger, the decline of religion
was but an expression of this disenchantment and, moreover, was irreversible.
Writing for an academic audience, Berger explained that modernity with its
secular centers of social life could not be overturned. In the modern industrial
society, he wrote in *Sacred Canopy*, the

> "liberated territory" of secularized society is so centrally "located,"
> in and around the capitalistic-industrial economy, that any attempt to
> "reconquer" it in the name of religio-political traditionalism endan-
> gers the continued functioning of this economy.... Any attempts
> at traditionalistic reconquista thus threaten to dismantle the ra-
> tional foundations of modern society.... The decisive variable for
> secularization does not seem to be the institutionalization of par-
> ticular property relations ... but rather the process of rationa-
> lization that is a prerequisite for any industrial society of the modern
> type.[29]

Speaking to the *New York Times* in early 1968, Berger said that "in a
surprise-free world" he saw "no reversal of the process of secularization....
The impact is the same everywhere, regardless of culture and local religion."[30]

Berger and Cox thus shared the dominant view that modernization and
secularization necessarily went hand in hand and were universal in their
manifestations, regardless of the cultural uniqueness of the place in question.
Berger also agreed with Cox about the notion of the self-secularizing elements
of the Judeo-Christian tradition. But for Berger, this inherent secularization
did not indicate a moral progress, in which human beings move from idolatry
to true religion. The self-secularizing elements of Judeo-Christian traditions

were for Berger embodied in the radical transformation of the relationship between the *nomos* (social order) and the cosmos. The Hebrews, Berger argued, brought about the separation between these two realms when their God became a transcendent one. Always outside both nomos and cosmos, yet directing both "worlds," Yahweh was linked with Israel only "artificially," through the Covenant. Christianity only completed this process: despite the doctrine of God incarnated in Jesus Christ and thus fully present in the world, Christianity kept the Hebrew Bible and with it the idea of a transcendent God. To be sure, Catholicism reestablished cosmic order by connecting the biblical religions with extrabiblical theological views. But with the Protestant Reformation, this was lost again. A case in point was the Lutheran doctrine of the two kingdoms, which provided the theological justification for the autonomous secular realm. In short, unlike Cox's, Berger's take on the self-secularizing aspects of the Judeo-Christian tradition was fundamentally sociological in character: it was focused on the changing relationship between the social order and the sacred order.

The secularization processes Berger historically traced in the Judeo-Christian traditions reached their peak with modernity, with the further fragmentation of the social world into separate realms. During this process, "the sectors of society and culture are removed from the domination of religious institutions and symbols." And although "the relationship between socio-economic modernization and political secularization . . . is not a simple one," there is a tendency, Berger wrote, "toward the secularization of the political order that goes naturally with the development of modern industrialism."[31]

In the end, secularization pervaded all levels of life in modern industrial societies in an unstoppable fashion. In the political sphere, it was most clearly expressed in the separation of church and state. In the sphere of culture, secularization was manifested in the separation of education from the jurisdiction of ecclesiastical authority, the decline of religious contents in the arts, in philosophy, and literature, and the rise of science as an autonomous form of inquiry. The outcome of this process (which contemporary sociologists of religion designate as a process of differentiation) was an individual who looked on the world without religious interpretations or outside the religious frameworks. Government was no longer explained in terms of the divine right of kings but the will of the people, and the economic realm was not governed by religious norms but by market principle. In modern societies, in Berger's terms, religion had ceased to be the guiding norm of the nomos. Its decline occurred on the individual and collective level of life. In the subjective side of this process, Berger saw the individualization of religion. In its collective aspect, Berger wrote, secularization brought the demonopolization of religious traditions as the exclusive authority of social life. Religious traditions lost their "common, binding quality" and became "a matter of the 'choice' or 'preference' of the individual or the nuclear family."[32]

In Berger's secularization thesis, the decline of religion in modern societies was therefore characterized by an omnipresent deinstitutionalization or "demonopolization" of religion. These processes had an effect on both the individual's understanding of world and her living in it with other people. By losing its authority, the religious tradition was in the position of having to market itself. The result was pluralism, with privatized religion and the freedom to choose one's own religious tradition.

Berger differed from Cox regarding the meaning of this freedom. Cox thought it brought people one step closer to the early church and universal community. For Cox, freedom was a moral condition and moral possibility. For Berger, freedom was first and foremost the liberty to follow one's own inclination in the increasingly competitive religious realm—the possibility to have and to demonstrate one's religious preference. Already in the 1960s, Berger talked about religion in economic terms. In addition, Berger saw the privatized religion that is a matter of choice as something "quite 'functional' for the maintenance of the highly rationalized order of modern economic and political institutions."[33] Nevertheless, and very much unlike Cox, Berger was quite concerned that pluralism and its resulting freedom posed a serious problem for modern individuals. He thought that

> the pluralistic situation, in demonopolizing religion, makes it ever more difficult to maintain or to construct anew viable plausibility structures for religion . . . it becomes increasingly difficult for the "inhabitants" of any particular religious world to remain *entre nous* in contemporary society. . . . As religious contents become susceptible to "fashion," it becomes increasingly difficult to maintain them as unchangeable verities.[34]

Once religion loses its legitimating power, any "particular choice," including the one of religion, "is relativized and less than certain."[35] Or, as Berger clarified later in his work, pluralism not only permitted choice but forced one to choose. And when the individual approached everything with the questions of "what to choose" and "how to choose," convictions became a matter of taste, and commandments became suggestions. With all these choices, nothing can be taken for granted.[36] No ultimate meaning can guide individuals in their actions; people no longer share the same source of values and norms.

What Berger sensed was that pluralism could cause a crisis in having and upholding shared principles and institutions in social life. This was a rephrasing of an old sociological question—how do we organize society with individuals who share almost nothing? In addressing the question about the outcomes of freedom for social life, Berger did not display optimism and the hopefulness present in the social movements of the 1960s or Cox's theological understanding of secular-as-sacred. Further, Berger arguably did not share their philosophical anthropology, if for no other reason than because he is a Weberian. However, Berger was just as confident as Cox and others that the pluralization of the world represented progress toward the freedom of choice. Like others, Berger also did not doubt the reversibility of secularization. Predicting for the American newspaper that, by the year 2000, traditional, institutionalized religions will be only a relic from the past, Berger also envisioned these religions as future sects, which would exist isolated from, in opposition to, the secular world.

It took Berger only two years, 1967–69—between the publications of his *Sacred Canopy* and his *Rumor of Angels*—to move from seeing the sky emptied of angels to hearing their silence.[37] And while he later gave up his claims about the irreversibility of secularization and its inseparable link to modernity,[38] Berger's understanding of the deinstitutionalization of religion—his association between the dethroning of religious institutions and authorities and the individualization of religious identities so that one has a freedom to choose one's own religion—has remained central to his thought until today.

Conclusion

Berger and Cox wrote about secularization in the 1960s with different ultimate questions in mind. After all, one was a sociologist and one a theologian. At that time, however, they did share two major arguments—about the deinstitutionalization of religion and its irreversibility. In this they represented broader movements of learned opinion, and were very persuasive to their respective audiences. In the context of 1960s, in which a number of revolutionary movements disputed the authority of social institutions, religious life was yet another realm wherein institutions were challenged.

In Berger's writings, the notion of deinstitutionalization was explicit; in Cox's and in the works of a number of other theologians, this notion was implicit and inherent to their views of the content of traditional religiosity. But—what is most important for this essay—Berger's and Cox's secularization theses were persuasive not because of some, to use Berger's words, broad allegiance to a scientific progressivism, or because everyone indeed saw traditional religion as declining. They were persuasive because they happened in a context in which deinstitutionalized religion—"religionless religions"—was increasingly becoming the *ideal* of religious life. It was shaping not just practical religious expressions in the 1960s but scholarly views of the decline of religion as well. Berger and Cox, in other words, did not simply describe what they saw but also what they assumed. Their views carried an inherent understanding of the deinstitutionalization of religion as *progress*, which brought about freedom for individuals to choose. Their prophesies of godlessness were—while with different contents—prophesies of freedom.

Berger's and Cox's views of the potential consequences of the processes of the deinstitutionalization were different. Berger's sociological perspective compelled him to contend that the freedom pluralization brought was a burden for human beings as creatures of meaning and for societies as places in which meaning had to be institutionalized. Cox's optimistic theological lenses allowed him to conclude that such difficulties were secondary to the possibility of human beings achieving freedom and (religious) maturity. The "secular city" was, for him, a place where the bondage of religious institutions and traditions was abolished in order that true tolerance could be experienced. Berger saw pluralism as the freedom of religious choice; Cox saw this as a dangerous liberation, but a liberation nonetheless, for the real engagement with God.

Recent debates about the secularization theory—which was The Theory of the 1960s[39]—have neglected its link with the period's focus on the deinstitutionalization of religion, and the period's optimism and hopes for freer individuals and freer societies. Yet Berger and Cox implicitly or explicitly talked about these questions, and these questions constituted a broader intellectual climate that shaped the social movements of the 1960s. The understanding that freedom (of religion) and the deinstitutionalization of religion are mutually related originated at least partly in the Protestant Reformation and was very present in the American prophesies of godlessness. But the embodiment of religionless religion reached its peak precisely in the 1960s, and as an idea *and* an ideal of religious life, constituted the secularization thesis, whenever this thesis referred to the questions and the prophesies of freedom.

NOTES

I am grateful to Christy Hall for her generous and thorough editing of this essay and to James D. Hunter for his questions and comments.

1. See appraisals of *The Secular City*, by Harvey Cox, *Sociological Analysis* 27, 1 (spring 1966). See Harvey Cox, "Response to Commentators," *Sociological Analysis* 45, 2 (summer 1984): 107–13; 109.

2. See Robert S. Ellwood, *The Sixties: Spiritual Awakening; American Religion Moving from Modern to Postmodern* (New Brunswick, N.J.: Rutgers University Press, 1994), 131.

3. See Bryan R. Wilson, review of *The Sacred Canopy: Elements of a Theological Theory of Religion*, by Peter Berger, *American Sociological Review* 33, 5 (October 1968): 844; Erich Goode, review of Berger, *Sacred Canopy*, *Journal of Health and Social Behavior* 9, 4 (December 1968): 352; and Gillian Lindt Gollin, review of *A Rumor of Angels*, by Peter Berger, *American Sociological Review* 35, 3 (June 1970): 554.

4. For the account of these contradictions as well for tracing the sensibility of the age as the sensibility of confidence, I am greatly indebted to Howard Brick's *The Age of Contradiction: American Thought and Culture in the 1960s* (New York: Twayne, 1998).

This section's title comes from a remark by a renowned sociologist, made about religion in relation to the processes in the Roman Catholic Church of the 1960s (from a private conversation with the author).

5. Robert Wuthnow, *The Restructuring of American Religion* (Princeton: Princeton University Press, 1989), 159.

6. See Ellwood, *Sixties*, 127.

7. On the 1960s commentary on the *aggiornamento* in the Roman Catholic Church, see Martin E. Marty, "God-Talk in the Sixties," *New York Times*, March 16, 1969.

8. See Andrew Greeley, "There's a New-Time Religion on Campus," *New York Times*, June 1, 1969. Even among the Christian denominations, the more successful ones were those that emphasized inner spiritual life than highly ritualized religious expression; see Beth Bailey, "Religion," in David Farber and Beth Bailey, eds., *The Columbia Guide to America in the 1960s* (New York: Columbia University Press, 2001), 301.

9. Wuthnow, *Restructuring* 152.

10. Quotations all from Greeley, "New-Time Religion on Campus."

11. The latter is the title of Robin Morgan's article published in the late 1960s, referring to a "condemnation of the male-led New Left and its sexist practices," in *Columbia Guide*, 229.

12. See Peter Berger, foreword to Arnold Gehlen, *Man in the Age of Technology* (New York: Columbia University Press, 1980).

13. In his appraisal of Cox's book, theologian Christopher F. Mooney recognized the affinity between Cox's optimistic celebration of the "dignity of human endeavor" and "one of the deepest spiritual needs of the modern Christian," adding that this affinity "is the true source of the extraordinary popularity of Harvey Cox's book"; see "A Theologian's Appraisal," *Sociological Analysis* 27, 1 (spring 1966): 43–45; 43.

14. Brick, *Age of Contradiction*, p. xii; italics are mine. See also James Patterson, *Grand Expectations: The United States, 1945–1974* (New York: Oxford University Press, 1996), and Todd Gitlin, *The Sixties: Years of Hope, Days of Rage* (New York: Bantam, 1987).

15. See Farber and Bailey, *Columbia Guide*, 359.

16. The 1960s gave rise to discussions of theories of abundance, starting with Kenneth Galbraith's *The Affluent Society* (Boston: Houghton Mifflin, 1958). See a discussion of Galbraith in Jeff Madrick, "A Mind of His Own," *New York Review of Books* 52, 9 (May 26, 2005). See also Loren Okroi, *Galbraith, Harrington, Heilbroner: Economics and Dissent in an Age of Optimism* (Princeton: Princeton University Press, 1988).

17. Theobald and Riesman in Brick, *Age of Contradictions*, 3; 5.

18. See Greeley, "New-Time Religion on Campus."

19. Ellwood, *Sixties*, 131.

20. See Harvey Cox's rebuttal of this label in Elizabeth Gehrman, "Symposium Re-enters 'Secular City,' " *Harvard Gazette Archives*, March 3, 2005.

21. See Harvey Cox, *The Secular City: Secularization and Urbanization in Theological Perspective* (New York: Macmillan, 1966).

22. Ibid., 4; 34.

23. Ibid., 1–2; 15.

24. Ibid., 30.

25. See Mooney's view of the reasons for the popularity of Cox's book, "Theologian's Appraisal," 43–45; 43.

26. Ibid., 27–28.

27. Cox, *Secular City*, 3.

28. Ibid., 145.

29. See Peter Berger, *The Sacred Canopy: Elements of a Theological Theory of Religion* (New York: Anchor Books, 1990), 132–33.

30. "A Bleak Outlook Is Seen for Religion," *New York Times*, February 25, 1968.

31. Berger, *Sacred Canopy*, 107, 130.

32. Ibid., 133.

33. Ibid., 134.

34. Ibid., 151.

35. Ibid., 152.

36. Ibid., 151.

37. See Marty, "God-Talk in the Sixties."

38. See Peter Berger, "Protestantism and the Quest for Certainty," religion-online.org, www.religion-online.org/showarticle.asp?title=239.

39. I thank Kevin Schultz for this remark.

10

The Seventies and Eighties:
A Reversal of Fortunes

Joseph E. Davis and David Franz

One bright afternoon in the spring of 1969, three coeds dressed in "shabby and tattered garments" entered the usually quiet Social Science Building at the University of Chicago and proceeded to the Department of Sociology. They had no conventional student matters on their minds. Their business was more radical, though not in the usual sixties sense. They did not come to occupy any office, make any demands for justice, or decry the war. They were neither Black Panthers nor members of the Weather Underground. Their group was the Women's International Terrorists Corps from Hell (WITCH). And their mission that fine day was to put a hex on the Sociology Department. Firmly planted outside the office door, they raised their voices and called down their curse.[1]

The hex had no discernible effect, but the WITCHes had made quite an impression. They were a spectacular manifestation of a rebirth of interest among young people not only in witchcraft, divination, and other occult practices but in religion and spirituality more generally. This resurgence began to gather momentum in the late 1960s, and its flowering would have a powerful influence on perceptions of godlessness in America over the next two decades. For conservative religious leaders, occult groups like WITCH, along with many other new religious movements and forms of spiritual experimentation, were one of the signs of crisis in the churches and in the spiritual life of the nation. These leaders responded by reviving a religious tradition of prophetic statement and public activism that had been largely dormant for half a century. For many scholars of religion, on the other hand, the sudden surge of religious energy challenged taken-for-granted predictions of religious decline and fed a growing skepticism about the triumph of scientific rationalism and the predictions of social science.

In the 1970s and 1980s, the crosscutting trajectories of these two traditions of thinking about godlessness in America went in directions wholly unforeseen. Evangelicals and Fundamentalists, cowed and withdrawn from public life, suddenly and forcefully returned from their self-imposed exile. They entered the 1990s with new confidence and renewed hope. Social scientists, by contrast, so long secure in their basic presuppositions about the direction of social change, suddenly lost confidence and began to bicker among themselves. By the 1990s, consensus on their "secularization thesis" had collapsed. Nobody had anticipated such a reversal of fortunes.

Swallowed Up by Godlessness?

The 1960s appeared to be a period of rapidly spreading secularization. Although religious leaders such as Martin Luther King Jr., the Berrigan brothers, and William Sloan Coffin played prominent roles in the civil rights and peace movements, the counterculture, for all its search for meaning, was markedly secular. "Establishment" religious institutions were among the explicit targets of youth disenchantment. Protestant theologians of many stripes grappled with the meaning of belief in a "world come of age" and, at the extreme edge of accommodation, proposed a form of Christian atheism under the rubric of the "death of God."[2] In the immediate aftermath of Vatican II, the Catholic Church in America appeared in crisis and poised for a dramatic decline. Looking toward the year 2000, prominent futurist Herman Kahn predicted a continuing trend toward a culture that is "increasingly sensate" and characterized by being "empirical, this-worldly, secular, humanistic, pragmatic, utilitarian, contractual, epicurean or hedonistic, and the like."[3] Sociologists saw no "reversal of the process of secularization" going forward and even suggested that by the twenty-first century, "the traditional religions are likely to survive [only] in small enclaves and pockets."[4]

Then the unexpected happened. Over a fairly short period of time, beginning in the late 1960s, a host of new religious groups, utopian communes, and personal growth movements appeared among middle-class youth at elite universities and beyond. These groups covered the spiritual waterfront. Some were inspired by Eastern philosophies, such as the Hare Krishna movement and the Divine Light Mission, and followed one or another swami or guru from Asia. Some emerged from the Christian tradition, including the Jesus People, the Catholic charismatic renewal movement, and Jews for Jesus. Still others were quasi-religious human potential groups, such as *est*, Scientology, and Silva Mind Control. The significance of these groups and movements, many of which proved to be short-lived, would be debated well into the 1980s, but the sheer scope of religious activity and expressions of "new religious consciousness" had a seismic effect on perceptions of secularization.[5]

At roughly the same time, yet another development began to challenge the reigning assumptions about religious decline. Sixties discussions of secularization in the United States tended to focus on the mainline or liberal Protestant churches. Few studied the conservative churches; most assumed that the same processes of decline were also at work eroding the numbers and influence of the evangelicals and Fundamentalists.[6] Events, however, soon made conservatives impossible to ignore. While evangelical institution building, publishing activities, and campus evangelicalism had been little noticed, evangelicals' broadcasting activities and apparent political influence were much in the news by the mid-1970s. Seemingly out of nowhere came the TV evangelists, hosting popular shows and building large, sophisticated communications networks. Equally surprising was the evangelical political mobilization, symbolized by Jimmy Carter's announcement of having been "born again," the resounding defeat of the Equal Rights Amendment, and the emerging militancy of groups like the Moral Majority. The raw numbers, too, supported the impression that people still took religious commitments very seriously. Dean Kelly's 1972 book *Why Conservative Churches Are Growing* showed that personally demanding evangelical and Fundamentalist churches had been growing at a sustained pace since the late 1950s.[7] To considerable media attention, the pollster George Gallup reported in 1976 that one-third of the American population identified themselves as "born-again" or "evangelical Christian." Ruminations about religious revitalization and even a "new spiritual awakening" replaced proclamations about the death of God and quieted talk of being "swallowed up by godlessness."[8]

The new outbursts of popular spirituality and new public presence of conservative Protestantism led many social scientists to call into question their longstanding assumptions about the direction of religious change. So, too, the changing state of the Cold War balance of power prompted new thinking about the future of faith at home and abroad. The dramatic public role of religion in international affairs in the 1980s, from the Islamic revolution in Iran to the emergence of Solidarity in Poland and the influence of liberation theology in the Sandinista revolution in Nicaragua, and elsewhere, had the same effect.[9] One strand of this scholarly reaction called for an end to the forecasts of secularization inherited from the nineteenth century. New data and new readings of older data proved that the taken-for-granted thesis about the progressive eclipse of religious institutions and erosion of personal belief was a "myth" and needed to be abandoned. Another strand retained the secularization thesis but with many important modifications. The intellectual climate that sustained the basic tenets of secularization theory had changed, and changed dramatically.

While scholars were growing increasingly skeptical of their prophesies of godlessness, conservative Christian leaders were reviving theirs. For these leaders, the 1960s showed that godlessness in the form of liberalism, secular humanism, and the occult was on the rise. Moral relativism, irrationality, and all manner of vacuous spiritualisms were capturing the hearts of young people. Moral decay, from legalized abortion to homosexuality and rampant divorce, was eating away at the very fabric of American society. The devil was having a field day, and while many believers were concerned, they were quiescent about the decline of religious-moral influence in national life or unprepared for the intellectual challenge of responding to it. With a sense of growing despair, Fundamentalist and evangelical Christians stepped forward to fight back. Influential leaders like televangelist Jerry Falwell and theologian Francis Schaeffer emerged to both interpret the signs of the times and call believers to action. Each in his respective way revived the jeremiad tradition of religious criticism and cultural-political activism to powerful effect.

Born in Ignorance, Dying in Knowledge

Secularization, as a social science theory, emerged hand in hand with theories of modernization in the nineteenth century. The idea that faith was destined to disappear was much older, of course; it dated to the radical Enlightenment and its critique of religion.[10] Such early philosophies, however, did not propose *scientific* explanations for their predictions of religious decline. That awaited the coming of positivism, the new science of society defined by Auguste Comte and his predecessor, Henri de Saint-Simon, in the mid-nineteenth century. Positivism, modeled on the natural sciences, was inspired by Comte's discovery of his "law of three stages." According to this law, history had reached its third and highest stage, the positive or scientific, spelling the end of the second or metaphysical stage. In this third stage, religion would be superseded by science, empirical and ethically neutral, as it freed human affairs from ecclesiastical authority and supernaturalism and redirected intellectual energy toward human well-being. Traditional religious views of the world and individual theistic faith, which had been "born in ignorance," would eventually "die in knowledge."[11]

As we have seen, Comtean positivism, with its prediction of inevitable secularization, was a theory of modernity and of social differentiation. In their more systematic and influential theories of religion and modernization, Emile Durkheim and Max Weber, the principal founders of sociology, also emphasized social differentiation and the key role of secularization as cause and effect of differentiation. Neither Weber nor Durkheim shared Comte's positivist critique of religion as ignorance, but both believed that traditional religion would undergo drastic and irreversible decline. In Western industrial societies, Durkheim argued, specialized professions and institutions evolve to address discrete functions, such as education, health care, social control, and welfare, formerly carried on within the ambit of the churches. This differentiation of spheres and loss of core functions over an ever-widening domain of public life leads to a decisive decline in the formal and formative influence of religious institutions. Over time, Durkheim predicted, the residual role of historic religion (the Judeo-Christian tradition) would continue to erode, leading, perhaps, to its eventual extinction. In Weber's more historically specific theory, the rise of a rationalist and intellectualist view of the world would be fatal for the future prospects of religion. Propelled by the Protestant Reformation and the subsequent scientific and industrial revolutions, rationalist thinking would work to undermine supernatural explanation and sanction, and would generate deep skepticism toward all metaphysical beliefs. Further, rationalization, according to Weber, would drive the institutional differentiation of competing and internally autonomous "value-spheres." In these pluralistic spheres religion would be replaced by forms of organization dominated by bureaucratic-technical rationality. This does not necessarily mean the total disappearance of traditional religion. The "old churches" would remain, Weber predicted, as a refuge for "those who cannot bear the fate of the times."[12]

In these theories of secularization, some version of which most social theorists (and leading intellectuals) of the late nineteenth and early twentieth centuries shared, there was a strong presumption of historical inevitability and a conviction that modernity and religion are inherently antagonistic. Typically, as with Comte and Durkheim, the death of the "old gods" is identified as an integral feature of the progressive evolution of human societies from simple to complex forms. Modern science has given us the tools to discover the stages through which human history unfolds and reveal the processes that drive social change. Scientific research, to quote Weber, reveals "the steady progress of the characteristic process of 'secularization,' to which in modern times all phenomena that originated in religious conceptions succumb."[13] In the struggle between modernity and traditional religion, religion inescapably loses.

This grand thesis, as later scholars would argue, appears to have been so taken for granted that it simply did not require investigation. Knowing religion's future apparently canceled any need to attend to the empirical details. Only in the 1960s did sociologists begin making efforts to get "beyond the classics" and elaborate more systematic and empirically grounded versions of secularization theory.[14] These diverse efforts retained many of the old propositions, though they generally allowed for the persistence of individual religiosity as privatized spirituality or civil religion.[15] At the same time, a few lone voices registered the first rumblings of discontent, a reassessment that would gain momentum in the 1970s. In that decade and the following, the enduring social scientific consensus on secularization began to break apart as the assumptions that had sustained it came under increasing fire.

The emerging critique of secularization theory was inspired in part by the dramatic appearance of new religious movements and the religiously inspired political activism that thrust evangelicals and Fundamentalists into public view. By itself, however, empirical counterevidence cannot explain the profound shift in intellectual climate. As José Casanova would later write, "similar counterevidence has existed all along and yet the evidence remained unseen or was explained away as irrelevant."[16] Something more was in the air, deeper changes that had quietly altered established frames of reference. The terms in which the classical model was critiqued, and rejected or modified, suggest that social scientists were losing a faith of their own.

For many scholars, the classical model of secularization came to be regarded as a pernicious "myth." How, they asked, could we have ever believed in such a story? The answer was that secularization theory was not a scientific paradigm at all. Rather, it was a dogma, a nineteenth-century ideological project sustained "by a deep and abiding antagonism to religious belief and various expressions of organized religion."[17] The theory remained largely unquestioned because it fit so well with the secularist bias of academics. The most prominent group leveling this charge was the religious economists. They came to regard the "founders of social science" as a "laughing stock" for their "failed prophesy" about the "death of faith."[18] For these scholars, discrediting the classical model cleaned the slate so that the real (nonideological) science of religious economies could proceed. But the very vehemence and indiscriminate nature of this backlash is revealing. It belies a prior and very basic crisis of confidence.

Across the board, social scientists quietly had been losing faith in the Comtean account of the triumph of reason and the role of the social sciences in it. Even those who remained defenders of the secularization thesis dropped key elements of the classical model. By and large, they abandoned the teleological and social evolutionary frameworks for understanding history that had long underwritten key concepts in the social sciences.[19] While continuing to look for general trends and comparative patterns, few claimed any longer that social science could identify deterministic laws or stages of historical development. Defenders of secularization no longer saw the theory predicting the "disappearance of religiosity, nor even of organized religion."[20] They allowed that there can be periods of resacralization and that science and rationalization do not necessarily obliterate morality, questions of ultimate meaning, or supernaturalism. Indeed, social scientists reclaimed heretofore deemphasized ideas from the founders of sociology, including Durkheim's emphasis on the functional necessity of the "sacred" and Weber's emphasis on the human desire for meaning, to reassert the importance of myth in social life and reject simplistic notions of a unidirectional disenchantment of the world.

The grandest assumptions of the classical model ceased to be intellectually compelling ideas. If anything, social scientists had themselves become disenchanted with their mission and now set their sights on a far less ambitious program. This change reflects the wider revolution in sensibility among intellectuals in these decades, which called into question all the modern historical and philosophical schemes of progress and perfectibility—what Jean-François Lyotard called "metanarratives"[21]—as theoretically unwarranted and historically implausible. There was a sharp retreat from any sort of prediction about where social processes would "inevitably" or "irreversibly" lead. "Contingency" was the new watchword. Research centered on investigating the far more flexible and provisional "variation in patterns of religious change."

Prophesies of godlessness, however, by no means disappeared. Jerry Falwell revitalized the old jeremiad tradition and sparked a revival of political and civic activism among conservative Christians. Another key prophet was theologian and cultural critic Francis Schaeffer. From his missionary outpost in Switzerland, Schaeffer worked out a comprehensive story of growing godlessness in America and the West that inspired not a political but an intellectual renaissance.[22] Together, these two scholars were instrumental in shaping the theological critique of a new generation of evangelicals and Fundamentalists.

America, You're Too Young to Die!

The jeremiad tradition in America dates to the famous letters and sermons of the ministers and magistrates of the seventeenth-century Puritan colony in

New England. As a rhetorical formula, the jeremiad was widely used by Protestant leaders in succeeding generations to decry the decline of piety and
moral vigor among the faithful, to lament the disorder and woes that had come
and would come as a consequence, and to call for a return to former greatness,
both within the church and in national life.[23] The power of the jeremiad lies in
its ability to mobilize energy for revival by amplifying anxiety over current
misfortunes while at the same time showing how these very calamities are
a sign of God's election. Thus a call for personal repentance is intertwined with
a reaffirmation of hope that the community might be spared further punishment and God's favor restored. Rising social protest movements, the Vietnam
War, and resulting disillusionment with government further exacerbated
a sense of decline and a widespread urge for change. In his rise to national
prominence in the 1970s, Jerry Falwell, pastor of the Thomas Road Baptist
Church in Lynchburg, Virginia, pioneer of religious broadcasting, and founder
of the Moral Majority, proved to be a master of the jeremiad form in response
to the new environment.

Falwell's turn toward political action signaled that the implicit truce between Fundamentalists and the rest of American society since the 1920s had
come to an end. According to that truce, true Christians would concern
themselves with the saving of souls, and would stay out of the business of
reforming society. Falwell himself was once firmly committed to such a position. His early sermons warned of the dangers of mixing religion and politics.
In 1965, for instance, he delivered a widely distributed sermon, "Ministers and
Marchers," in which he argued:

> As far as the relationship of the church to the world, it can be ex-
> pressed as simply as the three words which Paul gave Timothy—
> "preach the Word."... Nowhere are we commissioned to reform the
> externals. We are not told to wage wars against bootleggers, liquor
> stores, gamblers, murderers, prostitutes, racketeers, prejudiced per-
> sons or institutions, or any other existing evil as such. I feel that we
> need to get off the streets and back into the pulpits and into our
> prayer rooms. I believe we need to rededicate ourselves to the great
> task of turning this world back to God. The preaching of the gospel is
> the only means by which this can be done.[24]

But just over a decade later, Falwell had changed his view. He now preached
that "the idea that 'religion and politics don't mix' was invented by the devil to
keep Christians from running their own country." He labeled his "Ministers
and Marchers" position "false prophecy."[25]

When Falwell tells the story of this shift in his thinking, the urgency of the American situation coming out of the 1960s and early 1970s plays a crucial role. In his autobiography, *Strength for the Journey*, he writes:

> If ever there was a time when God needed a job done, it was during the 1960s and 1970s. The future of our nation was at stake.... I sincerely believe that Satan had mobilized his own forces to destroy America by negating the Judeo-Christian ethic, secularizing our society, and devaluing human life through the legalization of abortion and infanticide. God needed voices raised to save the nation from inward moral decay.[26]

He also recounts nightly prayer times with his children in the 1970s when he would tell them that it was "very doubtful that America will remain a free nation for another ten or twenty years."[27] America had lost its way, and God was judging the nation for its sins.

Falwell's dire assessment of the situation led to action. In 1979 he took his Liberty Baptist College Choir on an "I Love America" tour. It began on the steps of the Capitol in Washington, D.C., and included visits to forty-four state capitals. Falwell's message on those occasions expressed his profound apprehension about where things were headed:

> "We have to pay the price for freedom," I said over and over again to those who stopped to listen. "If we're not willing to pay the price, God will give us what we want. Remember! He repeatedly sold His people into bondage.... I think our country is now at the point where we could fall. I don't think that is alarmism; I think that's fact, unless we repent now. The question is, if we repent and get right with God, will God bring us out? I really don't know."[28]

Similarly, in the summer of 1980, Falwell headed up an arena tour with the choir. In Harrisburg, Pennsylvania, thousands of people filled the Zembo Temple for one of these rallies. The event featured many opportunities for the gathered to celebrate America, but ended on a less cheerful note with "America, You're Too Young to Die!" a multimedia presentation of music, pictures, and drama. Falwell described it as a "sobering indictment of the sins of the nation and the dramatic call to spiritual renewal."[29] Images of Charles Manson, Times Square sex film marquees, and aborted fetuses flashed across the screen, documenting American's iniquities, while pictures of mushroom

clouds and Soviet troops warned of impending national catastrophe. The im-
mediacy of the communist threat was brought home by the words of Gus Hall,
head of the Communist Party USA, projected on the screen: "I dream of the
hour when the last Congressman is strangled to death on [sic] the guts of
the last preacher."[30]

Domestic immorality and foreign threats, however, were merely symp-
toms. The more basic crisis, for Falwell, concerned the churches themselves.
Liberalism had eaten the heart out of much of the mainline. "The ultimate
product of theological Liberalism," he wrote, "is a vague kind of religious
humanism that is devoid of any true Gospel content."[31] No wonder, then,
given this spiritual emptiness, that all manner of pagan spiritualities were
attracting the young. Yet even more critical to explaining American decline was
the complacency of "Bible-believing Christians" and the "pro-moral" majority.
Those who should be serving as the spiritual bulwark against the liberal,
secularist elite were missing in action. The conservative activist Paul Weyrich
helped convince Falwell that the faithful could be mustered to revitalize
America's civic republican values. They only needed a leader. "Jerry," Weyrich
said, "there is in America a moral majority that agrees about the basic issues.
But they aren't organized. They don't have a platform. The media ignore them.
Somebody's got to get that moral majority together!"[32] Even in the liberal
churches, Falwell believed, "the leaders do not really speak for their people.
Many church members are deeply disturbed by the direction their churches are
taking."[33] There was hope after all. There was a new shift happening across
society—the "Reagan Revolution." In 1980, after he had founded the Moral
Majority, Falwell summed up his new vision and the new era: "If Americans
will face the truth, our nation can be turned around and can be saved from the
evils and the destruction that have fallen upon every other nation that has
turned its back on God."[34]

In his tireless efforts to mobilize conservative Christians, Jerry Falwell
appropriated and revitalized the classic jeremiad formula. He sounded the
alarm over spiritual and moral laxity while affirming a confidence in America
as a chosen people capable even now of repenting of its misdeeds and re-
newing its covenant. This potent mix of urgency and optimism, as so often in
the American past, did not go unheeded. Along with others, Falwell's message
helped reawaken the slumbering giant of conservative Protestantism and fuel
its outburst of organization building and activism in the 1980s. The political
jeremiad was not, however, the only form the revived jeremiad took in this
period. At roughly the same time, a quite different conservative Protestant
account was emerging from the most unlikely of places.

How Shall We Then Think?

Francis Schaeffer wrote more than twenty books before his death in 1984, many of them with the words "death" or "disaster" in the titles. Like Falwell, he operated in the prophetic mode, heightening the sense of crisis and impending judgment and challenging Christians to take action. He, too, was unsparing in his criticism of the liberal churches for abandoning orthodoxy, and he linked this failing to the rampant secularism, dehumanization, and moral evil pervading society. Late in his life, Schaeffer even joined Falwell as an active leader in the moral-political battles of American conservative Christians. But significant differences separated the two. For one, Schaeffer's style was bohemian, and he spoke readily of avant-garde art and film and of popular music. With his long hair, goatee, and knickers, he attracted a following of young people and was sympathetic to the counterculture and its critique of the "plastic culture." More important, Schaeffer understood the moral-religious crisis and its resolution differently. His jeremiad centered on philosophical ideas, not liberal elites. It was a cultural jeremiad, not politics. He introduced the term "worldview" into the evangelical lexicon and sparked a quite different and perhaps even more far-reaching revolution than did Falwell.

Schaeffer began preparing for the ministry at Westminster Seminary in 1935, not long after its founding. J. Gresham Machen, a central figure in the modernist-fundamentalist controversy of the 1920s and 1930s, had established Westminster to counteract the growing liberalism he had experienced while a professor at Princeton Seminary. But for Schaeffer, Westminster was not conservative enough. He joined a splinter faction and eventually graduated from the newly formed Faith Theological Seminary. Following other appointments, he and his family were sent to Switzerland in 1948 by the Independent Board for Foreign Missions. The board, a Fundamentalist body, charged Schaeffer with developing a children's ministry and with strengthening ties between "Bible-believing" churches across Europe. When he arrived, however, Schaeffer found his energies were more urgently needed to address the searching questions of young people. In 1955, he and his wife, Edith, dedicated themselves to this work full-time, inviting backpackers, students, and intellectual seekers of all kinds to stay in their home, which they called L'Abri, and take part in conversations about God and the meaning of life.

Through these conversations and in light of the upheavals of the 1960s, Schaeffer became convinced that the philosophical assumptions of secular humanism were creating a culture of meaninglessness and irrationality. With its roots in the Renaissance and the rationalism of the Enlightenment, secular humanism, by placing "man at the center," was pushing the West toward godlessness, a course that would lead, paradoxically, to antihumanism and irrationalism. This godlessness, in the encompassing narrative that Schaeffer was developing, took many forms. In art, for instance, it was represented by cubism, in philosophy by existentialism. It was manifested in the radical relativism and subjectivism Schaeffer saw in his visitors to L'Abri. Though many claimed to believe in God, Schaeffer observed that the status of belief had changed. God was not "there" but only "there for me."

The new spiritualities of the 1960s were an especially vivid expression of the irrationality of the godless culture. "The reason young people turn to the Eastern Religions," Schaeffer argued, "is simply that man having moved into the area of non-reason" will believe anything.[35] Similarly, the popularity of occult practices was evidence of a desperate search for meaning in a culture that denied God's existence. Schaeffer wrote:

> Though demons do not fit into modern man's conclusions on the basis of his reason, many modern people feel that even demons are better than everything in the universe being one big machine. People [turn to the occult] in the hope of some kind of meaning. Even if it is a horrendous kind of meaning.

Moreover, in Schaeffer's story, godlessness was having pervasive social and political consequences. *How Shall We Then Live?* for instance, his film series from the late 1970s, opens with scenes of young people throwing rocks, troops in riot gear, and burning buses. Schaeffer appears on screen to comment on the "violence and breakdown in society" that these scenes depict and the "authoritarianism that is rising to meet the threat of chaos." In the grip of secularism, things were falling apart. Beyond violence and civil unrest, he also identified divorce, abortion, pornography, and euthanasia as evidence of the new disorder.

These issues of American moral politics brought Schaeffer's world closer to Falwell's. He worked with C. Everett Koop on an influential documentary on abortion and euthanasia, and wrote a book—*A Christian Manifesto*—about American politics that was promoted on Falwell's television programs and inspired Randall Terry to start the militant antiabortion group Operation Rescue. Yet Schaeffer consistently insisted that the basic crisis concerned the philosophical "base"—assumptions about truth, humanity, and transcendence—not control of its institutional expression. In his grand narrative of Western culture, the high point was the Reformation and the recovery of authentic Christianity, leading to the great culture of Bach and Rembrandt, the principle of the rule of law, and the foundations of natural science. The erosion of this "Reformation base" and the contemporary ascendancy of secular humanism, including its byproducts of liberal theology and a culture of meaninglessness, was driven by bad ideas. In faulting Christian leaders for their role in the crisis, Schaeffer cited intellectual failure, not political quiescence: "The floodwaters of secular thought and liberal theology overwhelmed the church because the leaders did not understand the importance of combating a false set of presuppositions.... This was a real weakness which it is hard, even today, to rectify among evangelicals."[36] Even in *A Christian Manifesto*, his most directly political book, Schaeffer argued that "permissiveness, pornography, the public schools, the breakdown of the family and...abortion" are the product of a "shift in worldview...away from a worldview that was at least vaguely Christian...toward something completely different."[37] Politics, for Schaeffer, was a symptom, not a cause.

Schaeffer did not see the secular worldview as some recent invention. Nor did he think that it was only an elite problem from which the majority remained insulated and safely "moral." Rather, he viewed secularism as pervasive, calling it the "monolithic culture." Still, for all its power and destructiveness, secularism was simply an expression of mistaken philosophical ideas. And herein lay the hope for its defeat. False answers to the basic questions of human existence could be replaced with the truth. In his books and lectures Schaeffer displayed the method: Reveal the inconsistencies of secular philosophies, showing them to suffer from errors directly related to their departure from the worldview. of Christianity, which "is exactly in line with the experience of every man."[38] Ideas also form the basis of individual lives; "as a man thinks, so he is" was Schaeffer's formula. In conversations with secularists, then, Christians could work to bring their interlocutors to an awareness of how the secular worldview did not fit their own life experience—what Schaeffer called "taking the roof off"—whereas the Christian view did. By such "pre-evangelism," the work of revival and conversion could go forward and so reverse the tide of secularity.

Schaeffer's philosophical jeremiad, like Falwell's political one, inspired widespread mobilization. Schaeffer made intellectual life matter to evangelicals by drawing on their traditional commitment to evangelism and doctrinal purity and connecting these to concerns about social and cultural disorder. Against conservative Protestantism's antiintellectual tendencies, Schaeffer inspired a whole generation of evangelical scholars, some of whom, like Os Guinness, launched their intellectual careers from L'Abri, while others, like Mark Noll, were influenced by his American lectures and books. The story and image of L'Abri (spread in part by Edith Schaeffer's book *L'Abri*) also became a model for evangelical study centers and off-campus programs throughout the world. Influenced by Schaeffer, evangelical colleges—historically defensive, insulated institutions—increasingly came to see part of their task as equipping students to understand competing worldviews. Not all of these efforts embraced Schaeffer's goal of demolishing opposing worldviews for the purpose of "pre-evangelism." In a typical case of intellectual patricide, many of the evangelical scholars who were either inspired by Schaeffer or supported by institutions that were influenced by him would later draw on their academic skills to attack the errors and oversimplifications in his books.[39] Yet even if he is not always honored as such, Schaeffer was the patriarch of the evangelical cultural-intellectual resurgence that blossomed in the 1980s and continued to grow thereafter.

A Reversal of Fortunes

The best-selling book in the decade of the 1970s was Hal Lindsey's *The Late Great Planet Earth*, with more than two million copies in print by 1977. Reading "Bible prophecy" about the "final stages of history," in light of the 1948 reestablishment of the state of Israel and the geopolitics of the late 1960s, Lindsey argued that "we are watching the fulfillment of these prophecies in our time."[40] Events "in this generation" had launched the countdown toward the "climactic hour." For those with eyes to see, the signs of "His coming" were unmistakable. Jerry Falwell spoke in similar terms in the 1970s, as did many others. Predictions of coming hard times, apocalyptic crisis, and the end of the world were common.

But by the 1990s and the approach of the millennium, when such prophesies were widely expected, they were seldom heard. Lindsey, who continued to retell the same story about "earth's final hour," was toiling away in relative obscurity. The first of the *Left Behind* books by Tim LaHaye and Jerry Jenkins, about the "earth's last days," was published in 1996. In the same year, televangelist Pat Robertson came out with *The End of the Age* on the same theme. Both were big bestsellers. And both were novels. It is not that these authors had doubts that we were likely living in the end times.[41] But apparently it now required the expedient of thriller fiction to make the idea seem plausible to the rank and file.

This shift is suggestive of the social changes through which most evangelicals and Fundamentalists had lived. While deep moral, spiritual, and political concerns remained, they felt a new confidence in the future and their place in it. The mood of the whole country had changed. The sixties were long over, the evil empire had collapsed, the Reagan years had shifted the country rightward, and Jimmy Carter's infamous "malaise" speech was a distant memory. American society no longer appeared to be falling apart. Conservative Christians had found their voice in politics and on the airwaves, had created a vast network of new institutions and overseas missions, and were even a presence in popular culture. The Judgment just did not feel as near as it once did. In his study *The New England Mind*, historian Perry Miller writes that the jeremiad "could make sense out of existence as long as adversity was to be overcome, but in the moment of victory it was confused."[42] While few Fundamentalists or evangelicals would suggest they had reached a "moment of victory," by the 1990s no one was accusing them of withdrawing into their ghetto or failing to combat error. They had become, again, a force in American life, and the decline of the broad jeremiad marked their movement from the margins. The tradition had, in part, been undermined by its own success, having been powerfully reestablished and institutionalized in think tanks, advocacy organizations, and schools, which continued to recite variations the political jeremiad of Falwell and the intellectual jeremiad of Schaeffer, but in a less comprehensive mode, usually in public skirmishes over abortion and family values and in appeals to donors.

In the 1970s and 1980s, the fortunes of that other great tradition of prophecy, secularization, were not so auspicious. Writing in the early 1990s, José Casanova argued that, judging from recent debates among sociologists, the "appropriate question" with which to begin any current discussion of secularization theory was "Who still believes in the *myth* of secularization?"[43] How far a once proud, intellectually dominant idea had fallen! That such a question could even be posed is eloquent witness to the distance traveled from those heady days of the sixties when the death of God seemed such a sure thing and scholars had such confidence in their predictions. Maybe the curse of the WITCHes that day in Chicago had an effect after all.

Despite its setbacks, secularization theory did not disappear. Some social scientists remained unswayed by the attacks on the theory or by the empirical counterclaims, such as the religious economists' argument that the United States was more religious than it used to be. These social scientists continued to expound one or another modified version of secularization theory. They continued to think that the United States was basically a secular society and that some process—not a conspiracy of secularists—brought it about. Though the theoretical defenders of this proposition were relatively few, it seems safe to say that most scholars in the academy believed it. In other words, the *idea* of secularization remained widely held, despite the challenges to the scientific *theory* or *thesis*. Perhaps this just reveals the difficulty scholars have in breaking with deeply entrenched patterns of thought—or merely reflects the ambivalence and hostility that still characterizes intellectual attitudes toward religion. But there is more to it than that.

Secularization persisted because the idea is intertwined with liberal democratic theory and more generally with deeply held understandings of modernity and of progress in human affairs. Reassertions of religious vitality and activism, both domestically and abroad, challenged these understandings but did not dislodge them. Despite overt skepticism, the metanarrative of modern progress persisted as the background presupposition.

Scholars interpreted outbursts of religion as anomalies and characterized them collectively as instances of antimodern Fundamentalism. Such outbursts were troubling, to be sure, but in the bigger picture were futile. The clock could not be turned back. Or so the story went. Yet even in this wider, more general sense, all was not well with secularization. If the theorists felt besieged and now spoke of contingency and multiple modernities, so did others. The old confidence had been shaken. In the coming years, unforseen events would challenge that confidence to its very core.

NOTES

1. Andrew M. Greeley, "There's a New-Time Religion on Campus," *New York Times*, June 1, 1969, SM14.

2. See, for example, Thomas J. J. Altizer and William Hamilton, *Radical Theology and the Death of God* (Indianapolis: Bobbs-Merrill, 1966); Paul van Buren, *The Secular Meaning of the Gospel* (New York: Macmillan, 1963).

3. Herman Kahn and Anthony J. Wiener, *The Year 2000* (New York: Macmillan, 1967), 39.

4. Peter L. Berger, quoted in "A Bleak Outlook Is Seen for Religion," *New York Times*, February 25, 1968, 3. For one sharply contrary view, see Andrew M. Greeley, *Religion in the Year 2000* (New York: Sheed and Ward, 1969).

5. Charles Y. Glock and Robert N. Bellah, eds., *The New Religious Consciousness* (Berkeley: University of California Press, 1976.)

6. James Davison Hunter, "Conservative Protestantism," in Phillip E. Hammond, *The Sacred in a Secular Age* (Berkeley: University of California Press, 1985), 150–66. Stephen R. Warner, "Theoretical Barriers to the Understanding of Evangelical Christianity," *Sociological Analysis* 40 (spring 1979): 1–9.

7. Dean Kelly, *Why Conservative Churches Are Growing* (New York: Harper and Row, 1972).

8. The phrase "new spiritual awakening" is from Jeremy Rifkin with Ted Howard, *The Emerging Order* (New York: Putnam, 1979). The phrase "swallowed up by godlessness" is borrowed from Gabriel Vahanian, "Swallowed Up by Godlessness," *Christian Century*, December 8, 1965, 1505–7.

9. José Casanova, *Public Religions in the Modern World* (Chicago: University of Chicago Press, 1994), 3.

10. Ibid., 30–35.

11. This phrase is adapted from Callum G. Brown, "A Revisionist Approach to Religious Change," in Steve Bruce, ed., *Religion and Modernization* (New York: Oxford University Press, 1992), 39.

12. Max Weber, "Science as a Vocation," in *From Max Weber*, trans. and ed. H. H. Gerth and C. Wright Mills (New York: Oxford University Press, 1958), 155.

13. Max Weber, "The Protestant Sects and the Spirit of Capitalism," in ibid., 307.

14. Charles Y. Glock and Phillip E. Hammond, eds., *Beyond the Classics?* (New York; Harper and Row, 1973).

15. Philip S. Gorski, "Historicizing the Secularization Debate," *American Sociological Review* 65 (2000): 138–67.

16. Casanova, *Public Religions*, 11.

17. Jeffrey K. Hadden, "Toward Desacralizing Secularization Theory," *Social Forces* 65, 3 (1987): 587–611.

18. Rodney Stark, "Church and Sect," in Phillip E. Hammond, ed., *The Sacred in a Secular Age* (Berkeley: University of California Press, 1985), 147.

19. Phillip Hammond, introduction to Hammond, *Sacred in a Secular Age*, 1. Hammond writes: "A linear image dominates Western thought about society. Even cyclical views are cast in spiral form, thus helping to maintain the notion that social life is systematically 'coming from' somewhere and 'going' elsewhere."

20. Bryan Wilson, "Secularization: The Inherited Model," in ibid., 14.

21. Jean-François Lyotard, *The Postmodern Condition* (Minneapolis: University of Minnesota Press, 1984).

22. The evangelical flagship magazine *Christianity Today* suggested that, of his contemporaries, only Billy Graham rivaled Schaeffer's influence on evangelicalism; Michael S. Hamilton, "The Dissatisfaction of Francis Schaeffer," *Christianity Today*, March 3, 1997, 22.

23. Sacvan Bercovitch, *The American Jeremiad* (Madison: University of Wisconsin Press, 1978).

24. Quoted in Susan Friend Harding, *The Book of Jerry Falwell* (Princeton: Princeton University Press, 2000), 22.

25. Ibid.

26. Jerry Falwell, *Strength for the Journey* (New York: Simon and Schuster, 1987), 362.

27. Quoted in Jeffrey Hadden and Charles E. Swann, *Prime Time Preachers* (Reading, Mass.: Addison-Wesley, 1981), 159.

28. Falwell, *Strength for the Journey*, 357–58.

29. Jerry Falwell, *Strength for the Journey*, 356–57.

30. Dudley Clendinen, "Rev. Falwell Inspires Evangelical Vote," *New York Times*, August 20, 1980, B22.

31. Jerry Falwell, ed., *The Fundamentalist Phenomenon* (Garden City, N.Y.: Doubleday, 1981), 187.

32. Falwell, *Strength for the Journey*, 359.

33. Falwell, *The Fundamentalist Phenomenon*, 218.

34. Jerry Falwell, *Listen, America!* (Garden City, N.Y.: Doubleday, 1980), 18.

35. *How Shall We Then Live?* Gospel Communications, 1979. Further quotations in this paragraph are taken from this film.

36. Francis Schaeffer, *The God Who Is There* (Downers Grove, Ill.: InterVarsity Press, 1968), 7.

37. Francis Schaeffer, *A Christian Manifesto* (Westchester, Ill.: Crossway Books, 1981), 17.

38. Francis Schaeffer, *He Is There and He Is Not Silent* (Wheaton, Ill.: Tyndale, 1972), 61.

39. See for example, Ronald W. Ruegsegger, ed., *Reflections on Francis Schaeffer* (Grand Rapids, Mich.: Academie Books, 1986).

40. Hal Lindsey with C. C. Carlson, *The Late Great Planet Earth* (Grand Rapids, Mich.: Zondervan, 1970), 20.

41. LaHaye, for example, publishes a "Tim LaHaye Prophecy Library," which contains a number of nonfiction titles interpreting "Bible prophecy" to the effect that "the Rapture and Tribulation could occur during our generation."

42. Perry Miller, *The New England Mind: From Colony to Province* (Cambridge, Mass.: Harvard University Press, 1953), 33.

43. Casanova, *Public Religions*, 11.

11

From 11/9/1989 to 9/11/2001 and Beyond: The Return of Jeremiad and the Specter of Secularization

Joshua J. Yates

The year 1989 was not all it was thought to be. The farther away from it we move in time, the more confounding it becomes and the more quaint our initial excitement and hopes for it appear. At the time, in the wake of Soviet Communism's surprising demise, humanity seemed poised at the threshold of world-historical change. Dictators were toppled, often peacefully, and democratic capitalism spread throughout the globe. Intimations of perpetual peace once again stirred the imaginations of world leaders. Soon into the 1990s, there was also reason for American domestic ebullience due to the growing prosperity of the dot-com boom, the fading Japanese economic challenge, budgetary surpluses, and declining rates of crime, divorce, and people on the dole. At the start of the twentieth century's final decade, at least, human society appeared to have converged on, in Francis Fukuyama's provocative description, "the end of history." As we now know, our millennial confidence would be short-lived—if not misplaced.

The idea that history had ended did not mean an end to violent conflict in the world, even genocidal conflict.[1] Nor, for Fukuyama, did it mean liberal democracy would remain uncontested. Democrats themselves would likely find reason to question it from within. His was not a triumphant, utopian end to history. Still, like all modernization theorists before him, from Comte, Hegel, and Marx to the conventional social science and development theory of the mid-twentieth century, Fukuyama assumed an evolutionary trajectory to world history. These theories, whether of the "weakly" or "strongly" deterministic variety, understand all societies as passing through stages of development and moving ineluctably toward a more free, equal, just, and therefore, more productive and prosperous politic and economic system. The direction of history and its achievement in its final stage has gone by different terms—*civilization, enlightenment, progress,* and more recently, *liberal democracy.* All hold to a dichotomy between modern, developed, and open societies on the one hand, and traditional, underdeveloped, and closed societies on the other. Between these two developmental poles all societies are thought to travel the same road, if not at the same speed. "Developed" societies lead the way, but reach back to assist "underdeveloped" societies to overcome hurdles in their way. In the end, this universal evolutionary road will lead the world to political, economic, and cultural "convergence." For much of the twentieth century, the world was a battlefield between competing ideologies, struggling to define the terms of this grand convergence. By century's end, the contest appeared all but over. Fukuyama was among the first to say what many already believed: Marx had misread the directions—the universal road of development did not lead to communism but to liberal democratic capitalism. This, accordingly, was widely believed to be the symbolic significance of 1989.

Yet as the 1990s proceeded, followed by the first decade of the new millennium, the promise of 1989—of a new world order—appeared farther and farther off: the old world remained as full of disorder, conflict, and danger as ever. Newer, bleaker, and even apocalyptic images proliferated, replacing *The End of History* with best-selling nonfiction titles including Moynihan's *Pandemonium,* Brzezinski's *Out of Control,* Barber's *Jihad vs. McWorld,* Huntington's *The Clash of Civilizations,* and Kaplan's *The Coming Anarchy.* An era that began with the tearing down of a wall in Berlin to shouts of solidarity and freedom and the end of one war ended with the catastrophic collapse of walls in Manhattan to cries of grief and outrage and the call for a new war. Domestically, the culture wars raged and intensified as Red and Blue Americans became increasingly polarized, provoking fears in some of yet another wall— that between church and state—might also be in danger of coming down. In a word, from 11/9/1989 to 9/11/2001, history made a comeback.

It has been against the unruly and surprisingly obdurate contours of the globalized modern world that classic modernization theory, so long an unquestioned assumption in Western public policy and scholarly discourse, exhausted itself—and with it, the so-called secularization thesis at its heart. The worldwide resurgence of religion and its reappearance in the public square has animated concerns about the intransigency of jihad, civilizational clash, and anarchy.

Under intense scrutiny since the 1970s, the secularization thesis of evolutionary, inevitable godlessness found itself increasingly put on trial (not unlike the way the language of belief was in the 1920s) and found by most accounts to have been wrong, if not also expressive of wishful thinking. After a century of globalizing modernity, the world appears to be as religious and god-filled as it ever has, perhaps even more so. And this has largely come as something of a surprise. Present-day scholarly prophesies are no longer of a godless world of secularization but of a god-filled world—indeed, a world overpopulated by jealous gods.[2] By the end of the 1990s, the language of the inevitable, evolutionary, and secular modernization had been largely replaced by the language of "desecularization," "resurgent religion," and "multiple modernities." In the words of Peter Berger, a repentant one-time secularization theorist, the evidence amounts to "massive falsification of the idea that modernization and secularization are cognate phenomena. At the very least they show that counter-secularization is at least as important a phenomenon in the contemporary world as secularization."[3]

Against the fundamental convergence predicted by modernization theory, and so bravely reasserted by Fukuyama, the new theoretical discourse posited a messy world, full of discontinuities, disjunctures, and divergence. Seen from this angle, the significance of 1989 might be found not centrally in the fall of the Berlin Wall but rather in the victory of the Arab *mujahedin* in the mountains of Afghanistan and in the formation of the Christian Coalition in the United States.

Curiously, while many Western intellectuals were busy consigning secularization theory to the scrap heap of outmoded ideas, the mere specter of secularization continued to mobilize the faithful. In a typical case of historical irony, fear and resentment of what the secularization thesis purported to describe underwrote the ascendance of counter-secularization movements around the world. In the period stretching from the fall of the Berlin Wall to the fall of the World Trade Center (and its immediate aftermath), no prophecy of godlessness has been more conspicuous in this regard than the resurgence of the Puritan jeremiad in American public and political life.

The Return of the Jeremiad

Whether known by name or not, the jeremiad is familiar to most Americans and has a long and illustrious cultural history. It is recognizable as a bitter lament enumerating manifold social ills and collective troubles. The jeremiad finds its original referent in the Lamentations of Jeremiah in the Hebrew Bible, but as we have seen, its origins as cultural practice in American history arise with the Puritans. In sermon after sermon, Puritan divines cautioned their congregations of the temptations of the flesh, worldly backsliding, disregarding the demands of the covenant God made with the ancient Israelites and, by extension, with them. These divines consistently warned of God's coming judgment. Increase Mather, among others, preached that "the day of trouble is near" and exhorted the faithful with the penitential mantra *remember* the covenant, *repent* from sin, and *return* to God.

The Puritan jeremiad eventually became a rhetorical tradition, outliving and transcending its Puritan origins. From the abolitionists and temperance teetotalers to the Social Gospelers and Progressives, religious and irreligious alike, Americans have invoked the literary form of the jeremiad time and again to rail against the wrongs of the day. Throughout the middle decades of the twentieth century and up to the 1970s, however, the specifically religious version of the jeremiad—the one concerned with the temptations of an encroaching godlessness—seemed to go silent in American public discourse. It is no coincidence that these decades featured the high tide of secularization theory as the zeitgeist of American elite culture. These heady times reached their zenith in the late 1950s and early 1960s when *Time* magazine, a handful of influential post-Christian theologians, and nearly all of academic social science agreed that God was dead. By the final decades of the twentieth century, then, when the Puritan brand of jeremiad returned with an ardor and intensity equal to anything in its past, most observers were quite unprepared to understand its significance. *Time* may have reversed its earlier conclusion, hailing along with *Newsweek* and George Gallup the year 1976 as the "Year of the Evangelical," but to the heirs of Comte and champions of modernization theory, the revival of the Puritan jeremiad represented, at best, a longing for meaning among alienated consumers and, at worst, a retrograde reaction to the winds of social change then sweeping American culture as it transformed itself from an industrial to a postindustrial society.

For those reinvoking the jeremiad, the rift between their belief and the public life of American culture had grown to such an extent that it now threatened the self-selected segregation that had defined their place in American society for a generation. Quietism was no longer an option. To be sure, an increasingly godless society would not let them remain segregated, but many believed in the jeremiad's warning that to remain passive in the face of such a slide into immorality would bring their nation, and ultimately their own communities, to ruin.[4] The seeds of the classic jeremiad were thus repotted during the 1970s and 1980s in a hothouse of religious institution building: from the establishment of hundreds of evangelistic parachurch ministries to the creation of scores of special interest organizations dedicated to fighting abortion or saving the traditional family to a growing private and home-schooling movement to the founding of a number of global media empires, all largely outside the American mainstream. By the 1990s, the jeremiad tradition had become institutionalized to such an extent—and with enough political proficiency—that standard social theory could no longer conveniently account for it. The return of the jeremiad was no hiccup in the history of progress; it was a straightforward and unwanted contradiction of the secularization thesis, the first tenet of modernization theory.

In the wake of the ensuing theoretical turmoil, social science has be-grudgingly struggled to come to terms with the empirical reality of an assertive and increasingly public conservative religiosity that has mobilized itself around the fear that secularization theory was in fact true, or at least would be true if the faithful did not *remind* their fellow citizens about their covenantal heritage, call for national *repentance*, and *return* their country back to God.

Under the heading "Remember, Repent, Return," the evangelical political organization America 21 updates the classic jeremiad, imbuing it with alarming implication:

> On September 11, 2001, for the first time in our history since the War of 1812, America was attacked on our own soil by a foreign armed force. One of the unmistakable lessons of that terrible day is that America has lost the full measure of God's hedge of protection. When we ask ourselves why, the scriptures remind us that ancient Israel was invaded by its foreign enemy, Babylon, in 586 B.C. Despite the repeated warnings of its prophets, Jerusalem was destroyed by another invading foreign power in 70 A.D. Jesus warned Jerusalem that all the innocent blood shed since the time of Abel would be visited on that generation. Psalm 106:37 says that these judgments of God under Deuteronomy 28 were because of Israel's idolatry and its shedding of innocent blood. Israel, the apple of God's eye, was de-stroyed because they forgot their history, their covenant with the Lord, and they failed to tear down their high places of idol worship and repent.[5]

The lesson could neither be clearer nor more severe. If America is to avoid a similar fate it must "*Remember* the legacy of our heritage under God and our covenant with Him, *Repent* of where we have lost our way, and as II Chronicles

7:14 says, 'Turn from our wicked ways,' and *Return* to a right relationship and the protections God provides under His Covenant" (emphasis in original).[6]

Not all partisans of jeremiad give such explicit articulation of its constitutive components, but nearly all cover variations of its basic themes. The political activist organization American Values contends that "America today is in a virtue deficit," whose result has been potentially disastrous for the nation. Out of this deficit a host of social problems has arisen, including "hostility towards organized religion, sexual exploitation, the homosexual agenda, the demise of the family, and the culture of death." For American Values and its constituency, "these are disastrous trends for our country. If they aren't reversed, America—this great experiment in self-government—will be in jeopardy."[7] Beverly LaHaye, founder of Concerned Women of America, writes:

> Today, the future of America hangs in the balance. It is up to you and me—the Christians throughout this great nation—to get on our knees and pray, educate ourselves, and mobilize the members of our churches to action. Our nation's fate is at stake. The challenge is before us. The question each of us must answer is this: Will I accept this challenge?[8]

Dr. James Kennedy, pastor of Coral Ridge Ministries and founder of the Center for Reclaiming America, adds an apocalyptic edge to this jeremiad:

> No one living in America today can deny the fact that we are standing on the sheer precipice of some sort of national disaster. We have been pounded by every calamity known to man. Just think of the storms that have struck the nation in the past twelve months. These are warnings, foretold by the Bible, that God is reaching the end of His patience with us. How long will we resist Him? How long will this nation continue its sin? Unless we can restore some sense of moral vision and personal integrity and unless the people of this nation can come back to God's standards of righteousness, I believe I can say without stretching the truth at all, that within a very short time we will witness the end of life as we know it.[9]

But the ranks of those issuing various forms of jeremiad are not just staffed by Fundamentalist and evangelical Protestants. They are also filled by conservative Catholics, Jews, and Mormons. Father Richard John Neuhaus, editor of the neoconservative journal on religion and public affairs *First Things*, draws a particularly stark picture of the threat of godlessness for American democracy: "Unless there is a new and widely convincing assertion of the religious meaning of liberal democracy, it will not survive the next century." Neuhaus raises the stakes further: Should American democracy falter, the entire world could be thrown into a new dark age. Don Feder, president of the Anti-Christian Defamation League, is a conservative Jew who believes, likewise, "that if Christians should falter, America will fail—with disastrous consequences for Jews and Christian alike."[10]

As the presence of conservative Catholics and Jews suggests, what these leaders and their organizations are invoking is *not* the Puritan jeremiad in its classic form. While it retains its basic narrative structure, today's jeremiad radically departs from its forebear in several ways. Doubtless, the ecumenical character of the contemporary jeremiad alone would have been tantamount to godlessness for the Puritan practitioners of jeremiad. The covenant between God and the Massachusetts Puritans (as Israel's later-day surrogate) has been broadened to include all present-day U.S. citizens and is premised not on a particular sectarianism but on the "big tent" ecumenism of Protestant-Catholic-Jew. The public-political imagination of what may be better described as the neo-Puritan jeremiad offers a vision of liberal democratic institutions premised on that complex of values that now go under the heading "Judeo-Christian."

Perhaps the most distinguishing feature of today's jeremiad is the scope and intensity of its engagement with politics. Over the course of American history the partisans of the Puritan jeremiad certainly have had political interests. These interests, such as abolition, prohibition, and anti-immigration, were often pursued with tremendous conviction. These interests were, however, secondary to the importance of national revival. The archetypical response to perceived cultural crisis has, in this way, come in the evangelistic crusades and social reform movements. Put another way, Billy Graham, not Jerry Falwell, has been the rule. The question arises, then, in the words of historian George Marsden, "How did a soul-saving revivalistic movement that mostly steered clear of direct political involvement emerge at the end of the twentieth century as known especially for its political stances and influences?"[11] Why did jeremiad get political?

Many causes of the politicized jeremiad have been adduced, from the integration of the South following the civil rights movement to the social earthquakes of 1960s counterculture radicalism, to the demise of the Protestant establishment, to Cold War anti-totalitarianism, to the increasing size and scope of the federal government. No doubt all have played a role. Whatever the reason, it is clear that fear of an encroaching godlessness has been pervasive.[12] Of course, it is not the godlessness that threatened the sixteenth-century Massachusetts Bay Colony but that of the late twentieth and early twenty-first centuries that exercises today's partisans of jeremiad. It is the fear of an all-encompassing imperial secularization and the activism of its boosters that provokes the return of jeremiad.

Secular Humanism versus Judeo-Christian Values

Dr. Sam Weaver, evangelical commentator and frequently featured contributor on Renew America's website, summarizes the basic complaint. "The very foundation of American liberty and justice," he writes, "has long been under attack by the forces of secularism, relativism and the 'theories' and philosophies of men. The Judeo-Christian faith of our Founders has been all but annihilated by the powerful, concerted advance of the armies of the Enemy."[13] D. James Kennedy likewise complains: "While Christians have withdrawn into their holy huddles, the nation has been taken from us and transformed by secular liberals and humanists into a nation we no longer recognize." How has this come to pass? "Because we were not there to be counted," Kennedy chides, "and because we consoled ourselves with the silly notion that we could be a 'silent majority'—people who have a very different agenda for America have stripped the nation of its pride, dignity, and honor."[14] America 21 provides some examples of this agenda and warns about the activism of those who support it: "Radical forces are pressing our government for measures that will destroy the moral fabric of America, such as expansion of abortion rights, human cloning, and shutting God and the churches out of the public debate. Voting by these radical forces has increased dramatically since 1994."[15] American Values adds another voice to this chorus on its website:

> Recently, we have witnessed a substantial effort by secularist forces to prevent people of faith from continuing to acknowledge religion in the public square. At a time when Americans need to be reminded of our nation's moral roots and the virtues that spring from those roots, secularists have worked tirelessly for such things as removing the words "under God" from our country's most sacred oath, an education system that forbids any mention or recognition of faith, and the removal of Judge Roy Moore as Alabama's Chief Justice because he refused to remove a 10 Commandments monument from the state's Supreme Court building. Not only have the public expression and acknowledgement of religion and traditional values been banned, but in its place emerges the liberal culture, which targets our children. Hollywood serves up a steady diet of irresponsible sex and violence.

The pro-abortion crowd gives them condoms and birth control pills. And even worse, textbooks and liberal education bureaucrats are selling our children the liberal political agenda.[16]

At the heart of the liberal political agenda, the jeremiadists maintain, is a program of forced secularization. They resent what they perceive to be the hijacking of their society by a class of godless elites, technocrats, and New Left activists—from pro-choice feminists to environmentalists and homosexuals—who want to abolish any connection between traditional religious morals and public policy. This hostile takeover is thought to have come largely through nondemocratic means—via courts, mass media, and universities—and at the expense of the majority of Americans, who, it is believed, still largely hold to Judeo-Christian values (who are, according to Neuhaus, "incorrigibly, however confusedly, religious"[17]). Because this godless elite is seen to have a monopoly on respectable public discourse, millions (the purported moral elite) feel both alienated from the public life of their society and very often on the defensive. Citing examples of legal trends in Canada, Holland, and the Scandinavian countries, the Christian Coalition claims:

> For years our own government has flirted with passage of so-called "hate crimes" legislation that essentially criminalizes individual thoughts by way of adding extra penalties if biases, hatreds or intolerances are perceived in the commission of a crime. Its effect will be that of forcing people of faith, be it Christian, Jew, or Muslim—pretty much everyone expect secular humanists—to act contrary to their religious beliefs in the conduct of their everyday lives, or else become a criminal.[18]

The upshot, the Christian Coalition claims, is that while history is filled with examples of religious intolerances, "the greatest levels of intolerance today no longer come from the faithful, but rather from the anti-religious."[19] Don Feder supports this view: "Of course, as [Jewish] Americans, we are deeply troubled by the injustice done to Christians in a country founded on the tenets of Christianity, by believing Christians. It has been correctly observed that, for the elite, anti-Christian animus is the last acceptable form of prejudice."[20] Neuhaus concurs. In his widely influential book *The Naked Public Square*, he argues: "We insist we are a democratic society, yet we have in recent decades systematically excluded from policy considerations the operative values of the American people, values that are overwhelmingly grounded in religious belief."[21]

Again it is Sam Weaver who captures the spirit of a politically assertive jeremiad. He warns: "America's foundations are under all-out assault by forces

of atheism, secularism, relativism and multiculturalism. America's foundations are crumbling before our very eyes. What can the righteous do?" In
answering this question, Weaver is at pains to demonstrate that while a quick
glance at the Bible might suggest a strategy of passive dependence on God in
such times, this would be a mistaken reading. "Upon second thought," he
contends, "every Christian should follow the example of Christ." Citing various
passages throughout the New Testament, he continues:

> Whenever false doctrine, exercised in conjunction with selfish am-
> bition, becomes a threat to national morality, national liberty and/or
> justice, or national security, an active and determined stand *must be
> made*! I only wish that I had the time and the space in this column to
> document more of the false doctrines of secularism that are both
> perpetrated and perpetuated by elitist groups and individuals whose
> ambition is power and control. If we humble and passive followers of
> Christ had followed His example decades ago, then we would have
> driven these thieves and robbers out of our midst long before they
> totally corrupted our society and our culture![22] (emphasis in original)

For Weaver, as for all partisans of jeremiad, the days of quietism are over. To be
righteous can no longer mean living aloof from the larger culture, secure in the
religious subculture. "Passivism is passé!" Weaver exclaims. "The time for
action and activism is now! Let us work together in the Word and the Will of
God to restore the Foundation of this one Nation Under God!"[23]

Jeremiad as Mission Statement and Party Platform

In the early 1970s, when Jerry Falwell and Francis Schaeffer were among the
first in a generation to resort to the religiously inspired jeremiad, the challenge
facing the self-designated "moral elite" was that they had no public platform
from which to make their stand against the secular, "godless" elite. By 1979,
with the founding of the Moral Majority, this began to change, at least sym-
bolically. By 1989, if they were not yet on an equal footing, then the moral elite
had certainly gained ground, even amid defeat. Pat Robertson failed in his
presidential bid, the Moral Majority had all but collapsed by the end of the
1980s, and the Supreme Court nomination of the conservative judge Robert
Bork was blocked. Still, the concerns of jeremiad continued in a more de-
centralized and diffuse set of institutions working at all levels of public and
political life, each working toward a common set of bedrock moral issues, or
first things (to recall the title of Neuhaus's journal).

In this way, the locus of today's jeremiad is no longer limited to the pulpits of later-day Puritan divines or the subcultural ghettos of mid-twentieth-century conservative Christianity but has been institutionalized in a vast constellation of megachurch and parachurch ministries, special interest groups, religious schools, and the burgeoning homeschool movement, not to mention scores of religious media empires.[24] The neo-Puritan jeremiad has become standard boilerplate for thousands of organizations and associations seeking to bring Judeo-Christian values to bear on the many issues that presently embroil American public and political life.

In the 1990s, these organizations and their leaders seemingly burst forth into the public eye, enjoying if not widespread cultural revival, then certainly a new sense of power and influence. Nowhere did this newfound prominence seem more tangible than in politics. "Certainly, part of the answer to combating our nation's cultural depravity is continued faith in God and regular prayer," confesses Gary Bauer, former president of the Family Research Council and one-time Republican presidential candidate. But, he is quick to add, "part of the answer also lies in changing the government policies and laws which create an environment in which immorality and parental neglect are allowed to flourish."[25] James Dobson, perhaps the most influential of American evangelicals, is emphatic about Focus on the Family's commitment to politics under his leadership:

> We will continue to address the great moral issues of the day, even
> when they take us into the political arena. . . . As Christians, I be-
> lieve we are obligated to defend the principles of morality and righ-
> teousness in this representative form of government. . . . Thus,
> Focus on the Family will continue to lobby for and defend our fun-
> damental beliefs as long as I am at the helm of this ministry.[26]

Of such organizations perhaps few have been as emblematic, or as controversial, as the Christian Coalition. "We think the Lord is going to give us this nation back one precinct at a time," a Coalition activist exclaimed in the early 1990s. Rather than going for the White House all at once, their strategy would be "one neighborhood at a time, and one state at a time." To this end, the Christian Coalition established political technology training schools around the country in order to field as many as five thousand candidates at all levels by the end of the decade.[27] From the vantage of 2006, the strategy appears to have worked. From initial electoral success in Congress, which led to the "Contract with America" and welfare reform in 1994, to the successful judicial activism of recent years, to the election and reelection of George W. Bush, the institutional carriers of jeremiad have become a powerful political bloc, powerful enough to cause Ralph Reed, one-time head of the Christian Coalition, to proclaim: "We have finally gained what we have always sought, a place at the table, a sense of legitimacy and a voice in the conversation that we call democracy."[28] This political prominence continues today, with a new generation of political organizations like America 21 whose Pastor's Challenge recasts the classic formula of jeremiad in terms of electoral politics. Echoing the familiar refrain "Remember, repent, return," the Pastor's Challenge issues an urgent alert asking pastors to exhort their congregations to "(1) engage the battle through prayer; (2) review non-partisan voter guides suitable for distribution in your Church, and (3) use the site resources to learn how to vote." America 21 admits that only God can send revival, but believes "pastors can lead the turning in America that will stop her moral free fall."[29]

Alongside such broad-platform political organizations, the jeremiad has found a home in a host of more focused special interest groups whose reason for existence is to combat a secular counterpart. Opposed to the American Civil Liberties Union (ACLU) are the American Center for Law and Justice (ACLJ) and the Alliance Defense Fund; countering Planned Parenthood, there are groups like the Family Research Council and Focus on the Family; working against the National Organization of Women (NOW) or the National Abortion Rights League (NARAL) there is Concerned Women of America; for every secular liberal media outlet like *Newsweek*, there is a *World Magazine*. The partisans of jeremiad have even taken the battle of institutions virtual: RightMarch.com characterizes itself as the "'Rapid Response Force' against the ongoing liberal onslaught" and explicitly positions itself against what it describes as "the socialist wannabe's at MoveOn.org led by a coalition of 32 radical leftwing organizations—including Feminist Majority, Greenpeace, National Gay and Lesbian Task Force, National Organization for Women (NOW), and Jesse Jackson's Rainbow/PUSH Coalition."[30] The Alliance Defense Fund, founded by evangelical heavyweights James Dobson, Bill Bright, Larry Burkett, D. James Kennedy, Marlin Maddoux, and William Pew, exists to "not only tirelessly defend religious liberty, the sanctity of human life, marriage, and the traditional family, but to determine the most strategic and effective means to do so." It believes that core American values have come "under direct and relentless attack by organizations such as the American Civil Liberties Union (ACLU) and its allies who aggressively erect legal barriers to undermine the First Amendment's meaning. Freedom, as defined by these groups, bears little resemblance to the Founders' intent when drafting our nation's Constitution."[31]

What Jeremiad Wants: A Return to the "Founding"

The last point needs underscoring, for it illustrates the main objective of the neo-Puritan jeremiad. Very simply, its partisans want to return America to a nation that lives by (their understanding of) the principles of the Declaration of Independence, the Bill of Rights, *and* the Ten Commandments. To put it another way, they want to remoralize the American experiment in democratic self-government. In this aim, it is hard to ignore the distinctly civic republican sensibility reverberating within the calls of the contemporary jeremiad. Here is yet another way the contemporary jeremiad differs from the old. Moreover, today's partisans repeatedly turn not to the establishment of Puritan New England writ large but to the constitutionally secular republic of the founding. More precisely, they yearn for the days when the separation of church and state guaranteed by the First Amendment was anchored in a civic culture firmly committed to the Protestant ethic. "Traditional Values," the appositely named Traditional Value Coalition declares, "are based upon biblical foundations and upon the principles outlined in the Declaration of Independence, our Constitution, the writings of the Founding Fathers, and upon the writings of great political and religious thinkers throughout the ages." The concern is unmistakable. For the Traditional Value Coalition and their allies, "Bible-based traditional values are what created and what have preserved our nation. We will lose our freedoms if we reject these values."[32] Renew America is similarly emphatic: "This site is for ALL people who consider themselves loyal Americans. It has no philosophy, image, or agenda beyond this one unifying premise: America must return to its founding principles if it is to survive."[33] The Values Voters' Contract with Congress, sponsored by a number of the most influential of these political organizations, drafted its own "Declaration of American Renewal," which begins:

> We are citizens of the United States of America and subjects of the sovereign Creator, acknowledged in the Declaration of Independence as the Supreme Ruler and Judge of the World. We strongly affirm our allegiance to the Constitution of the United States, and are moved by our faith in God to join together now to defend government of, by, and for the people against the greatest form of assault it has ever faced: the destruction of our constitutionally-mandated republican form of government by judges who legislate from the bench and thereby subvert our liberty and our entire way of life.[34]

website after website prominently displays quotations from an array of founders. One prominent group features the words of John Marshall, the illustrious chief justice of the Supreme Court: "The American population is entirely Christian, and with us Christianity and Religion are identified. It would be strange indeed, if with such a people, our institutions did not pre-suppose Christianity, and did not often refer to it, and exhibit relations with it."[35] Another features words from George Washington's Farewell Address: "Popular government cannot exist without morality—and morality based upon biblical principles." Yet another displays a quotation from Samuel Adams, words expressed as the Declaration of Independence was being signed:

> We have this day restored the Sovereign to Whom all men ought to be obedient. He reigns in heaven and from the rising to the setting of the sun, let His kingdom come. He therefore is the truest friend to the liberty of his country who tries most to promote its virtue, and who, so far as his power and influence extend, will not suffer a man to be chosen into any office of power and trust who is not a wise and virtuous man. . . . The sum of all is, if we would most truly enjoy this gift of Heaven, let us become a virtuous people.[36]

What would a return to the principles of America's founding mean in practice? American Values, Gary Bauer's newly founded organization, describes more concretely the world to which the partisans of the jeremiad wish to take us:

> We work for a country where reliable standards of right and wrong matter again; where character counts; where virtue isn't seen as something old-fashioned but as something to treasure and pass on from one generation to another. We want America to be a country where once again women who choose to be mothers are not looked down upon or seen as being behind the times and wives are appre-ciated for their valuable contribution to America. We support mea-sures that protect religious expression, restore the freedom of states to allow the acknowledgement of God in public places, and allow the posting of the Ten Commandments in public buildings. We en-courage and support the heroic work being done by churches, non-profit groups and people of faith and compassion to reach out to drug addicts, prisoners, at-risk children, and women facing crisis preg-nancies and support public policies that give faith-based organiza-tions equal opportunity to apply for federal funding for these purposes. We are convinced that, if we do these things, we can start to reverse the terrible trends we have seen in recent years, and we can once again be "the shining city upon a hill" that our founders envisioned.[37]

Of course, the character of America's founding principles is precisely what is in dispute in the larger cultural wars. Every one of these issues has become a front in the battle to define American public life. It is a battle, moreover, that by necessity recruits the past to its cause, with each side enlisting the country's founders and claiming the mantle of original intent. While today's jeremiad still, however loosely, envisions a covenanted "city on the hill," it is a city whose creation is, rather inconveniently for its partisans, due as much to the efforts of Enlightenment Deists and Freemasons as to Presbyterians and Baptists.

The more sophisticated of jeremiad's present-day partisans are not blind to this fact. Indeed, they go to some length to show how they remain faithful to the founding spirit of 1776, while the "successor parties" of the Enlightenment have moved away from the position of their forbears. Thus it is argued that, for all their freethinking, the overwhelming majority of the founding generation held to the centrality of a transcendent or "higher" moral law, if not on the basis of faith or revelation, then on a belief in the correspondence of reason and natural law. Writing about the "uniqueness of the American experiment," Charles Colson, the former Nixon aide convicted during Watergate and now a leading light among American evangelicals, explains:

> When the republic was founded, the biblical tradition and the En-
> lightenment—two distinct and often antagonistic understandings of
> the world—seemed to find a patch of common ground. God's au-
> thority was acknowledged ("All men are endowed by their Creator
> with certain inalienable rights"), but sovereignty was vested not in
> God but in the people who consented to be governed. The subsequent
> experiment in "ordered liberty" was achieved because, while some
> saw their liberty secured by God and others by their status as human
> beings alone, all agreed to be bound together for the sake of that
> liberty.[38]

Alan Keyes, a conservative Catholic, one-time presidential candidate, and president of Renew America, agrees completely. He is certain that the majority of the founders would side with today's partisans of jeremiad, for they would share the fundamental belief that for liberty to endure, all earthly authority must ultimately be subject to a higher law. He writes:

> and here's the secret they [those who want to abandon a moral un-
> derstanding of law] don't want you to realize—this notion that we
> should banish God is actually a notion that we must banish law, that
> we must banish an underlying sense that there is an order that must
> be respected in human life and affairs.[39]

The consequence of this would not only be morally regressive, establishing a world where might makes right, but it would create the very world, according to Keyes, that "America was explicitly founded to reject."[40]

At stake for the partisans of jeremiad is nothing less than the future of America's experiment in democracy. They contend that the viability of a free society depends on a virtuous citizenry. Virtue, in turn, can only come from its correspondence with a higher moral law, and this is the crux of the matter. Today's jeremiad is ultimately aimed at forces promoting what is perceived to be a thoroughgoing rejection of this higher moral law in the name of pluralism and tolerance. "Once that moral strength has been degraded," Keyes contends, "then a people enslaved to its passions and its vices and its whims become the slaves of any who can manipulate those things." Again, the civic republican current in the contemporary jeremiad runs deep.

How serious do the partisans of jeremiad believe the situation to be? Very. In fact, the hour is late. "Our Constitution has already been subverted," Keyes pleads. "Do you understand?" "We have lost the Judeo-Christian consensus upon which our founders staked the success of this experiment," Dobson proclaims. Neuhaus believes this has been a direct consequence of an activist, and actively antireligious, Supreme Court: "Law, as it is presently made by the judiciary, has declared its independence from morality . . . morality—especially traditional morality, and most especially morality associated with religion— has been declared legally suspect and a threat to the public order." Others maintain that the problem is as much about American culture as about its judiciary or any of its political institutions, but nearly all share Neuhaus's fear, expressed in Tocquevillian terms: "What happens to the rule of law when law is divorced from, indeed pitted against, the first political institution [religion]?" The answer is certain: moral failure, and eventually the end of democracy.[41] "Without faith, there is no freedom," Keyes concludes; "without God, there is no liberty." "Can you see now why this is such a crucial battle?" Dobson implores his readers.

> If we fail at this moment of destiny, we will become a secularized
> nation like Canada or the continental Europe, whose laws are based
> on secular humanism, or worse, on post-modernism, which holds
> that there is no truth, no basic right or wrong, nothing good or bad,
> nothing evil or noble, nothing moral or immoral. Law then will be a
> whimsical standard that shifts with the sands of time.[42]

Again, evangelical Christians are not alone in either their worry or in their estimation of what's at stake in the struggle they lead. Don Feder, the outspoken president of Jews Against Anti-Christian Defamation, comes to the defense of his cobelligerents:

> [There is an] implication that it's all right for anyone to be involved in politics, except for conservative Christians. If environmentalists, feminists, or animal rights advocates do get-out-the-vote drives, registration drives, or political education, it's called democracy. When Christians do it, it's called theology. Suddenly, what's good for everyone else becomes sinister when conservative Christians do it.

Feder believes that the anti-Christian bias among most elites is not on account of particular theological positions—whether the Catholic belief in transubstantiation or the belief of some fundamentalists about the rapture. Conservative believers are being attacked because of the stances they take on basic moral and social questions. He writes:

> They're being attacked because they object to same-sex marriage; they object to abortion on demand; they support public displays of the Ten Commandments; they support voluntary school prayer or a moment of silent meditation at the beginning of the school day; because they want judges to interpret the Constitution rather than using the Constitution to legislate from the bench; because they object to, you might even say they were outraged by, what happened to Terri Schiavo. Christians are the last remaining obstacle to the triumph of secular humanist values.

Again, Feder is adamant: "If Christians falter, America will fail." The fate of the American experiment in democracy rests finally with the descendents of the Puritan jeremiad.

Despite the strangely mingled notes of militant triumphalism that have sounded in these years of jeremiad's political ascendancy, the partisans of jeremiad continue to feel embattled, beleaguered, and threatened by the forces of a godless elite who are believed to be bound and determined to subvert the divinely appointed moral order and religious conservatives' role of defending it. With every square inch of ground gained in the culture wars, they worry about an accompanying loss of terrain on other fronts. For every conservative Supreme Court justice who is placed on the high court, there is a judicial ruling perceived in some way to be undermining the place of religion in public life or the sanctity of human life or threatening the integrity of the traditional, heterosexual family. To be sure, the fear of moral failure and social decline are hardwired into the narrative structure of jeremiad, and therefore into its institutional carriers. But these self-styled religious patriots fear that they may rapidly be facing a line of no return in the political and cultural life of America. While most caution with Colson, "we dare not at present despair of America and advocate open rebellion," others ask with Dobson "the pressing question . . . where do we go from here?" Whence jeremiad? Because the rhetorical cast of jeremiad has always been given to metaphors of spiritual warfare and the apocalyptic struggle between the forces of light and darkness, it is hard to gauge what it will mean when today's faithful sing the old hymnody. Will calls of "Onward Christian soldiers, marching as to war" or "Stand up, stand up for Jesus, ye soldiers of the cross" continue in the long-standing theological tradition of "spiritual warfare," or will they become a prelude to real violence, battle hymns for a "morally justified revolution"?[43]

Jeremiad, Jihad, and the Specter of Secularization

However politically aggressive it may be, the likelihood of the neo-Puritan jeremiad inspiring violent revolution in order to establish a theocratic "Christian America" seems highly unlikely. Of course, the partisans of today's jeremiad are likely to continue playing political hardball in an effort to reassert Judeo-Christian moral positions as the law of the land. But such a project of remoralization as legal fiat has its inherent limits. Most conservative Protestants are, after all, Baptists who have a long, pre-Enlightenment tradition affirming the separation of church and state.[44] Again, the champions of jeremiad are overwhelmingly liberal democrats who want public culture to be based on Judeo-Christian principles traditionally understood. In the words of one recent pundit, what they want "would merely turn the clock back to the late 1950s. That may be a very bad idea, but the America of the 1950s was not a theocracy."[45]

Where today's partisans of jeremiad evidently show no reticence regarding violence is not in their social protest or political activism, but rather in their vision of American foreign policy. They are among the strongest advocates of state-sponsored violence abroad, whether to establish American-style liberal democracy in the Middle East or to defend American democracy at home against the threat of Islamic terrorism.[46] The apparent paradox here is hard to reconcile. If the partisans of the jeremiad are to be believed, America is sliding into moral ruin, and democracy is being undermined domestically by godless elites. However, when it comes to foreign policy abroad, America apparently remains a beacon of both liberty and faith—a city on the hill.

Making matters still more complex is the emergence of a new, historically alien, and therefore completely unexpected prophecy of godlessness, one that irrevocably grafted itself into American consciousness on September 11, 2001. As in the earlier quotation from America 21, the lethal and symbolic praxis of jihad on that date now figures prominently in the narrative of the contemporary jeremiad. Jihad has become Exhibit A in the case against godlessness. Like every other civilization in the history of the world that has turned its back on God, America is headed to its ruin—in the words of the conservative Judge Robert Bork, is "slouching toward Gomorrah"—and jihad is the price we must pay for our godlessness; unless, that is, we remember, repent, and return to godly values.

Revealingly, the rhetorical symmetry between the narrative of the jeremiad and that of jihad is striking. Here is the paradigmatic version of jihad: The Islamic *umma* (the Islamic supernation) has been defiled by *jahiliyya* society (the paganism of pre-Islamic Arabia attributed to modern secular nation-states, Western-dominated global culture, and the elites who run both). It has been defiled because of Muslims' failure to wage jihad. Thus, the jihadists call on the faithful to rise up and wage jihad to repel the "great *kufr*" (literally, unbelief) and restore the holy geography of believers. The objects of jihad, like that of jeremiad, are likewise secular elites *and* the faithful.

But the similarities do not end with parallels in narrative and thematic structure. Islam, too, underwent a long period of quietism in the mid-twentieth century, with radical Islamist undercurrents surfacing here and there, only to emerge with public and political assertiveness in the 1970s, most infamously with the 1979 overthrow of the shah and the establishment of the Islamic Republic of Iran.[47] The crowning event came a decade later with the liberation of Afghanistan from the Soviets in 1989. The ragtag *mujahedin* had defeated the world's atheist superpower (albeit with major backing from the impious Central Intelligence Agency). Battle-hardened and fresh from victory, jihad entered the 1990s with a fierce vigor. Determined to rid their respective national societies of unbelief and unrighteousness, Afghan Arab jihadis nevertheless met resistance and failure at nearly every turn. Just when the militancy of radical Islamism seemed doomed, a new, more desperate, and isolated brand of jihad emerged, rallying the faithful around the idea that victory would come only by taking on the other godless superpower: the United States of America, backer of all corrupt and apostate regimes in the Muslim world, as well as the Israeli occupation of Palestine. Like a bombardier sighting in, this globalizing jihad did so with increasingly deadly accuracy, from the first bombing of the World Trade Center in 1993 to the 1995 Khobar Towers bombings in Saudi Arabia to the 1998 bombings of U.S. embassies in Nairobi and Dar es Salaam (the first terrorist attacks indisputably traceable to bin Laden and Al-Qaeda) to the 2000 bombing of the *U.S.S. Cole* to September 11,

2001, and the more recent bombings in Bali, Madrid, and London, to name only a few of the more well known.

With the crucial exception of their radically different forms of political activism, it is hard to ignore the striking symmetry of discontent found in the prophesies of godlessness coming from jeremiad and jihad. The protagonists of both are the scripture-believing remnant, while the antagonists are the secular elites who deny any transcendent authority, let alone acknowledge the cultural authority of any given religious tradition. By contrast, the protagonists of both jeremiad and jihad believe in the adjudication of tradition based in the revelation of divine authority.

For the protagonists of both the jeremiad and the jihad, history is far from over. Still, Fukuyama may be right in once crucial respect. *The Last Man*, the second part of his contentious title, invokes the inevitable character type who lives at the "end of history," that is, Nietzsche's "last man." The last men are self-contented individuals who know better than to believe in the irrationalities of tradition, especially in religious tradition. Last men live "beyond good and evil." More than anything else, the espousers of jeremiad and jihad fear the ascendance of such last men. Indeed, they fear becoming last men themselves and have developed a language to stand resolutely against such a fate. This is the religious aspect of their activism. In this way, these religious fears largely buy into the idea of a culture war at home and a clash of civilizations abroad. At least in terms of the institutionalized stories they tell, both jeremiad and jihad represent self-reflexively modern religious orthodoxies in confrontation with an increasingly global, secularizing modernity. Both, significantly, see the West as the source of imperial godlessness.

This strange symmetry of discontent reveals something about the character of religion in the global modern world. Despite all the god-talk, there is something not quite the same with these old-time religions now seemingly everywhere on the move. However resilient, however renascent, religion has been changed by its encounter with modernity. Although the social theory of secularization is in question, one wonders whether the Weberian language of disenchantment may still be pertinent. Weber predicted that as the world became more rationalized under the dislocating forces of modern capitalism and science, it would lose its metaphysical grounding for personal meaning and collective moral order. Today, it is precisely the plausibility of transcendently legitimated social orders, and the institutions that once underwrote them, that have been called into question, as the forces of capitalism and science penetrate more deeply (if unevenly and not without resistance) around the world. It is the *experience* of this loss of plausibility, along with the structural dislocations and inequalities that accompany it, that many so-called fundamentalists reflexively attribute to the spread of secularization. If it is not quite the "iron cage" Weber predicted, the disenchanting effects of modernity are both globally pervasive and locally acute.

This is nothing if not ironic. Just as the public and political assertiveness of jeremiad and jihad force conventional standard social scientific analysis to reconsider its latent secularist bias, the fear of secularization, in terms of the experience of disenchantment, contributes to that religious resurgence. Put differently, the specter of religious "fundamentalism" under the banner of jeremiad and jihad will no doubt continue to undermine the old confidence in secularization, just as the experience of disenchantment keeps secularization's specter alive.

NOTES

1. "History" for Fukuyama is "history understood as a single, coherent, evolutionary process, when taking into account the experience of all peoples in all times." See Francis Fukuyama, *The End of History and the Last Man* (New York: Free Press, 1992), xii.

2. See Timothy Shah and Monica Duffy Toft, "Why God Is Winning," *Foreign Policy* (July–August 2006), 39–43.

3. Peter Berger, ed., *The Desecularization of the World: Resurgent Religion and World Politics* (Grand Rapids, Mich.: Eerdmans, 1999), 6.

4. While there can be no doubt that *Roe v. Wade* was the symbolic pole around which the religious Right eventually mobilized itself, there were other, earlier events that set the stage for *Roe*. As historian George Marsden has argued, the 1978 IRS decision to deny racially segregated schools tax-exempt status contributed to the growing resentment among southern Fundamentalists of increasing federal government intrusion, imposed by no less than secular northern elites. See Marsden, *Fundamentalism and American Culture*, 2nd ed. (Oxford: Oxford University Press, 2005), 237.

5. America 21, www.america21.us/home.cfm.

6. Ibid. It is difficult to know how representative or influential groups like America 21 are, but it is clear they are representative of a class of political activist organizations on the religious Right. All organizations quoted in this chapter are ranked among the top twenty Christian political organizations by the *Church Report*, a magazine for church business administrators and parachurch executives. See www.thechurchreport.com/content/view/1256/32.

7. American Values, www.ouramericanvalues.org/issues_culture.php.

8. Beverly LaHaye, "How Christians Make an Impact on Their Government," in Richard D. Land and Louis A. Moore, eds., *Citizen Christians: The Rights and Responsibilities of Dual Citizenship* (Nashville: Broadman, 1994).

9. James D. Kennedy and Jim Nelson Black, *Character and Destiny: A Nation in Search of Its Soul* (Grand Rapids, Mich.: Zondervan, 1994), 17.

10. Richard John Neuhaus quoted in Damon Linker, "The Christianizing of America without a Doubt," *New Republic*, April 3, 2006, 3; Don Feder, "If Christians Fail, America Fails," interview in Christianity *Today*, www.christianitytoday.com/ct/2005/125/22.0. These quotations reflect the contemporary jeremiad in its starkest forms. Like all cultural scripts, the jeremiad possesses many permutations and variations. There are, for instance, jeremiads of the Christian Left, just as there are jeremiads emphasizing culture over politics.

11. Marsden, *Fundamentalism and American Culture*, 232.

12. Few things made this fear more acute and personal than the Supreme Court's decision to remove the Bible from local public schools, while making it legal for *Playboy* to be sold at every corner convenience store (ibid., 245).

13. Renew America, www.renewamerica.us/columns/weaver/030915.

14. Kennedy and Black, *Character and Destiny*, 274.

15. America 21.

16. American Values.

17. Richard John Neuhaus, "The End of Democracy? The Judicial Usurpation of Politics," *First Things* 67 (November 1996): 20.

18. Christian Coalition, www.cc.org/noapp/commentarydetail.cfm?id=8.

19. Ibid.

20. Remarks announcing the formation of Jews Against Anti-Christian Defamation, National Press Club, Washington, D.C., April 14, 2005. See www.jews4fairness.org/who.php.

21. *The Naked Public Square: Religion and Democracy in America* (Grand Rapids, Mich.: Eerdmans, 1984).

22. Renew America.

23. Ibid.

24. Pat Robertson's Christian Broadcasting Network alone boasts a 2004 revenue of $186,482,060. Focus on the Family's 2005 revenue was $135,848,520; see "The Top 10 Power Brokers of the Religious Right," AlterNet, www.alternet.org/story/38467.

25. Mass mailing letter from Gary Bauer, Family Research Council, July 9, 1998.

26. "Dr. Dobson Answers Questions about Focus on the Family's Twentieth Anniversary—and His Future," *Focus on the Family*, April 1997.

27. James Davison Hunter, *Culture Wars: The Struggle to Define America* (New York: Basic Books, 1991), 296.

28. Dan Balz and Ronald Brownstein, "God's Fixer," *Washington Post Magazine*, January 28, 1996.

29. America 21.

30. Rightmarch, www.rightmarch.com/about.htm.

31. Alliance Defense Fund, www.alliancedefensefund.org/UserDocs/defendingfirstliberty.pdf.

32. Traditional Values, www.traditionalvalues.org/defined.php.

33. Renew America.

34. www.declarationproject.us/read.php.

35. Wall Builders, www.wallbuilders.com.

36. www.traditionalvalues.org/defined.php.

37. www.ouramericanvalues.org/issues_culture.php.

38. www.firstthings.com/ftissues/ft9611/articles/eodmaster.html#colson.

39. Alan Keyes, address, "War on Christians" conference, Washington, D.C., April 11, 2006; see www.renewamerica.us/news/060411conference.htm.

40. Ibid.

41. Neuhaus, "The End of Democracy?" 20.

42. "Restoring the Foundations: Repealing Judicial Tyranny," www.family.org.

43. In its Pastor's Challenge, America 21 elides moral reform with direct political (military?) action in an educational video about Pastor Peter Muhlenberg, the Lutheran minister turned Revolutionary War hero. We are told that true faithfulness and patriotism at times of crisis may well mean exchanging our clerical robes for breastplate and sword.

44. There is a great deal of historical and sociological evidence supporting the view that today's partisans of jeremiad do not want to institute a theocracy or even to reconnect church and state. For starters, as the sociologist Christian Smith has amply demonstrated, most average evangelicals would not endorse such a move even if the elites of the religious Right wanted it; see Smith, *Christian America? What Evangelicals Really Want* (Berkeley: University of California Press, 2000). There is also no evidence that these elites do want it. However they may romanticize the American founding as essentially a Christian project, they believe that central to the project was a deep commitment to religious freedom. On this principle, the partisans of jeremiad differ radically from the followers of other forms of militant religion, such as radical Islam, to which they are often compared. George Marsden, again drawing on Smith's research, puts it this way: "Above all—and most important in making the comparison to militant religious movements elsewhere more misleading than clarifying—is that when American Evangelicals speak of a 'Christian America,' the first thing they are likely to speak of is religious freedom as being at the heart of the American Experiment" (*Fundamentalism and American Culture*, 251).

45. Ramesh Ponnuru, quoted in Ross Douthat, "Theocracy, Theocracy, Theocracy," *First Things* 165 (August–September 2006): 23–30.

46. See Charles Marsh, "Wayward Christian Soldiers," *New York Times*, January 20, 2006.

47. Just as Jimmy Carter, the first "born-again" American president since Andrew Jackson, entered the White House, radical ayatollahs were busy mobilizing their brethren to fight America, the "Great Satan," overthrow the domestic infidels, and reinstitute *shar'ia*.

Conclusion: Prophesies, in Retrospect and Prospect

Christopher McKnight Nichols and Charles Mathewes

From the time of the Puritans to today, Americans have been devout believers who are deeply anxious about their believing. With each new era, every new stage in the nation's history, these anxieties translated into prophesies of godlessness and godliness. The serial predictions explored in this book, spanning four centuries, arose in successive waves. By tracking these prophetic scripts and their reincarnations in virtually every generation—sometimes returning to the same phrases—we have tried to establish that these prophesies have been very powerful, and are very American. They have been adapted to dramatically different contexts and challenges by Americans of almost every political bent and religious (or irreligious) persuasion.

Today, questions about America's moral and religious future are just as anxiety-inducing, and just as pressing, as they have been in the past. From the pages of prominent newspapers to academic conferences, to church study groups, to presidential debates, concerns about the nation's moral and religious condition, today and in the future, continue to generate new predictions and new uses of the long-standing rhetorics of ascension and declension.

While we do not aim to make prophesies of our own here, the conclusion seems a good moment to make some observations about how the patterns we have found in this history appear today and have implications for the future. We suspect that this history is far from over, and we will be wise to attend to whatever lessons we can learn from the past for the years to come.

Additional Themes in Retrospect

In our introduction, we identified several central themes and scripts that pervaded the history captured in this book—most important, themes of ascension and declension, the rhetoric of jeremiad, and the ideologies of civic republicanism and Enlightenment rationalism. But now at the end, we can note certain other issues and ideas that have emerged more subtly from our study.

First and foremost, "democracy" as a concept and in practice has been and continues to be a crucial concern in debates about the nation's moral and religious future. It engenders questions such as: what is the true meaning of democracy? Is it related to religious belief or not? What is the real nature of democracy and religions or religious belief? From Washington to Bryan to Falwell, many have tied religion and democracy together, asserting that without the former, the latter would collapse. Others, such as Jefferson and Emerson, thought the reliance was mutual; still others thought them antithetical.

Second, from the informal inventions of early America through the formal laboratory discoveries of the present, virtually no one has been publicly against science, and the improvement of life that it promises. Scientific advancement and American progress seem to go hand in hand. Thus, the nation has never embraced Ludditism in any significant ways. But by the late nineteenth century an ideological dualism emerged in many projections about America's moral future—a seeming war between science and religion was emerging, and this came to be perceived as an inevitable and perhaps intractable conflict, which in turn changed how scientific progress was represented by secularists, Fundamentalists, and the vast group in the middle.

Third, pluralism has developed slowly throughout American history. Tolerance has been invented and learned, and the nation's immigrant character has repeatedly strained received understandings of the social contract. Some of the best minds have seized on this as the fundamental American exercise; others continually see a false toleration, born of indifference, as the enemy of religious seriousness. From the Puritans to William James to Harvey Cox and Peter Berger, the question of pluralism has been a highly contested subject.

Fourth, the impact of America's culture of voluntarism on religious belief is visible throughout this history, inflecting the various prophesies in complicated ways. Membership and participation in American civic life has always been articulated as a voluntary phenomenon, in two senses. On the one hand, such participation is optional—at least in America's most noble self-understanding, it cannot be compelled by the state or some institution; people are free to join, or not, but they cannot be coerced. On the other hand, participation must be *willed*—it must be chosen, and rechosen, at every moment. This can put enormous psychological pressure on the citizens' character, and some worry that it leads to deformations in the American psyche. (Most recently these worries have focused on Americans' work habits, which differ dramatically from Europeans'.) The two facets interact in deeply interesting ways in society, and also appear as interlaced themes in many observers of the nation. As Tocqueville correctly observed, America has been and perhaps always will be defined by the voluntary activities of its people; the nation seems inherently "associational." And individually, Americans have traditionally focused the nature of believing on the free choice of the individual's will and on the ability to choose to associate. From almost the beginning, this voluntarist strain in religion has provoked some to worry that *chosen* convictions are not, properly speaking, convictions. In such critics' eyes, *true* convictions never present themselves under the guise of a choice, a lifestyle option; a true conviction forces its adherents to profess that they have not "chosen" this, but that the facts of the matter, or reality itself, have *compelled* their assent. The slipperiness of the will, the evanescence of choice, has influenced those who have pondered the future of American religion. Recently, such concerns have been couched in the language of "commodification" of belief or the "therapeutization" of the self, while some defenses of American character have emphasized the "hybridity" and "dynamism" of this self.[1] But the concerns go much further back than recent debates about "consumerism." Indeed they lurk at the heart of the formative American understanding of agency.

Fifth is the subterranean but powerful presence of what we can call a distinctive American Gnosticism: a hyperprivatized, deeply interiorized, radically individualist philosophy. More broadly, the nature of religion in America in general can be understood as gnostic in several ways. While patently Christian, as we have seen, American religion often has exhibited a strongly individual, internal character that, in keeping with the Greek meaning of *gnosis*, has relied on developing transcendent understandings through personal experience. This has been particularly true in homegrown religious traditions such as Mormonism, Christian Science, and Pentecostalism, as well as in the way liberal Protestants have tended to predict a more tolerant, more interior national religious life and in the way politicians have tended to view and expand the concept of separation between church and state.

Sixth and finally, there is the pivotal role the "vital center" has played in the making of these prophesies, and their reception—or rather, the role this center has *not* played. For this center has as good a right as any group to be labeled a "silent majority." They have often been the primary actors who have enacted, defied, or become evidence for future forecasts. Their increasing or decreasing religiosity, morality, and often liberalizing cultural behaviors also have been prime reasons for the production of the prophesies we have examined here. What the historian Arthur Schlesinger Jr. termed the Cold War period's "vital center" of liberal anticommunists seeking freedom and adherence to American ideals can be extended and pushed back into earlier predictions and eras, as ordinary Americans confronted such seminal events as the Revolution and the Civil War and such divisive social issues as heresy, slavery, evolution, secularization, feminism, and communism.[2] For all the fractiousness of American politics, there has always been a common ground over which advocates for all sides have fought—and a common audience that they have wanted to sway. The extremity of those advocates' rhetoric may be related in some complicated way to the moderation of this vital center.

No doubt there are other important themes embedded in the prophetic scripts analyzed throughout this book. These are simply those we ourselves have noted. Others will find their own. We have only begun this conversation, and we look forward to the assessments of others.

Some Concluding Questions

Here at the end of the book, some pivotal questions remain to be raised, if not answered.

First is the surprising role that imagined atheists have played in American public life. We emphasize *imagined,* since actual atheists have been few and far between in American history. And yet this bogeyman has figured prominently in many nightmares, especially in the twentieth century and today. Indeed it is noteworthy that, in the face of rising pluralism and toleration, atheists alone have been left out in the cold. Since the 1950s, American tolerance of various religions, ethnicities, races, and sexual orientations has increased remarkably, but atheists are the sole group that is less tolerated now than it was a half century ago.[3] "American tolerance" has boundaries, and for those who find themselves on the outside, this "tolerance" can be actually intolerant. Indeed, some have argued that it is doubly frustrating for the unconscious way it refuses to recognize the limits it places on legitimate belief and behavior. This has something to do with the pervasiveness of voluntarism that we noted. This voluntarism entails a common-sense epistemology that is dangerously unaware of its own limits, and can lead to intransigence, intolerance, and an inability to imagine that others quite literally see things differently from the way you yourself do.[4] This voluntarism implies a necessity that citizens repeatedly recommit themselves to the polity and the polity's mission. Intertwined with this engagement seems to be an impulse that every generation *choose* America, and in so doing form views of America's God, which has something to do with a fact often apparent throughout this book—namely, the fact that fears of godlessness are, in good civic republican fashion, often deeply entangled with fears about the moral decay of the polity, and indeed identified with them. Despite protestations to the contrary, American tolerance generally remains open to almost all beliefs, even (perhaps especially) the most attenuated, while those who eschew the language of belief entirely seem unwelcome in the public square.

These tensions around atheists are only likely to grow in America in the coming years, for several reasons. First of all, since the end of the Cold War, there has been a surprising increase in the numbers of overt atheists in America. Since 1990, those professing "no religion" have risen from 8 percent to 14 percent of the population.[5]

Furthermore, changes on the geopolitical stage may have implications for new prophesies of godlessness. Whereas from the 1930s through 1989, Americans imagined their enemies as deeply "godless" (first Germany and Japan, then the godless atheism of the communist Soviet Union), the apparent "opponents" of the twenty-first century, today most notably Islamist terrorism, are suffused in religiosity and the languages of political theology. If totalitarian godlessness encouraged American views of the importance of godliness in much of the twentieth century, what might an inversion of this formula mean for the twenty-first? It will be interesting to see what happens to civic culture when affirming America's godliness no longer seems to be the way to distinguish "us" from "them, the enemy."

Finally, in the past several years polemical "new atheists," for example, Richard Dawkins, Sam Harris, and Christopher Hitchens, have emerged as a vocal force in public life, for the first time, perhaps, since before World War II. They hope for a godless future, and attack all believers mercilessly, and without distinction, in a way that has often led others to label *them* "fundamentalist." The recent upsurge in atheist critiques of religion seems rhetorically to mimic some of the worst intransigencies of the dominant antisecularist pietism; for example, columnist Katha Pollitt, neatly employing her own stereotypes, wrote:

> If we look at who actually becomes a Christian fundamentalist, we
> will find . . . lots of anxious workers and small business people, as well

as a good many ex-alcoholics and ex-addicts and other casualties of contemporary life, who are attracted to the practical support system, emotional fellowship, and structured ideology provide by their churches.[6]

And in his book *Letter to a Christian Nation*, Sam Harris attacks moderate religious believers as essentially fellow travelers who protect their more hard-core coreligionists.[7] Such attacks are depressing, to be sure, but entirely of a piece with the severity of the "faithful" versus "atheist" polemics in which religious believers have indulged over the past century and beyond.

Instead of the battles of the past—belief versus unbelief, science versus faith—a new strategy and style appeared over the last few decades, and especially the last decade. During this period Americans heard renewed outcries about an impending godlessness as part of debates about the politicization of religion, and in particular the role of evangelical Protestants in American politics. As evangelicals have reemerged from their (apparent) dogmatic slumber and forcefully entered the political fray, people across the political spectrum have questioned the future of American faith and morality. The hot-button political issues of abortion, gay marriage, environmental conservation, and (more recently) "just war" are as imbued with ascension and declension narratives as ever in the past. If the recent past is prologue, this large bloc of citizen-voters likely will continue to try to shape the future of American politics and society. How will this play out? Americans of many faiths historically have voted their self-interest, as we have seen, but they have also tended to agree that religion and politics should mix only cautiously, if at all. What does the future hold, if the future holds—as it appears to—a strong evangelical bloc?

Finally, and on a slightly different track, what makes these scripts' endurance most astonishing is that they have rarely shared the same intellectual foundation. Every generation has prophesied godlessness on the basis of the most advanced social science, philosophy, politics, or theology they could muster. In other words, they have not just repeated themselves but have relied on new and innovative theoretical foundations to make their case. Moreover, while this tells us much about America, it also suggests something about the modern intellectual enterprise, both theology, of course, and the social sciences more broadly. What assumptions are so deeply embedded in Christian theology and Enlightenment and post-Enlightenment social science that, despite the constantly changing foundations, prophesies of godlessness continue?

There is one, last, deep irony in this book's argument. We claim to analyze a set of certain rhetorical scripts that, we assert, are deeply rooted in the

American political, cultural, and religious imagination. If we are right about the profundity of these scripts, our efforts to bring their history to public attention will have very little impact on the frequency and shape they take in the future. Efforts to resist the temptation to engage in these prophesies, even if fully illuminated, may well be stymied by the energies driving their articulation. In short, if our argument is right, it is likely that things will go on as they have gone on for centuries. If we had hopes that this book would radically reshape or even end these scripts, we now recognize that it would succeed in this aim only if it failed in its analysis.

Whether this happens or not remains to be seen, and is not ultimately the purview of this book. We have studied the history of prophesies—their past, not their futures. Rather than attempting comprehensiveness, we have opted for illustration and depth of individual analyses. In many ways, the historical evidence in this book serves as a stern rebuke to virtually any confident prognostications of coming godliness or godlessness.

Echoes of the old predictions reverberate today. The form, function, and meaning of Americans' prophesies of godlessness are as important and relevant in the present as they have ever been in the past. Americans have demonstrated a remarkably consistent penchant for reflecting on the meaning of their lives, and of their nation, in terms of the future of religion and morality. In a nation whose founders explicitly rejected the establishment of an official state church, Americans take astonishingly diverse paths but continue to measure their lives and times by remarkably common ethical standards, many of which are derived from an array of religious sources. Without a full understanding of this history of serial predictions and prescriptions to embrace, endure, or reject a coming godlessness, the prophets of tomorrow are likely to be just as confident and loquacious as their ancestors were; and just as misguided, as well.

NOTES

1. For a pessimistic view of some of these trends, emphasizing the shallowness of such convictions, see James Davison Hunter, *The Death of Character: Moral Education in an Age without Good or Evil* (New York: Basic Books, 2000); for an optimistic view, emphasizing the good of choice, see Alan Wolfe, *The Transformation of American Religion: How We Actually Live Our Faith* (New York: Free Press, 2003).

2. See Arthur Schlesinger Jr., *The Vital Center: The Politics of Freedom* (Boston: Houghton Mifflin, 1949).

3. See Penny Edgell, Joseph Gerteis, and Douglas Hartmann, "Atheists as 'Other': Moral Boundaries and Cultural Membership in American Society," *American Sociological Review* 71, 2 (April 2006): 211–34.

4. For more here, see Stanley Fish, *The Trouble with Principle* (Cambridge, Mass.: Harvard University Press, 1999), and Nathan Hatch, *The Democratization of American Christianity* (New Haven: Yale University Press, 1989).

5. U.S. Census Bureau, "Population," question no. 79, Self-Described Religious Identification of Adult Population: 1990 and 2001, *Statistical Abstract of the United States: 2003*; available at http://www.census.gov/prod/2004pubs/03statab/pop.pdf.

6. Katha Pollitt, introduction to *Nothing Sacred: Women Respond to Religious Fundamentalism and Terror*, ed. B. Reed (New York: Thunder's Mouth Press, 2002), xiii.

7. Sam Harris, *Letter to a Christian Nation* (New York: Knopf, 2006).

Index